ALL THE
CENTURIONS

WILLIAM MORROW

An Imprint of HarperCollins*Publishers*

ALL THE CENTURIONS

A NEW YORK
CITY COP
REMEMBERS
HIS YEARS
ON THE
STREET,
1961–1981

ROBERT LEUCI

HarperCollins books may be purchased for educational, business, or sales promotional use. For information please write: Special Markets Department, HarperCollins Publishers Inc., 10 East 53rd Street, New York, NY 10022.

FIRST EDITION

design and title page photograph by deborah kerner /
  dancing bears design

Printed on acid-free paper

Library of Congress Cataloging-in-Publication Data
Leuci, Bob, 1940–
    All the centurions : a New York City cop remembers his years on the
street, 1961–1981 / Robert Leuci.—1st ed.
        p. cm.
    ISBN 0-380-97626-9 (alk. paper)
    1. Police—New York (State)—New York.   2. Police patrol—New York
(State)—New York.   3. Criminal justice, Administration of—New York
(State)—New York.   4. Leuci, Bob, 1940–   I. Title.
HV8148.N5L39   2004
363.2'092—dc22   2003071013

04   05   06   07   08   WBC / RRD   10   9   8   7   6   5   4   3   2   1

FOR KATHY

It was the best of times,

it was the worst of times,

it was the age of wisdom,

it was the age of foolishness,

it was the epoch of belief,

it was the epoch of incredulity,

it was the season of Light,

it was the season of Darkness,

it was the spring of hope,

it was the winter of despair,

we had everything before us,

we had nothing before us,

we were all going direct to Heaven,

we were all going direct the other way—

— CHARLES DICKENS,
A Tale of Two Cities

CONTENTS

ALL THE
CENTURIONS

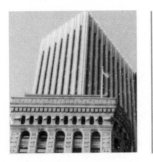

THE BIGGEST, BADDEST GANG IN TOWN

t's the fall of 1961. I'm twenty-one years old and part of a phalanx of gray-uniformed recruits marching into an out-of-date building on Hubert Street in lower Manhattan, the NYPD's police academy. What I remember most are glimpses of things antiquated and worn and the smells, the pleasant aromas of cinnamon and leather that have lingered for more than a hundred years from the lofts nearby that were used as storehouses for bales of spices brought by nineteenth-century sailing ships. I felt the mix of excitement and unnamed anxiety that comes when you are about to enter an unfamiliar world, knowing full well that you are a long way from belonging there. I was at the start of a journey and willing to go wherever the trip took me. Soon enough, mysteries began to slip away and the trip became more important than the destination.

In the academy, time flowed gently—class work, the gym, and the pistol range. Every day we took a certain greedy pleasure in knowing more about the life we were going to live than we had the day before; and after a time the weight of a gun belt felt natural.

We recruits got the feeling that there was nothing about police work the instructors didn't know, they were so confident, so sure of their view of the world. I'd ask a question and they would stand smirking at me with a fixed serenity. Though I looked for signs of uncertainty, none were there. I marveled at the number of medals they carried on their chests, and how their eyes shone when they repeated over and over, "Pay attention here and now or you'll pay a price later."

Most of us were in our early twenties, a time for illusions and wild imaginings, when dreams are new, dazzling. I was sure it would last forever; we all were.

As those first days turned to weeks and then to months, I found what I was looking for—acceptance, connection, kinship—call it what you like—belonging just to belong, that kind of thing. It is a very particular sort of yearning, a curious personality trait that has afflicted me my whole life.

You have to learn to compartmentalize your life. You must separate the street world from your world. Do not bring the job home, they told us. When you are all alone on patrol and need help, you will learn to love the sound a siren makes.

THE BABY WAS so small, two or three months old, and it cried a lot. Lover-boy wanted to have sex with the baby's mother; he wanted the baby to stop crying. He thought the bottle of sweet wine he gave it would end the crying. The baby went into convulsions, and I didn't have to wonder anymore how I'd behave at my first arrest.

It was an old story: a single mother, her baby, and a drunk, horny boyfriend. The first time you see such a thing it's a shock—the language, sounds, gestures. The veterans spoke to me slowly, gently, so I would understand that this arrest could turn a long night into an eternity.

I was on a training mission in Harlem. The veterans were telling me, "Rookie, here's your first arrest. You want it, you got it. This guy's going to be a pain in the ass to collar. Look at him."

We were standing in the kitchen, and cops and ambulance attendants seemed to be everywhere. The mother left with the medical people and the baby. I stared at the boyfriend. He seemed cool, aloof, detached. A small smile, his brains all down in his dick.

That first time and forever after you know you're part of something extraordinary. You begin to gain experiences that give you knowledge and pride. I don't mean all the bullshit macho stuff. Instead it's a real sense of accomplishment. Down deep you feel as though you're some kind of hero, the man in the white hat, the marshall of Dodge City.

"You're under arrest," I told him.

He said, "For what?"

It was a good question. "Don't worry, we'll figure something out," one of the veterans said.

When I tried to handcuff him, lover-boy went off and started throwing punches. He was tough, fast, strong, and a lot more rugged than I thought. There were cops in the apartment, cops waiting in the hallway, cops on the stairway, and they were all getting a laugh at my inability to handcuff this character.

Finally, two or three of them jumped in and gave me a hand; it was over in a flash. A veteran Harlem cop, a huge black guy, grabbed my shoulder.

"Kid," he said, "this is the street, not the Golden Gloves. There's no referee out here. Remember," he said, "you belong to the biggest, baddest gang in town. You need help, don't wait—ask."

IN THE DETECTIVES' squad room bright and early the following morning, I stood looking at a precinct detective who was wearing brown brogans, black ankle-length socks, a T-shirt, and boxer shorts. He was chomping on a cigar, banging away at his typewriter.

His face was covered with stubble and there were bags under his eyes. He wasn't a bad-looking guy. He did not seem at all happy.

It was early February, a cold and windy morning. I had dressed warmly, way too many layers for that sauna of a squad room.

My prisoner sat in the holding cage across from the detective. His legs and arms were crossed like a Buddha's, his head was down, his eyes at half-mast, all the fight in him gone.

"A real pain in the ass," the detective said. "When I was printing him, he broke free and tried to dive out the window. Your shit-bird smashed our fucking window. We were freezing in here all night."

The detective told me that he had been forced to spell out to my prisoner why it was a bad idea to break a precinct window on a cold night. "Spell out" was an interesting way to put it. The prisoner looked as though he had been stunned and then hypnotized.

"Your guy's wanted in the two-oh [20th Precinct] for an A&R [assault and robbery]," he said. "You made a good collar."

"So what do I do with him?"

"When you get to court, someone from the two-oh will pick him up and rebook him. Broke our fucking window, this prick."

A sudden change came over the detective; he became affable and friendly, giving me these strange inquiring looks. "How the hell old are you?"

"Twenty-one," I told him. Then he said something I didn't understand.

"What?" I said.

"Nothing personal, but you look like you're in high school. Not old enough to be a cop."

In truth, up until my thirtieth birthday I was carded in New York City. And although that might seem to be a compliment, I never took it that way.

"Maybe you should grow a mustache," he told me.

"Maybe," I said. "Yeah, maybe I will." I knew I couldn't grow a mustache if my life depended on it.

"You'd better get going," he said in a helpful tone. "The wagon will leave without you."

In those days the department had a small truck they called the wagon that transported newly arrested prisoners. It was green and black with gated doors, no springs, no windows, and wooden benches that were bolted to the floor.

Department policy mandated that the arresting officer always ride with his prisoner. So I was shocked to see a pair of detectives push their prisoners into the wagon and say, "See you guys later."

No riding in a cold old shit-box wagon for them. They followed in their own car.

So there I was, bouncing around with a crew of junkies, stickup men, hookers, and other perpetrators of unspeakable and horrifying crimes, none of them having showered in the last month, all of them throwing me tense and agitated glances.

We stopped at precinct houses along the way, picking up prisoners and more cops and detectives. After stops at the BCI (Bureau of Criminal Identification) and photo, we arrived at the Manhattan Criminal Courts Building. The drive had pretty much done me in and the day was barely beginning.

After delivering my prisoner to the corrections department, I went off to the complaint room and then to arraignment.

The place was a zoo. Manhattan cops had been busy the night before and there were a couple of hundred new arraignments. Everywhere I looked were assistant district attorneys, Legal Aid attorneys, private counsel, court officers, correction officers, victims of crime, cops and detectives from half the commands in Manhattan, social workers, bail bondsmen, probation officers—all of them moving at top speed. It seemed incredible that any form of justice could be done in all that craziness.

All the seats were taken so I stood along the courtroom wall watching. I was amazed at the skill of the judge, the lawyers, the DAs, and the court clerks. Everything seemed to work efficiently, not only the various officers of the court, but also the complainants, the victims of crime. When their names were called, they moved to the bench with their heads up, knowing the drill, as if they had done this many times before.

The detective from the 2-0 appeared beside me. "You're the rookie from the two-eight that pinched our guy," he said.

"It's me."

He was an attractive man, cheerful and bright, well dressed and friendly.

"Well, go get him. I spoke to the clerk, we're all set. Bring him up and I'll take him off your hands."

He grinned at me and wagged his head. "Who told you to make this collar?"

"Nobody, I wanted to make it."

"Good," he said, "good for you. Go get him and you can get out of here and get back to school. Tell all your friends about your first day in court."

He looked at me as if he knew me, had always known me. It was a feeling that took some getting used to because I didn't take to strangers easily; a kind of neighborhood thing.

This was a new value system—every cop is your brother: that was the idea, an attitude that took hold in your heart and mind and gave you a certain power, a feeling that these men around you were your only possible friends.

I got back to the academy sometime later that afternoon and my class sergeant told me to stand up. "Leuci here," he said, "went out last night on a training mission in the two-eight. He made an arrest. It's my understanding that it was a family dispute. Not a major arrest, but a collar nonetheless. Let's all give him a hand."

My classmates sat there for a second, staring at me. Then they brought their hands together in exaggerated slow motion. Clap, a long pause, and then—clap again.

ONE MORNING NEAR the end of recruit training, I was sent out to direct traffic at Fifty-fourth Street and Madison Avenue. It was important for recruits to gain experience in all phases of police work, the reasoning went. It turned out to be a day full of surprises.

The ex–middlewight champion Rocky Graziano snuck up behind me, lifted my summons book from my back pocket, and walked off with it. I ran after him and was thrilled to meet him. I wanted to talk to the champ about life, his life, his fights, the great Sugar Ray Robinson. He hunched up, feigned a punch, handed me back my book, turned, and walked away. From the corner of my eye, I spotted my father watching me from a storefront doorway.

The cop who normally handled the intersection explained the wisdom of letting the traffic signals do the work. Miraculously, I didn't make a total fool of myself, blowing my whistle and screwing up the morning rush hour.

MEANWHILE, THE ACADEMY training was winding down. We spent more time at the pistol range and in the gym boxing, and less and less hours in the classroom. We were close to the end of it, and all of us were smoldering under the need to move on.

Two weeks later I graduated from the academy and was assigned to the 100th Precinct in Rockaway Beach, Queens.

I was suddenly anxious. For weeks in class we had all speculated about where we would be assigned. I imagined myself in "Fort Apache, the Bronx" or one of the Harlem precincts. I anticipated learning the job quickly, arrests every day, careening around in a patrol car, the siren blaring, being first on the scene, always first. Or taking a bullet, being cut by a knife, something minor in the thigh, and being promoted to detective on the spot. Or beating a fireman into a burning building and saving a child or leading an elderly couple to safety.

All those heroic scenarios would be no more than figments of my imagination, the stuff of dreams and fantasy. I had been assigned to one of the least active precincts in the city. As soon as I could get to a telephone, I called the office of the Tactical Patrol Force to plead for an interview.

———

THIS WASN'T A new idea, the TPF. I'd always hoped I could get assigned there. It was the department's most elite patrol unit.

The collar insignias on TPF uniforms were highly polished silver, not the usual brass. Their tailored uniforms were always clean and smart. TPF did not work any particular precinct but moved through the high-crime areas of the city. Most members were under thirty years old, ex-marines and paratroopers, all with an appetite for the things that active street cops enjoyed, the jobs that most other cops avoided as a matter of course. In TPF you were very much set apart from the rest of the department's patrol force. TPF was my idea of what it meant to be a patrol cop.

In a precinct there were fixed posts like school crossings, guarding dead bodies, and sometimes—horror of horrors—traffic duty. In a precinct you were expected to be a part-time social worker, caring for the lost, the sick, and injured. But that wasn't all of it, or even most of it. Precincts were full of old-timers, "hair-bags" they called them, men who had done and seen enough. Aggressive patrol was not what they wanted.

I had other reasons for wanting to be assigned to TPF. I dreamed of being a detective, and TPF was a fast track to the Detective Bureau. I envisioned all sorts of possibilities for myself. I didn't want a conventional life; I wanted adventure, where tomorrow and the day after that would be different from today. *Adventure.* The very word has an uplifting feel to it, a means of escaping the ordinary.

I walked into the TPF office and immediately regretted the impulse that had brought me there. Even the clerical men were over six feet tall.

A lieutenant named James Sullivan interviewed me. Everything about him was perfect—his posture, sitting or standing, was perfectly straight.

Behind his desk someone had drawn a line on the wall.

"Go and stand by that line," he said. I was five-nine.

"I'm not six feet tall," I told him.

"Really," he said, "I never would have guessed."

"That doesn't mean I can't do the work."

He smiled. It wasn't a friendly smile; I don't think it was meant to be. "Look," he told me, "first of all we don't accept probationary officers."

Probationary officers were newly appointed cops who were on trial for one year. I had six months to go.

"You have to have some street experience to work here," Sullivan said. "And most important, as far you're concerned, TPF has a minimum height requirement and you don't make it."

"I'll bet there are exceptions," I said. Lieutenant Sullivan and I were the same height.

He asked me where I had been assigned, and when I told him the 100th in Rockaway Beach, he nodded. "You'll get sand in your shoes, get comfortable, and never want to leave that place. The one hundred is a retirement home."

"I'm way too young to retire."

He lost interest in talking to me, I could tell.

"Stay in touch with us. Things change in this job, you never know. Give us a call in a year," he said. I looked up at that line on the wall and figured that my chances of growing three inches in six months were slim at best.

As I was leaving the office one of the clerical officers followed me to the door. "Leuci," he said, pronouncing my name correctly, which I never did, Le-u-chi, the accent on the u. I pronounced my name Lu-cy. My father constantly instilled in us the importance of being American. I never knew why exactly. I suppose he had his reasons, something about not wanting to be judged as an ethnic.

The clerical man's name was Joseph Borelli. He was a mild-mannered, bright guy who years later would be chief of detectives. On that day he was a clerical officer and the TPF's delegate to the Columbia Association.

Every ethnic group in the department had an association. The most powerful, with the most political clout, was, of course, the Irish officers' Emerald Society. The German officers had the Steuben Association, and there was the Polaski Association for Polish officers, the Shomrim Society for Jewish officers, the Guardians for black officers, the Hispanic Society for Latin American officers, and the Columbia Association for Italian Americans. The Saint George Association was for everyone else.

Borelli asked me if I was a Columbian. I told him I'd joined while I was in the academy. He said they could use more Columbians in TPF. I told him I didn't think there were many of us over six feet tall. He told me to stay in touch, that they were expanding the outfit. "Stay active in the precinct," he said, "stay out of trouble, and whenever you do something special, let us know."

"Something special?"

"Yes. Can you do that?"

"Sure."

The next day, in my new blue uniform, I reported to the 100th Precinct in Rockaway Beach, Queens.

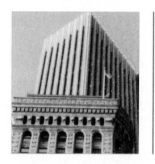

HEAVE
HEAVEN

had slept for a while, trying to prepare myself for my first late tour, and awoke groggy and dull. I put on insulated underwear while watching *The Lucy Show* on the TV. My mother asked if she should pack something for me to eat. I told her I wasn't going off to summer camp. I asked her why my newly washed underwear had turned pink. She laughed. My mother had this wild, cascading sort of laugh. She was a fine housekeeper, an even better cook, and she was a remarkably beautiful woman. She also had the extraordinary habit of turning much of my laundry pink.

I arrived at the station house around eleven o'clock.

to heave or to coop—to find a place to hide and sleep.

I was one of the first rookies to be assigned to the 100th Precinct in ten years. Not knowing what to do with me, they assigned me to a sector car with a salty cop named Larry.

Larry taught me many things about being a cop; he also taught me about the Second World War, and what it was like to fight it.

Normally it took some time before a rookie was assigned a seat in a sector car and never is a seat given to a recent academy graduate. For your first weeks and months on patrol you are assigned a foot post. In February, the 100th Precinct had no foot posts on late tours—a break for me. I wouldn't freeze my ass off walking some godforsaken uninhabited street.

Located on the Rockaway Beach peninsula, the 100th had on its eastern end a neighborhood called Arverne, once a cozy summertime neighborhood with large wood frame homes and cottages, but no more.

In the west were the sections of Breezy Point, Neponsit, and Belle Harbor. The southern end of the precinct was the glorious Atlantic Ocean.

In Neponsit and Belle Harbor lived lawyers, judges, doctors, and politicians. From 110th Street to 116th Street along Rockaway Boulevard were a line of Irish bars and restaurants. White summer cottages with blue shutters on the side streets, and for a long strip the precinct was only two blocks wide, with Jamaica Bay on one side and the Atlantic Ocean on the other. Imagine walking a boardwalk post in February, listening to the crashing green waves and your chattering teeth, so cold you thought you had to pee all the time, panicked you'd pee in your pants.

Larry said that in the summer months the precinct jumped. The beachfront bars and restaurants drew a hearty clientele of off-duty cops, fireman, sanitation workers, and their friends and family, and they caused all kinds of problems. He also told me that for all the activity during the remainder of the year, you might as well have been a cop on the tip of Alaska.

On the other hand, Arverne did offer some work. There were city housing projects, and the once large, proud old homes had been turned into SROs (single room occupancies). He said that the poor blacks and Puerto Ricans who lived there were too treacherous to make it in Harlem or Bedford-Stuyvesant, or in the South Bronx for that matter.

In the locker room I watched the veterans dress quickly, uniform trousers and a sweater, gun belt, blackjack, summons and memo book under a tunic. No one wore insulated long johns.

I was assigned a car and given a ring. On the hour, or five, ten, or twenty minutes past the hour, you called the precinct. For example: Leuci, sector 1, car 351: ten rings, 4:00 A.M. meal.

I was the driver for the first four hours and the recorder for the second four.

Larry introduced himself in the locker room and caught a glimpse of my insulated underwear. He told me I wouldn't need it; the car had a good heater. "What if we have to get out of the car, ya know, traffic duty or something?" He smiled and nodded. Larry did a lot of smiling and nodding that night.

The sector cars were lined up in front of the precinct. Larry told me to get in our car and check the gas and the siren.

"The siren? What for?"

"The guys that have the sector before us, a couple of comedians, they leave the siren on; you start the car and *waaaaa, waaaa, waaaa.* Supposed to be funny."

Six cars rolled out. There was legionary feel to it, warriors sent out to do combat. All the men were older, smart and savvy in ways I would learn that I was not. Still, I was in the best physical shape of my life, and I believed in myself, in my ability to handle anything that might come our way.

> a flute—a bottle of Coke, the Coke poured out and
> booze poured in.

As soon as we rolled out Larry directed me to the parking lot across from the precinct. He pointed at a station wagon—his car— loaded with cans of paint, drop cloths, and a ladder. He had a painting business on the side and said that when it got warm, he'd have some work for me.

"Great," I told him, "that's exactly how I'd like to spend my summer."

He took an inflatable pillow and an alarm clock from the station wagon and tossed them into the car's backseat.

A bit over six feet, Larry was reed thin; he had an impressive crown of white curly hair that needed to be trimmed. "Okay," he said, "time to roll. Let's check this sector out."

We quickly fell into the earnest rhythms of patrol, up one street, down the other. Occasionally we shone the spotlight into a deserted alleyway. Hissing noises came from the radio, but no calls. I pointed out that more cats and dogs were roaming on the street than people.

During the first hour I peppered Larry with questions, none of which he wanted to answer. He'd turn and glance at me with bored, questioning eyes.

As I drove I began to imagine myself answering hot calls: a robbery in progress, shots fired, and the most urgent of all, assist patrolman. In my reveries I was always the hero. I'd build up a big reputation, just the way the top cops did. Soon enough the brass would take notice and realize they were wasting my talent. "He's a natural," they'd say. "Make that man a detective." That was the way to make it in this job. That's how it would work for me.

"Larry," I said, "how do I go about getting a steady seat in a sector?"

We drove in silence for about five minutes. Then: "I walked for two years, filled in when I could find a seat. This is your first tour," he said, more to the empty street than to me.

"Okay," I said. "All right."

"Look," he said finally, "you get a chance to ride, there are certain things you have to do."

"What's that?"

Larry spelled out the list.

1. Give out traffic summonses, one or two a night, minimum.
2. Take care of the sergeant.

3. Never miss a job that comes over the radio.
4. Take care of the sergeant.
5. Make sure you're the first in your sector to find storefront glass that's been broken.
6. Take care of the sergeant.
7. Occasionally make an arrest.
8. Take care of the sergeant.

Larry's talk was tough and offhanded and it had nothing to do with causes or reasons, just with directions. He was also reluctant to make eye contact.

"I have no idea what you're talking about," I told him. "What do you mean, 'take care of the sergeant'?"

In a soft and understanding way, Larry said, "This is your first night. Relax, you'll see."

That night no cars were moving, and no people were walking the streets. All was calm. I lost myself in a fantasy of what life would be like working in a quiet precinct night in, night out, eternally circling in a silent patrol car.

Within the confines of the entire sector there was but one open business: Ciro's, an Italian restaurant, pizza parlor, and bar in the eastern end of the sector.

Suddenly a burst of static came over the radio and then a call, our first call of the night. It was a 10-2: return to the precinct.

Flutes. They wanted us to pick up two flutes. "Where the hell are we going to find a music store open this time of night?" I asked him.

"Ciro's," Larry said. "Ciro has flutes."

Telling me to wait and pay attention to the radio, Larry left the car and walked into the resturant. Five minutes later he returned with two Coca-Cola bottles filled with booze. It was some time around two in the morning when we returned to the station house.

"Go on," he said. "Go in the house and take care of the sergeant."

I handed the Coke bottles to the sergeant behind the desk. He smiled, muttered a quick thanks, and then buried his head in the blotter.

We circled the sector one more time, made sure that Ciro's was closed and quiet, then Larry directed me over the Cross Bay Bridge onto Cross Bay Boulevard. He pointed to a trail junction at the foot of the bridge.

"In there," he said. "Drive in there."

It was the Jamaica Bay bird sanctuary. A sign said No Hunting or Fishing.

I felt foolish driving down a dark trail, wondering where the hell we were going but afraid to ask. It was a narrow, winding dirt road. The car's tires sloshing through ruts filled with water, we moved like a black and green spirit in the night. When we came to a clearing, Larry told me to park.

"Keep the engine running," he told me. "You did a good job," he said.

"Thanks."

"You're going to ask me what we're doing here?"

"No."

"Why not?"

"Because I figure you're about to tell me."

"It's heave time," he said. "We're going in, take a little rest, a couple of hours. Your meal hour, my meal hour, we take a little snooze."

"Snooze?"

"Yup."

"No shit?"

"No shit."

"I'm not tired," I said. "I slept all day."

"Good, then you can listen to the radio. Remember," he said, "you only answer calls for our sector. No one else, understand?"

"Sure."

Larry opened the car door and stepped outside, took off his tunic and gun belt and tossed them into the backseat, walked off a few feet and urinated in the weeds. Then he let himself into the car's back-seat, blew up his pillow, and set the alarm clock. Using his tunic as a blanket, he was snoring in less than a minute.

That clearing was very dark, with evil shadows. I took my gun from its holster and laid it in my lap. When I was a kid they said that wild animals, rabid dogs, and mutant rats lived in the bird sanctuary.

Sitting there was not an easy thing; my adrenaline was still pump-ing, but I had to sit still listening to the static from the otherwise silent radio. Larry slept peacefully. It was difficult to judge how slowly time was moving, but it certainly did drag. Not to be be-lieved. Not at all to be believed. It seemed the entire precinct was asleep.

"In the one hundred precinct, car two-seven-four, call your command."

No answer.

Then the disembodied voice on the radio came louder, a bit of a catch in his voice. "In the one hundred precinct, that's car two-seven-four, your command. Call your command!"

Still no answer.

"In the one hundred precinct, any car available—K?" Pleading.

I sat frozen, hoping Larry would wake up and tell me to take the call, but he didn't.

Then at long last a responding voice. "Sergeant's car in the one hundred to central-K. We'll handle that call."

"Call the command, Sarge."

"Ten-four."

It began to snow, big flakes softly covering the car, coating the windshield, while in the backseat Larry snored. Gusts of wind shook the car. I imagined a heavy snowfall wafting down, covering the sec-tor car and sealing us in. Someone over the radio hummed taps, and the central operator barked out, "Cut it out."

"I never heard it. I was awake, and I didn't hear it."

"You were sleeping."

Central had called with a job, but I hadn't heard it. Larry's arm came out of the backseat; he picked up the radio and answered, "Three fifty-one—K."

"See the woman" was how the call came over the air.

"The one thing I hate," Larry said, "is to get roused out of a good nap."

It was near 5:00 A.M. and the snow had stopped falling, but there was a cutting wind that turned the roads icy. Larry collected himself, then he took the wheel. Suddenly he was wide awake. Hitting the siren at intersections, flashing lights, he drove fast, on his face a sort of sad resignation.

Other sector cars called over the radio asking if we needed help. Larry told them we'd handle it. In ten minutes we pulled up in front of a small run-down apartment building. A somber, heavyset black woman, her arms folded, stood waiting at the curb smoking a cigarette.

Larry surveyed things for a second. "Let me handle this, okay. I've been here a hundred fucking times."

I asked if he thought the woman waiting was the woman that called. "She's the super of the building. She called all right," he said.

Out of the car, Larry hitched up his pants, then reached into the backseat for his nightstick. I already had mine.

"They're at it again," the woman said. "You gotta take him this time, Officer. I mean enough is enough. I got working people living here. It's the middle of the night, working people gotta get some sleep."

Larry took the woman's arm and began walking toward the building. I noticed the way he held her, bent his head toward her, the caring way he listened, how he nodded his head, how she deferred instantly to him. I followed a few steps behind, waves of apprehension rolling through my stomach.

As soon as we got to the front door steps we could hear them, and inside the building the shouting became more passionate. Someone threw something against a wall; a child began to scream.

Larry knocked on the apartment door. "Police," he said. "Open up, Stanley."

I heard someone moan soft and low.

"Open the goddamn door, Stanley. C'mon, open up."

Then a man's voice: "Nobody here called the police."

I said, "Somebody did." And Larry looked at me, putting his finger across his lips. "I'll handle this," he said.

"Stanley," he said, "you don't open this door right now, when I get in there, I'll fucking kill you. One," he said, "two . . ."

The door opened slightly, and Larry pushed it and walked into the room. I followed behind him. From where I stood I could see an unmade bed and a lamp on a table in the corner. A thin man sat on the edge of the bed, his face scrawny and rawboned in the dim light. He was being held firmly in place by three blond-headed young girls, one on each arm and one around his legs. The girls were clearly sisters and were all under thirteen. Draped onto a closet door was a woman five feet nothing tall, chubby with disheveled red hair, wearing a stained green dress. Her teeth jutted out and her face was white as death.

"I didn't call the police," she said. Her voice was tiny, helpless, and tears were in her eyes. She had somehow curled herself around the edge of the closet door. Even in the dim light I could make out ugly welts on her face and neck.

"It was the nigger," Stanley said. "The nigger bitch called the cops." He had a high-pitched voice like a bad-tempered drunk. "I didn't call you," he said. "What the hell are you doing in my house?"

Larry took a step toward him, a smile on his face, his manner solicitous. "Someone called the police, Stanley, said there was trouble in here, someone was getting hurt."

"Bullshit."

"A fact," Larry said. He looked around as if weighing options.

The girls didn't acknowledge either Larry or me, but they were watching, waiting. Then the oldest smiled at me. It was a sweet smile, and I think of it now as terribly sad, tragic and confused.

"One of you girls want to tell us what happened?" I said.

Negative sounds and wagging heads came from all three.

"I'll tell ya what happened," Larry said.

"Nothing happened," the woman said, and Larry said, "Sure it did."

Stanley was watching Larry with sleepy eyes, and I was watching Stanley, watching the girls and Stanley. All three were barefoot, wearing filthy T-shirts that hung to their knees. None of them looked as though they had bathed in a week. The stench in the room was awful, something I had never smelled before, a sourness I would smell many more times in the years ahead.

"Anne here," Larry said, "the lady in the closet, the girls' mother and Stanley's wife, caught our boy fooling with one of the little ones. Right, Stanley? Whenever that happens, Anne goes after him and Stanley kicks the shit out of her."

The three girls looked up at him with anxious, bewildered eyes. Stanley tried to get to his feet, but the girls held him tight, held him down.

I felt more and more as if I understood nothing of what was going on. It was clear that Larry knew things I didn't.

"You've done it before, Stanley," Larry said, "I know you have. I warned you, didn't I, Stanley? I gave you fair warning, told you 'You do that again, I'm going to drag your sorry ass to the ocean, toss you in, and watch you drown.' Bobby," he said, "handcuff this piece of shit and throw him in the car."

I didn't know what to say. I took my handcuffs off my belt. Stanley's mouth contorted into a desperate grin, he yipped like a puppy, and the three girls started screaming, shouting at us, and calling Larry a motherfucker. The sound of those girls, first wailing, then pleading, then cursing us, astonished me. I couldn't believe it.

"Do it," Larry said. "Cuff him."

Stanley didn't resist. He rolled over and offered me his wrists. I put a jacket over him and started for the door.

Larry was bent over Anne, nodding his head and whispering. The girls were screaming like banshees but they made no move toward us. I was afraid they might, and wondered what I would do if they did.

When I got to the street and tried to put Stanley into the sector car he resisted, not a lot, just a little. "Man," he said, "your hands are shaking. What are you, some kind of auxiliary?"

"Just get in the car."

"An auxiliary, that's what you are. A trainee, a police scout or something."

"Get in the fucking car or I'll bust your jaw." He smiled at me and got into the backseat, and I felt like a cop.

Larry drove up the street to the beach, made a quick U, then headed for the boulevard.

"I knew you weren't going to take me to the beach," Stanley said.

"Shut up," Larry said, and that's all he said.

We were heading out of the precinct, that much I knew, heading east to the outskirts of the city.

We reached Beach 9th Street just as the sun was starting to rise. Beach 9th Street was out of our sector, out of our precinct, and was almost out of New York City. It was quiet, cold, and there were gulls walking along the shore. Larry told me to take Stanley's handcuffs off and I did. If Stanley was frightened, he gave no sign of it.

"Get out of the car, Stanley," Larry said.

Stanley didn't move.

I expected Larry to turn and grab him, but no. I wondered if I should do something. We all sat still for a moment. "I'm going to tell you one more time, you get out of this car or I'll shoot you right here."

I was out of my depth, but I knew I couldn't take much more of this. Larry described how he'd blow a hole in Stanley, then put a gun in his hand and get a medal, maybe a promotion.

I started to say something and Larry glared at me. I decided to remain quiet and watch, and mostly the one I watched was Stanley. He did it quickly, opened the door and got out. Larry followed him. When I opened the passenger door, Larry bent down and told me to stay put and listen to the radio.

"Look," I told him, "if you don't want to, I'll lock this character up." He told me it wouldn't do any good. They'd locked him up a half-dozen times, they always cut him loose.

"What the hell are you going to do?"

Stanley hadn't walked off; he was standing alongside the car. "Shoot the prick, whadaya think?"

"C'mon."

"Why, you mind?"

"Why would I mind?"

"If I shot him?" He looked at me to see if he had gotten to me.

I couldn't figure what this scam was about: the ride out of the precinct, sitting on a windblown beach at sunrise, stupid fucking Stanley standing there with the most ridiculous expression on his face, Larry saying he's about to commit murder.

Larry made a half turn; he grabbed Stanley by the jacket and shook him. I was engrossed with the way Larry looked, not crazed exactly but right at the edge of losing control. I got out of the car. My legs were shaking, my hands too. I didn't say anything.

Stanley began crying. He tried to spin away but Larry held him steady. Larry made a fist and raised his hand. I'm thinking, *Man, don't hit this little shit, you'll kill him.*

He threw Stanley down onto the beach like a sack of coffee. The wind picked up.

"If I hear, one more time, that you abused that woman or any of those kids, so help me God, I'm going to kill you."

Stanley never said a word: he simply kept crying, turning his head this way and that, rolling around in the sand like a wounded seal.

"Stanley," Larry shouted, "did you hear me?"

Stanley was sobbing and going through his pockets, and Larry said again, "Did you hear me?"

Stanley said, "Yeah, yeah, I hear you, I do. Listen, man," he said, "I don't have any money, how do I get home?"

Larry started to say something but stopped himself. He bent over Stanley, grabbed him, and lifted him to his feet. He slapped him, an open handed slap, then he walked wearily back to the car and got in.

I was standing over Stanley, looking down. "You'd better pay attention to this guy," I said.

"You're telling me."

"Don't ever make us go back to your house."

Stanley nodded. Then he said in his small, insipid voice, "Officer, could you please lend me a dollar, some change, so I can make a call."

"Fuck you, Stanley," I said and walked back to the patrol car.

In the eastern sky the cloud cover washed away and the morning sun came shining through. As we drove off Larry handed me the radio, "Okay," he said, "put us back on the air."

I called central saying, "Three-five-one in the one hundred back on patrol, K."

"Disposition on the last job, three-five-one?"

I looked at Larry and he shrugged his shoulders. "Tell 'em, 'condition corrected.'"

I did just that.

Larry kept switching hands on the steering wheel, and as we

passed the boundary into our own precinct he threw his cap into the backseat. He turned to me. "Are you all right? I'm worried about you."

I had no answer.

AFTER LATE TOURS, I'd get home and my mother would make breakfast for my father and me. He would leave for the office around ten or eleven in the morning and rarely got home before eleven o'clock at night. The business of organizing unions kept him out late.

Over breakfast I told him about my night as best I could, not saying too much. It was hard to talk about heaving, so I kept that to myself.

My father read four newspapers a day and watched the news on TV every night and was worried about me. He was the kind of guy who liked to talk about the oppression of poor people and the workingman. Back then, I believed he was as detached from what was going on in the real world as a cave drawing. He was a committed liberal, and as far as I was concerned, his politics were weird.

The ethos of the McCarthy era had shaken my father badly. There was nothing he wanted more than to be considered a good American, and what he read in newspapers and watched on television every day during the fifties defined people like him as anything but. He stopped reading the *Daily Worker*, dropped his allegiance to the Socialist Party, and became a Democrat. Later, he saw the riots, assassinations, and drug culture of the sixties as frontal assaults on his family, and his politics moved further right. By the end of his life he gave up on both the Democrats and Republicans and voted Libertarian.

Anyway, back then my becoming a policeman frightened him, but I didn't know what to do about it. He'd grown up in a tough neighborhood in Brooklyn and as a kid saw plenty of violence on those Brownsville streets. I wondered what he thought I did at night riding around in a police car. Something heroic, something useful?

There was no advice he could give me on how to be a good cop, no talk about keeping my nose clean and not sleeping on the job. Unlike so many of my contemporaries, I had no cops in my family. My father had no close friends who were cops, and the ones he knew, he'd met at union demonstrations and strikes. On the streets that had molded him, cops and gangsters were the kinds of people you stayed away from.

When I first told him I was thinking of becoming a cop, he said that I should go back to school and finish my education. Then he said, "Look, I guess it isn't so bad. Cops and firemen were the only people who had jobs during the Depression. So if you want to be a cop, go ahead. Just be a good cop, don't be a schmuck, treat working people fairly." My father loved using words like *schlemiel* and *schmuck* and *putz*.

After breakfast I went up to my room and napped. I woke late in the afternoon and waited around until it was time to return to the precinct, where I could nap again if I liked. I started calling the TPF office every day, all but begging for another interview.

central—communications over the police radio.

fixer—a fixed post, a location you could not leave (e.g., a broken storefront window, a school crossing).

I remember it was a beautiful spring day, full of sparkling sunshine, clear and breezy but not cold, the smell of the ocean in the air. It was a terrible day to die.

It was the first day of March 1962, and I was into one of my first sets of day tours. I had a fixer in front of the station house, a school crossing. One of the children tugged on my coat and said, "Officer, ya know what, an airplane fell down."

I said, "What?"

The captain of the precinct, John Mink, bolted out of the station house shouting, talking fast, so frightened you'd think that the end of his world was at hand. On that day he was carried on a swell of horror, stunned and dismayed. He hollered out for me to get a car.

"A plane crashed, a jetliner full of people, a plane just crashed in Jamaica Bay. Drive like hell," he said. "Use the siren and lights."

We were the first car on the scene. A 727, an American Airlines flight, had come down only minutes after takeoff. There was no fire that I could see, no smoke. The plane sat in Jamaica Bay near the bird sanctuary and not all that far from the road. I looked across a long brush- and cattail-covered field that extended out toward the bay to the crash site. I could make out the fuselage and tail section flashing in the sun.

I scrambled out of the car, and as I began to run into the field, Captain Mink cried out to me, telling me to hold it, not to go there, it could explode.

I stopped, turned, and headed back to the car. For a second I glanced back over my shoulder, thinking of all those people—ninety-five of them—dead in that airplane.

I heard the sounds of the sirens coming in, the wailing fire trucks; cattails swayed in a light breeze. I saw a fireman step off his truck and cross himself, and thought that maybe I should too. It seemed impossible that only minutes earlier there were families with children on that airplane and they had been soaring like a bird.

In no time at all the area was full of emergency units, fire, police, and medical personal. The 100th would be used as a temporary morgue. A motorcycle cop gave me a ride on the back of his bike, which at the time was prohibited and I'm sure still is. I remember how thrilled I was speeding along the boulevard, how reassuring the feel of his leather coat in my hands. I directed traffic all that day, sending cars off the Crossbay Bridge, diverting them to the Marine Parkway Bridge. I remember how some people opened their car windows and cursed me, saying, "What the hell for? A plane crashes and we gotta drive all over the fucking city?"

———

ON MY NEXT set of late tours, sitting in a patrol car with Larry, watching the sun rise over the Atlantic Ocean, sipping a coffee, smoking a cigarette, he said to me, "Ya know, I've been doing this job close to twenty years and I could have made a lot more money doing something else. I wouldn't leave this for all the money in the world."

It was a brief respite from a busy night, at least a busy night for the 100th Precinct, and I'll never forget the lush pleasure of the smell of fresh coffee and cigarette smoke and the Atlantic Ocean at daybreak. Even across the chasm of our ages and experience we had become friends.

"Amazing," Larry said, "an airplane falls right out of the sky and you're there to see it."

"Beyond amazing," I told him.

We sat still and quiet, caps off, tunics open, listening to static from the radio.

"You think you'll like the job?" he said.

"I think I'm going to like it a lot."

"Good, that's good. Ya know," he told me, "the beauty of this job is that you get to see and do things, all kinds of things, beyond anything you can imagine. Someday you can tell your grandkids all the things you saw and did."

That's what the job did for you, it gave you a history. It turned you introspective; you learned that life is fragile and fleeting. You saw unbelievable car wrecks—one second life is going well, all it seems is in order, then some drunk comes across the center median and what's left is a blur of blood, bone, and gasoline. Somebody goes crazy in the middle of the night and picks up a knife. The chaos of a family fight, people who had a whole lifetime of feeling pissed off, all that boiling over in one moment of insanity—shrieking, cursing, imploring, assuring, threatening, crying, sad and dangerous people with physical and psychic wounds. When you're new at the job it's not easy to understand any of that, but you try. Soon you understand why the veteran cops laugh and shake their heads and look knowingly at each other. You learn a little more each day: when to talk, when to be silent, how to stand. You try and learn the words that reassure and loosen people up, make them trust you.

"Time goes by," Larry said, "take my word for it, the first ten years in this job drag, but the second ten go like a shot."

At that moment in that sector car, Larry seemed to be far away from me, years. Nevertheless, there was something we shared, a certain kinship and a connection. I see him now, as I watched him then, more than twenty years my senior, his silhouette framed in the sector car window, his tunic open at the collar, a cigarette dangling from the corner of his mouth, his eyes staring at something far beyond anything I could see—maybe some flashbacks, memories, movies going round and round in his head.

the bag—your uniform.

the bow and arrow or rubber gun squad—alcoholic or seriously mentally challenged cops who, the brass thought, were too dangerous to carry a gun. They worked inside the station house, carrying a rubber gun in their holsters.

on the arm—food or merchandise free to cops.

Larry was a wonderful teacher, a thoughtful, remote sort of man, and he lectured me about patrol work, about studying for boss, about making detective, about eating on the arm or for half price, about turning a dollar, about women.

I listened, paid attention, and asked questions. I understood that I could never get from him what I wanted most, enthusiasm to find collars. Larry was indifferent, he'd done it all, been a plainclothes cop awhile, active, made lots of collars, worked gambling enforcement and prostitution. He no longer had an interest in doing any of that.

bagman—a cop who picks up money, usually for a boss.

Larry's Dos and Don'ts

Never allow anyone to threaten you and walk away. Confront them. You need help, call for it. You have to be the master of your foot post or your sector.

Never take traffic money, period. I don't, and I don't work with anyone that does. It's way too dangerous. You never know who's inside a car.

Never get involved with a woman from the precinct; don't dirty where you eat, period.

When there's a fight in a bar and an arrest should be made or a summons issued, call the sergeant. Take care of him; let him handle it.

If a landlord calls for help evicting someone, or a sheriff needs a hand in an eviction and wants you to stand by, they'll offer you twenty bucks. You can take it if you want.

If someone offers you a free meal, that's okay; take it but leave a big tip.

An accident on the highway, you call the tow truck, that's ten, twenty, as much as fifty dollars a hook. It's a standard procedure; take it if you want. I don't, that's traffic money too. If you go for it, make sure you take care of the sergeant on patrol.

Some guy's getting a blow job or getting laid in a car. Say he's parked at the bird sanctuary or one of the beach parking lots, and say he's married and it's not his wife he's fucking. Say he offers you some money. Don't go near it. Some do; I don't, and you shouldn't either.

I carry jumper cables. Say a car breaks down, needs a jump, you give it to them. They offer you a couple of bucks, it's up to you, take it or not.

Don't shoot at anyone running away from you; it may be legal but it's a bad practice.

Ciro closes up his joint, wants someone to walk him to his car. He'll give you a sawbuck, take it, it's okay.

We don't give traffic summonses to firemen, most city employees, and never to another cop or federal agent.

There are guys in this precinct who work traffic on the late tour. They won't go in to heave until they've made a hundred bucks apiece for the night. Let them know right away you don't do that. Make it clear, no problem, okay?

Serious money is made here in the summertime. Playland opens, and there are all kinds of health code violations, all sorts of problems with the bars along the beach. Don't worry about any of that; that's the bosses' business. They have a guy, an ex-detective, that handles all that. You'll never get near it.

Larry always made a few bucks, but then so did every other cop in the precinct. All of them had big families. Larry had four kids, and the wages were low, almost impossible to live on, so they took some money and free food and some discounts from the local merchants. Almost all of them had second jobs. Larry painted houses on his off time, so he never wanted to make an arrest because that meant he'd have to go to court, and he couldn't afford the time.

I was unmarried, young, and living at home, with my future ahead of me. I didn't want to spend my career trying to make a dollar here or there or cruising around until it was time for a nap. I didn't tell Larry that I thought turning a dollar was outrageous; I knew better. I also knew that none of this behavior existed in TPF, and that it was there, in that elite unit, that I would work.

flop house—a precinct where cops who've been in
trouble are sent.

to fly—to be transferred for a short period of time
from one precinct to another.

AS THE WEATHER warmed the precinct became more active, and
the daily boredom dissipated considerably. With the arrival of summer, cops from all over Queens were flying into the 100th Precinct.
Most were uncontrollable, wilder than any of our own, and I
couldn't help but wonder what the department had in mind sending
them to our command. They were drinkers, troublemakers, and
money guys. Their war stories were astounding. It was obvious that
their own commands would not miss them and Rockaway Beach
would have to live with them for three months. The precinct added
more sector cars and assigned the 100th Precinct cops to work with
the summer visitors.

One night I was teamed with a cop from Long Island City who
told me that he would teach me the ways of the world. This guy got
off on hassling lovers: driving into parking lots, sneaking up to cars
like a pervert, shining his flashlight through windows, then banging
on the car roof with his flashlight and screaming about how sodomy
and adultery were crimes in this state. He liked to drink, and he
drank all the time. His drink of choice was Coca-Cola laced with
cheap rye whiskey. After a couple of hours of catching his act, I
asked him to take me back to the precinct.

In the station house I told the desk officer to relieve me from radio car duty. I said I was carsick.

"Carsick?"

"Motion sickness, it happens sometimes."

He assigned me a foot post, and when I came in that morning I
went straight to the roll-call man and told him never to put me with

any of those out-of-command cops again. I started to explain the incidents in the parking lots. When I came to the part about the low crawl up to the lover's car, he shook his head, letting me know he'd heard enough.

"You'll be glad to hear we're getting a group of recruits right out of the academy. I'll assign you one. How's that?"

And so it was that a recruit whose name was Jerry Schremph saved me from working an entire summer with any number of lunatics.

JERRY COULD MAKE anyone feel slow, soft, and lazy. By my recollection, at the time I was twenty-two and he was twenty-four, except in his company I felt half his age. The man was stranger than anyone I had ever met, and let me tell you, the competition was pretty stiff.

We were sitting in a jeep assigned to beach patrol. "Partner," he said, grabbing my wrist and lifting my arm so I could see, "you should be working out, doing curls with some weight, push-ups, and leg raises. You are not very strong."

We had been working together for a month and I didn't know if he believed me anymore; I doubted it, but I always answered, "Sure, sure. I work out whenever I can."

He dipped his chin into his chest and smiled, saying, "Well, you know what they say. They say that hope is the sum and substance of all life."

"Jerry," I said, "you're unusual. You know that, don't you? You are exceptionally weird."

Before joining the department, Jerry did three years in Turkey with the air force and he told me he never once lifted a woman's skirt. I asked him if there were whores in Turkey. He said, "Not many, no, not a whole lot."

"So what about other women, ya know, civilians, women in the towns and cities. There's got to be plenty of women there."

"It's a Muslim country," he told me, "and it's not too cool to fool with a Sunni Muslim woman."

I said, "Yeah, sure, but you were in the military, the air force. Are you going to tell me you didn't find one sweetie?"

He said, "I never looked for a whore."

"You were there, what, two, three years? How'd you stay mellow and manageable?"

"I did meet a girl from a good family," he told me. "She gave me a copy of the Koran."

"Yeah, but you were in the air force. Being in the air force away from home, I figured was dope, sex, and rock and roll."

"The Turks put you in touch with your ancestors you try and pull that crap," he said.

His stomach resembled a small rocky ladder. He did two hundred sit-ups and ran ten miles a day. He was in great shape, and he could quote Thoreau.

The police department was a place full of young and older men, and like anyplace where you go from here to there, assignment to assignment, partner to partner, he could have been just another buddy in a long series of partners who walked with me and rode with me during heated sticky days and chilly nights. Except he wasn't. Jerry Schremph's face, his manner, the way he moved and laughed is scorched into my memory. I can close my eyes now and imagine him standing there watching me, his soft laugh in my head.

"I'm not just any partner," he once told me. "You remember that. You know I can protect you, and no partner you'll ever have can protect you the way I can." He was right. What partner would devote himself to my mental and physical well-being; probably none would dedicate himself the way Jerry did to changing my view of things— both mystical and real. We were about the same age, but he had a long history of travel and enlightenment. I was a neighborhood guy, full of illusions and innocence; he had seen Troy and Istanbul. Jerry had this personal philosophy that the world was full of vermin and violence and evildoing and that some of us were preordained to stand between the righteous and the degenerate. I'd pretend to understand what he meant.

With his fair skin, freckles, and pleasant smile, he sometimes seemed a bit too sweet. But his face would harden and his eyes would get wide when he stared at the troublemaking drunks and the copfighters. In the summer at Rockaway Beach, there were problems for cops everywhere.

Most of the other cops in the precinct wanted to settle in, even the newcomers—especially the newcomers. They all nourished dreams of steady seats in a sector car, free meals, quiet late tours, and tanned and horny cop groupies (a female phenomenon, by the way, that was totally new to me but would not remain so). On late tours, Jerry and I covered the entire precinct; we let everyone else sleep. The old-timers loved us.

We both wanted to be part of the real action in Manhattan, the Bronx, or Brooklyn. Neither of us had joined the police department to sit on our asses. It was not some vague yearning; we worked at it all the time, made arrests whenever we could, covered as many jobs as possible. We were putting our hearts and souls into being good cops.

So there we were, sitting in a sector car, two rookies just months out of the academy. I was the recorder, cap off, my head back, my arms spread across the top of the seat. Jerry was behind the wheel, driving, speed-rapping about skydiving, how it was the greatest kick ever.

"A bird, you spin through the sky like a hawk, at one with your God and the cosmos." He almost screamed with glee.

I was playing with the radio, turning up the squelch, reminding him that we'd missed lunch.

"Whadaya say, come with me next weekend. You'll love it. I promise you'll get off on this."

"Bullshit. Not next weekend, not ever."

"Try it. Give it a shot. Live a little."

I always figured that what you did with yourself in the solitude of your head was nobody's business. In the solitude of my head, I was afraid of heights and hated airplanes.

It was around two in the afternoon, a couple of hours more or less to go. Central came on and told us to check, see if an ambulance and oxygen were needed at a cottage near the beach.

We hit the siren and lights—something we did every chance we got.

A seventyish woman stood in the cottage doorway, throwing her arms out, then pulling at her hair, jerking her head back and calling out, "Hurry, please hurry. Tom," she screamed, "Tommy."

I pushed past her into a dark kitchen lit only by a TV that squatted on the counter. The volume was off and the shades were drawn. I couldn't hear any sound, not the noise from the street, nothing.

Tom's elbows were on the table, his chin resting on his fists. When I walked toward him, he pitched forward, his face slamming onto the tabletop, making a horrible splat. I lifted him from under the armpits and laid him on the green linoleum floor. A scar ran the length of his cheek, dividing it. His eyes were closed tightly and he was bare-chested and covered with tattoos. Over his right nipple was "Death," in the center of his chest "Before," and over his left nipple was "Dishonor."

A marine, Jerry said. Then he ran from the room, telling me he was going to call for an ambulance with oxygen.

For a fraction of a second I focused on Tom's motionless chest, his eyes shut with pain and fear. Within that moment of time I wallowed in thinking myself a distinguished healer. I pinched his nose, opened his mouth, removed his dentures, and blew. I remember no taste, nothing; only a sound, a deep hollow whispering from him. In that kitchen there was no air and I sweated freely. I blew into his mouth and pounded on his chest and felt movement from him, and then a hand, Jerry's hand, his lips next to my ear, his breath on my neck, his voice a soft, soft whisper. "I called for an ambulance, but I think it's too late."

I shook him off and kept working, harder, faster, until soon it seemed even to me that I had crawled to the very edge of madness. Two hands on my shoulders now, yet I didn't turn. I was with Tom, fighting to keep him in this world. Then an unfamiliar voice talking to me with genuine concern and tenderness.

"Let me take over. I've got oxygen here. You've done good, kid, all you can. Let me take over now."

Jerry stood on the porch of the cottage smoothing out the page in his memorandum book. Emergency Service officers, the sergeant and ambulance attendants, were with Tom in the kitchen. It was a fly sergeant, not from the 100th, one of the summer hummers from outside our command.

"You did real good work in there," Jerry said. "All that could be expected and then some."

"Sure," I told him, "whatever."

The door swung open and the Emergency Service officer stepped out. His name was Paul and he carried the oxygen tank in one hand and a clipboard in the other and said to me, "You know, the old guy was a DOA. What I'm trying to say," he said, "what I'm trying to tell you, rookie, is that you were blowing for a half hour into the mouth of a dead man."

"Get in here," the sergeant called from inside the cottage.

Jerry and I walked into the kitchen, and I could see that something was going on with the sergeant; he was on his knees, kneeling next to Tom. The pockets of Tom's slacks had been turned out.

"One of you," he said, "go into the living room and sit with the wife. You," he said to me, "you get me some soap." Jerry gave me one of his cool half smiles, and I got nervous because he seemed to know something and I didn't know nearly so much as he did. There was a language that he and the sergeant understood, that Jerry probably picked up in the air force, the same language the sergeant had learned in the street. *Language*, I thought, *is the key*.

When I gave the sergeant the soap we did not speak. He rubbed the soap onto Tom's fingers. There were two rings there. I watched the way he rubbed the soap around those rings and slid them from Tom's hand. He told me to make sure that Tom's wife stayed in the living room because she would not grasp that part of his job. It was one of the things I'd learned at the academy, the sergeant at the scene of a DOA is responsible for safeguarding valuables. What I couldn't understand was why this guy, this sergeant, summer visitor to our precinct, couldn't tell Tom's wife his responsibilities. Tom's wife, I figured, would understand. I realized what he was doing, and I looked past him, over his shoulder at the TV on the counter. All I thought about was the way it was with us, me and Tom. I saw his face closed down, his eyes shut like a pair of clams. The sergeant looked up and smiled at me a moment, waiting, I figured, for a sign from me that we were making some sort of an agreement. He turned from me to look at Tom, then back to me again, his face now a question.

Later I remember sitting in the cruiser, staring out over the ocean, Jerry trying to tell me again that the world was full of evil and violence and that some of us were destined to stand between the righteous and evildoers.

I told him I was glad, so fucking happy to be away from that cottage and that sergeant, away from Tom. I said I felt like a vulture. But how could I have stopped that guy? What was there for me to do? I told Jerry about the guy from Long Island City who crept up on lovers in parked cars. I said I didn't do anything but turn and run.

Jerry came out of his mystic bag, telling me that there were demons and shitheads in this world that you can't run away from. "Demons and shitheads," he said, "must be faced head-on."

"I hate it when you talk like that. What do you mean? Be clear."

"That sergeant, the cop in the parking lot, they sound like bad guys. But I'm telling you, they ain't nothing compared to what can come crawling out of the woodwork in this here city if you let them."

"I don't want to have to deal with any of that," I told him. "It's not me."

He half laughed and waved me away saying, "You'll learn. You'll have to."

"And what about you? I didn't see you charging in there like the Light Brigade."

"I didn't see the sergeant do anything wrong. If I had it would have been a different story. And that guy, the cop from Long Island City, if it was me, I'da put an end to his bullshit real quick."

I didn't believe him. In those days—and it hasn't changed all that much—a young cop did not stand up and face off with an older cop in a situation like that. It just didn't happen.

> 10-13—an "assist patrolman" radio call; no other call
> got half the response of a 10-13.

The Russians were moving missiles into Cuba. In June, the Supreme Court banned school prayer, and James Meredith was preparing himself to be the first black to register at the University of Mississippi.

Jerry and I, along with everyone else in Rockaway Beach, detected not one sign of the stirring civil rights movement. Other than a job or two that took us to Arverne, ours was an all-white world.

I had convinced Jerry to place his name on the TPF waiting list too, but our hopes were beginning to fade. We made a stolen car arrest and I called TPF to let them know. A burglary arrest and then some assault collars—I called TPF after each one. We had the precinct clerical man write TPF a letter outlining our heads-up police work and requesting interviews for both of us. No response.

Jerry figured it was because we were both under six feet tall. I didn't know what to think.

It was midsummer and party time at the beach; jukeboxes were playing the Twist and Mashed Potato and Elvis's "Return to Sender" and my personal favorite, Ray Charles doing "I Can't Stop Loving You." The 100th Precinct was hopping.

Jerry and I tooled around the boardwalk and beach in a jeep that we were constantly burying in the sand and having to have towed out. We were having a blast.

Cop-fighters were everywhere, and strangely enough, they were mostly relatives of other cops and firemen. All the saloons along Rockaway Beach Boulevard and the White House Tavern on 110th Street (a huge open place with a deck that exited right onto the beach) could be counted on for at least one signal 10-13 every other day. A case of beer and the hot sun brought all the sentimental Irish singers out swinging.

One afternoon when I was on duty at a school crossing, watching a group of summer-school kids and their flirtatious, dark-eyed mothers, Jerry called to me from the radio car. First he said that there was a fight at the Emerald Isle. A moment later he shouted that it was a 10-13 and we were off.

These characters were Teamsters, ironworkers, and city firemen; they loved to fight, and most of them—drunk or sober—could hit like mules. You had to watch your ass or you'd end up on your back with a broken jaw while listening to the strains of "Irish Soldier Boy."

That afternoon they were going full bore, and it would take a dozen cops swinging sticks and blackjacks to rein them in. City employees were involved, and one or two were sent to the hospital. In the end no arrests were made, and the sergeant worked out the particulars with the bar owner. Seconds after the fight, there was booze and beer all over the bar, with Irish music blaring and pretty women dancing—alone, in pairs, or in groups of three. The women enchanted me; a couple asked us if we'd come back after work, but Jerry expressed no interest whatsoever.

The school crossing was a fixer, so we scooted on back. You never leave a fixer for any reason, except, of course, a 10-13. I was standing in the intersection crossing the last of the kids. Jerry was talking to a half-dozen pretty Puerto Rican mommas when he called me over.

On the beach and in the bars, Jerry would affect a casual, blasé attitude toward the airline stewardesses, college girls, and nurses who seemed to be horny, out on the make, and everywhere. But show him a Latin lady and he'd light up. And on that afternoon we were surrounded.

He pointed to a dark and brooding but pretty woman who was standing in the doorway of a standard New York City public housing project, a building of orange-red brick with heavy doors and lightless hallways in which the air was always heavy with the cooking smells of fiery bean and pork dishes and the music loud, a wonderful commingling of salsa with Sam Cooke and Diana Ross.

"That woman," Jerry said, "told me she wants to talk to you."

When I spoke to her she told me she had been a witness to an arrest Jerry and I had made a week before in front of the project. She said she watched me every day crossing the children for summer school. She said she had some serious problems of her own and asked if I'd help her. She said I should come up to her apartment because she didn't want to be seen talking to a cop in the street. Her English was practically nonexistent, and I had to struggle with the dozen or so words I knew in Spanish.

We ended up in the kitchen of her apartment. Her neighbor, she said, was baby-sitting her children and her husband was out partying. I remember pale light coming into the room through curtained windows, the smell of strong coffee, candles burning, and the aroma of cocoa butter.

She talked very quickly in broken English, telling me about her husband, how he spent every Friday night and all day Saturday get-

ting drunk and gambling at a place she described as a casino. It was a
house near the beach. A black Cuban named Felix, who came from
the Bronx, ran it. She was full of anger, telling me how her family
was suffering. I remember that she had a gorgeous smile and an
amazing body for a mother of four.

Her husband's name was Luis, and he blew his entire paycheck
every week. When she'd ask him for the money he no longer had,
he'd beat her.

"Can you help me?"

"Yes."

"*Por favor.*"

"I'll help."

She took a pad and wrote the address and apartment number of
the building where the gambling took place. "Good," I told her,
"good."

As I sat and copied her notes into my memo book she left the
room. I remember a candle in a jelly jar in front of a statue of the
crucified Christ in the kitchen window.

She called to me and I got up from the table and walked to a bedroom where I found her naked on the bed.

I was twenty-two years old, already awed by the things I'd seen
and done. Outside this job yawned the great, horrible abyss of the
ordinary life. From where I stood, there could be no doubt: I had the
greatest job in the world.

> PMD—Public Morals Division; plainclothes cops who
> investigate gambling, prostitution, and all the
> violations of the public morals code. They are not
> detectives, not a part of the Detective Bureau, but
> simply police officers who work in civilian clothes.

The house was in Arverne, a run-down wood-frame Victorian at
the end of a street that dead-ended at the beach. For a few nights we

played hide-and-seek with the gamblers. On our next set of day tours we drove straight to the building. Jerry went into the basement, and I went up the fire escape. Looking through a window I could see it all, and it was exactly the way my Latin lady from the projects had painted it. I saw a craps table and a roulette wheel; the place was a casino.

Uniform cops don't get involved in such things, so we followed the rules and turned in a report to the lieutenant on the desk. It was his job to notify the Public Morals Division. He took the report and smiled at us saying, "You guys are kidding me, right?"

"It's there," I told him. "We've seen it."

It needs to be said here that nationwide, the units that investigate gambling are historically the most corrupt. Across the country these units are required to enforce laws that nobody wants enforced—against gambling, prostitution, after-hour clubs, and so on. Often the type of report we turned in went nowhere other than some PMD cop's collection files.

A PMD folktale:

Three PMD cops are killed in a car wreck. They go to meet Saint Peter who is guarding the pearly gates. Peter, they say, we've got to get into heaven. He'll never let you in, Peter tells them, He knows what you do. Ask Him again, Peter, plead our case, we're good men. Sure we've done some things we shouldn't have, but we're good men. I'll try, Peter tells them. Peter tells God about the three PMD men at the pearly gates. Sure, God says, I'll be glad to give them a second chance. Let them in. Peter leaves and returns a short time later saying, they're gone. The policemen? asks God. Yes, says Peter, and so are the pearly gates.

— BRIAN MCDONALD, *My Father's Gun*

shoe fly—a ranking supervisor who investigates police misconduct.

A week went by, two weeks, a month, nothing happened, and on every Friday night the casino's going strong. Whenever the woman from the projects saw me, she'd tell me that her husband was still losing his paycheck. She'd ask if I'd like to come up to her apartment for coffee, and then she'd whine that her husband told her the casino was protected, the owner paid the police.

The lieutenant on the desk laughed. "I turned it in," he told me. "You've done your job and I've done my job. We can't do anything more."

Then one afternoon, while waiting for service at a gas station not far from where I lived, I met a man named Joseph McGovern. Joseph McGovern was an important cop, an inspector who worked in the police commissioner's confidential investigating unit. Irish Catholic, tough as nails, disliked and mistrusted, a shoe fly. Who knew? I thought he was terrific and we exchanged cop stories. He lived not far from me in Queens and had an amazingly clear view of police work. I remember we went for a ride in his immaculately clean station wagon and he gave me a lecture on his immaculately clean view of the job. The man had a Bible on the dashboard of his car.

Not thinking twice, I told him about the casino, and how I'd turned in a report a month ago.

"How long ago?"

"A month."

"Tell your captain you're a friend of mine, tell him that you called me, tell him you gave me the information too."

When I did, I thought my captain would have a coronary.

"You did what? You called who? Are you fucking nuts?" Captain Mink wasn't happy. "Well," I said, "it's been over a month since I turned in the report." The capacity to appear naive, unsure, and innocent helped.

"Inspector McGovern is a friend of yours?"

"I suppose you could say friend," I said, hoping he wouldn't ask me too many particulars about the inspector. I didn't know much about him, but neither did my captain.

The casino was closed down the following week. And a week later, Captain Mink called Jerry and me into his office to tell us what a great job we'd done, how proud he was of us—the first gambling arrest of any consequence in the 100th Precinct in a decade. At some point he asked what he could do for us. Did we have an interest in a steady seat in a sector car? I told Captain Mink that we were both interested in the Tactical Patrol Force.

"Let me ask you something," he said.

A long moment of silence.

"Do you understand what TPF is all about? Steady six at night to two in the morning, no home, no precinct to call your own. Going from one high-crime area to another, every night a hassle. The thing is, they pay you the same if you're riding in a jeep along the beach or ducking bottles and bricks in Fort Apache, the Bronx."

"With due respect, captain, we know all that."

Another long moment of silence.

I remember the way he smiled at us, somehow proud that he'd been our commanding officer. "TPF is a squared-away unit," he said. "Knowing you two, you'll love it. It's the real deal, the genuine article. You want to be knock-around cops, TPF is the place to do it.

"By the way," he said, "you're both six feet tall, aren't you?"

A week later the orders were cut and the department Teletype carried the news. Jerry and I had been transferred to the Tactical Patrol Force, Jerry to Manhattan South and Brooklyn; me to Manhattan North and the Bronx.

When we were cleaning out our lockers at the 100th, we tried to be casual about it. I told him I'd call Borelli, the clerical man, to see if he could help us get assigned together. Jerry told me he'd already done that and was told we'd work together more than it appeared we would. TPF was a highly mobile unit and our initial assignments really didn't mean a whole lot.

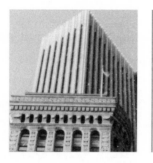 COMMANDOS

The Tactical Patrol Force had been formed in 1959 and was the creation of a police commissioner named Steven P. Kennedy. At first there were thoughts to name it simply Special Services, but having SS on the collars of New York City cops' uniforms would have been less than wise. Their nickname back then was Kennedy's Commandos.

Kennedy was one of the first police leaders to sense the youth rebellion that was emerging in America. He didn't like it. "Apply the law and apply it vigorously" was his stated philosophy. "It's not your job to become bemused with the vagaries of the 'why, oh why school'," he told cops. "The policeman has a job to do and if he does it honestly and intelligently, he gains respect. That's a damned sight more important than being liked." Recalling his own youth, Kennedy noted that the cops on the beat had never asked him, "What are your needs? . . . Are you happy?" It was, "Look, bud, do this." And if you didn't do it you got belted.

—JAMES LARDNER AND THOMAS REPETTO, *NYPD*

They say he was a real tough guy, not at all liked by the rank and file. Educated late in life, the sort of man who got off on the threatening impressiveness of his own vocabulary.

skel (from skeleton)—a wino, junkie, or just about anyone who is a potential problem in the street.

yom (from the Italian word melanzana, "eggplant," spoken phonetically moo-lan-yom)—a black person.

My first night in TPF, the day had been sunny and warm and I remember how we assembled, not in a precinct but on a street corner. I remember the tenements—run-down, ancient, sad-looking buildings—and the people giving us impatient, arrogant, and unbelieving looks. We thought we were there to help, but they saw it as an invasion of their neighborhood. Back then I didn't understand the rage I saw in their faces, the contempt. My father would have understood it; maybe he would have glanced around and understood what all those angry faces were thinking.

Werner Huber, a cop who was born in Germany, said, "A sniper on the roof of any of these buildings and we're fucked."

"Skel city," another of the cops said.

In TPF there were no school crossings, no aided cases, no guarding DOAs or broken storefront glass. In TPF there was only aggressive patrol.

Later that night, I was standing on a rooftop with a cop whose name was Pete Schmidt, both of us new to TPF, both of us picking up bottles and bricks and tossing them into the rear yard of the building. We were on Powell Street and Lavonia Avenue in the 73rd Precinct.

Brownsville, Brooklyn, not all that far from where my father was born. Only a few blocks from where, as a kid, my mother would drag me shopping for fruit and vegetables, going from pushcart to pushcart along Belmont, Blake, and Pitken Avenues. Into the dark basement shops of those buildings, buying packages of underwear and socks, the Jewish merchants seeing her coming, yelling her name, Lucy, Lucy. My mother's name was Lucy—Lucy Leuci—always good for a laugh. She had the smallest feet, so tiny she couldn't find her size in an everyday shoe store. But they had them, the Jewish shopkeepers had samples; samples came in my mother's size. They loved seeing her, shouted, "Lucy!" when she walked down the street. For a small woman my mother had a remarkable figure.

Now, all these years later, Pete Schmidt and I were standing at the edge of the roof of a six-story tenement in one of the most squalid and dilapidated ghettos of New York City. It was a long way from Playland and the Atlantic Ocean, but right next door to my childhood.

Pete was a big guy, six-one or -two, bulging with muscles. Before his assignment to TPF he'd worked the 7-5, a precinct that adjoined the 73rd. Pete knew all about the bottles and bricks that had been stashed along the parapet of a roof, knew that it would be wise to get rid of them.

Off the roof and onto the street, we patrolled the neighborhood. It was still light out and the night was fairly warm. There were people everywhere, standing on corners, sitting on stoops, angry faces lounging in doorways, all of them pissed off and put out, even the women. Nobody smiled.

What I tried to do was look friendly and slightly self-effacing, like I'm a nice guy, just here to do a job. Need me, call me; I'll be here for you. That kind of thing.

They didn't like us, simple as that. They felt we were intruding in their lives. And we were. TPF didn't only patrol the streets—we went into the alleyways, the basements, onto the rooftops, through the tenement hallways. It wasn't long before you realized that it didn't matter to these ghetto people what color you were. A cop could be white or black or Hispanic, they called us all pig and hated us because we were blue. This was not the 100th Precinct.

For part of the night three of us walked the post. I had Pete Schmidt on my right, a guy named Dave Jackel on my left. TPF was home to many German American cops. Dave was a student—he attended Columbia University during the day and worked TPF at night. A bright guy, and man was he big. Dave went about six-five, 250 or 260. With Pete at six-two and me, we made quite an interesting-looking trio walking down the street.

Later that night I found myself alone, standing on the corner of Powell and Lavonia, an infamous intersection, but I didn't know it then. What I remember most are the alleyways, rooftops, and backyards of the tenements, scary stuff, the sounds and smells and always the music, the sweet sounds of salsa and Motown wafting up to the rooftops, how it made the scary stuff go away.

Things happen quickly in the street, and you really don't know what you're doing most of the time, you're just doing, and afterward you can tell yourself any kind of bullshit you want, say you handled it well, it didn't bother you one single bit, that you loved doing this or that, that you behaved heroically, and that you're proud of yourself. Hanging around with other cops telling stories, I'd say, "You would not believe this shit" after I'd been in the job awhile, but that first night in TPF I felt like a total rookie.

A bottle came off a rooftop and hit about ten feet away. I walked out into the street and looked up. Somewhere up there, behind a parapet, concealed and silent, someone was using me for target practice. When a brick landed and exploded about twenty feet away, I went to the call box. The TPF lieutenant told me to patrol under the fire escapes. "Hang near the building line," he told me, "and don't call again unless it's an emergency." He said he was busy.

I got off the phone, walked about five steps, and got hit. It was a flashlight battery and it hit me square in the center of the back. I felt a sharp pain and thought I had been shot. Back at the call box I told the lieutenant, "Lieutenant," I said, trying to sound cool and under control but knowing my voice was full of fear and trembling, "they're throwing shit at me, for Christ sake. They hit me."

"Get in here," he said. "Get in here right now." His name was Epstein, one of the original TPF cops. When I got into the precinct he stood behind his desk and handed me a World War One helmet with a bulls-eye target on the top. He was smiling, one of those hard, ironic smiles that discards any and all good news. It was like hearing him say, "Now get the fuck back out there and stop bothering me."

Later that night I asked Dave Jackel what the hell he thought was going on.

"Going on?"

"You know, around here. They all seem to hate us. I mean all of them."

Dave thought about it a moment. "Yeah, well," he said finally, "if you want my opinion, there's shit going on in these neighborhoods. Shit none of us understand."

The next night I couldn't wait to get back out there. This time I ran up to a rooftop followed by Pete Schmidt. As I opened the roof landing door, I said, "Pete, tell you what, I catch some motherfucker up here, I'm gonna throw his ass off the roof." Three inches shorter than anyone else in the outfit, I thought it was important that I at least sound tough.

"Well," Pete said, "then you'd better slow down, you're gonna need my help."

We threw all the bottles, bricks, and flashlight batteries into the rear yard, and when we got to the roof of the building from which the bottle, brick, and flashlight battery had been thrown at me the night before, I tore down a few TV antennas and threw them into the rear yard too, saying, "Man, fuck these people, throwing shit at me."

Then I spotted a kid two or three buildings from where we were standing. He saw us, dropped the brick he was carrying, and took off back into the building. He was flying down the steps. I knew I'd never catch him, so I waited for him to hit the first floor and threw a battery at him. Missed. Maybe he was the sniper from the night before, maybe he wasn't. It didn't matter, I wanted some token of revenge.

> shooting gallery—an apartment, a basement, or the
> roof landing of a building, a place where junkies
> gather to buy drugs and shoot up heroin.

Back on the roof landing Pete pointed out all the empty glassine envelopes scattered about, the bottle caps, their bottoms blackened from where a match had been put to them, the half-empty paper cups of water. Every roof landing on the block was a shooting gallery and so were the basements. The sorrow, violence, and crime we associated with the heroin epidemic had already sunk its claws deep into the heart of Brownsville.

During this time I was still living at home, and the breakfast discussions with my father were becoming more and more heated.

"The yoms, Pop, they're crazy, they live like animals and throw shit at us from rooftops—I mean bottles and bricks. You know what a bottle or brick would do to you thrown from six stories up?"

"*Yom* is a dumb word spoken by stupid people. Don't use that word in this house."

"They're crazy, Pop."

"They're not crazy, they're poor and oppressed and they're angry. They take their anger into the streets. And let me tell you something else, it's going to get worse."

My father was kin to all the demoralized and poor and out-of-work peoples of the world; his instinctive belief in the class struggle drove me up the wall.

"The bosses and landlords screw these people over in ways you could never understand," he said.

"C'mon, you have to see how they live."

"I know how they live. You think we lived any differently?"

"Sure you did."

He smiled.

"Drugs, Dad. There are drugs everywhere—on the rooftops, in the basements, in the hallways. And where do they get the money for those drugs? They rob, they steal, they burglarize. The women are prostitutes. It's a hellhole."

"And, Mister Lawman, who do you think brought those drugs around?"

A shrug from me and a smile from him. "Everybody's fault but theirs, right, Pop? That's the way it is, everyone else's fault."

"I wish you had stayed in school" is what he told me.

In any number of important ways my father and I were very different people. He was an absolutely straight shooter, a devoted family man, and very much in love with my mother. As for me, I thought of myself as a player. I loved women—all kinds and all the time—and, if you want to know the truth, doubted that I could be monogamous. Nonetheless, I had been dating a terrific woman. Her name was Regina Manarin, and although I was too young, too self-involved, too selfish and wild to get married, I knew it was time I grew up.

"You're a mess," my father told me. "You'll always be a mess. You need someone like Gina. Don't screw this up."

Gina was born and raised in Germany of Italian parents; she spoke Italian, German, some Spanish and French. She introduced me to classical music and museums. I tried explaining baseball and football and played my Motown records for her. In May of 1963 I married Regina Manarin and left my father's house forever. It was a beautiful ceremony, my cousin Anita Caruso, a woman with a trained and magnificent voice, sang "Ave Maria."

IN LATE JUNE my TPF unit was ordered to the United Nations Plaza. The city was being racked by civil rights demonstrations; TPF was on the fly every day.

Young, yes, and according to my father politically uninformed, but even so, the protesters, hundreds of them, seemed to me to be out of control and about ready to metastasize into an all-out riot. Mixed among the pro- and anti-Castro Cubans were members of the Congress of Racial Equality (CORE) and Students for a Democratic Society (SDS) and the curious bedfellows the Black Muslims and the NAACP.

I remember thinking, *Who the hell started all this and when and why?* They seemed divided on every issue except their clear hatred of the police. *Amazing,* I thought, *a new wrinkle.* I had never seen anything like this before.

It started with a little pushing and shoving, some shouting and name-calling. Suddenly it was no longer a peaceful demonstration. These guys were serious. You couldn't help but feel you were in personal danger. Every cop there did. Lieutenant Epstein told me to hustle over the few blocks to the 15th Precinct. Make sure all was quiet there, he said. "Take a radio, stay there, and make sure you let me know what's going on."

Other than two cops behind the desk, the precinct was deserted. I remember standing out in front of the station house, the door locked and bolted behind me. The street was empty. Then a sound, a kind of howling, followed all at once by a massive crowd turning the corner and charging straight at me. I remember the fear in my chest, then it burned down to a smoldering pain in my stomach. There were no cops around, and it seemed to me that a thousand of these wacko characters were running straight at me, shouting, and all pissed off about something.

I called the lieutenant, held the radio in the air, saying, "Can you hear this?"

I imagined myself strung up in front of the precinct, and made up all kinds of crazy things I could do to drive them off, things I could not do. They were getting closer, and soon they were on me. They gathered in front of the station house, inching closer, hundreds of them calling me pig, my children piglets, and my wife a sow. My instincts were telling me to just take off and run like hell, but if I did that I could see the sorry details of my own future, a *Daily News* headline "Coward Cop Runs Off."

It was just about then that I saw four mounted cops turn the corner and gallop toward the station like the cavalry. It was a relief, sure, but it was much more than that. By that time people were pulling at me, grabbing my stick and radio, and I was moving around trying to keep my feet. *It's just a fight*, I told myself, *just another fight*. I was backed up against the door, my cap was gone, my shirt was torn; someone had tried to pull my shield off.

All of a sudden demonstrators were literally flying off the stoop of the station house. I stood still for a second and saw the giant brown rump of a horse, spinning, doing some kind of rodeo trick. I had grabbed onto one guy, his head bobbing, his shoulders rolling, a fighter, spitting, calling me motherfucker. He was big and strong and I was doing all I could just to hold on to him. Then all at once he flew from my hand, banged up against the wall of the building, the horse's ass in his chest. A smiling cop looked down at me, his face full and bright, his uniform sparkling, his boots and putties gleaming. I don't recall what he said exactly, but it was something like "Hey, pally, this is your collar, you got this asshole." The cop's name was Joe Nunziata, and he would be the most charismatic man I was ever to know. Back then he was just glorious, shouting at me, "Keep your head, stay cool, cuz."

"Some believe that the demonstrations may have passed, I tell you that preparations for 1964 are well under way, more and more and more and more."

—DR. MARTIN LUTHER KING JR., 1963

"Make sure you keep your head up and your eyes open, we have no friends out there."

— SERGEANT PETE BURKE, TPF

We didn't know it, but we were in the swelling core of change. The Vietnam War was intensifying, and in the city the flow of drugs and street crime was growing. The five New York City Mafia families were prosperous and strong. Tensions abounded everywhere—over the war, over civil rights, you name it, there was a demonstration for or against it, most of it undirected, some of it highly organized.

Police were the focus of everyone's attention. In the city and across the nation police officers were ambushed and even assassinated. All in all it was a fertile time for a closed society like the police department to become even more so. The world around you seemed like a rotten bunch of sold-out and whacked-out freaks. In such menacing times it seemed you could trust no one but other cops. The police were being savaged—attacked on the street, by the media, and by politicians who would rather be heard than right. They debased us and darkened us and ultimately united us behind a blue wall of silence. In our view, it did not take a whole lot of experience, seasoning, or education to know exactly where the true villains resided.

GINA AND I moved into a garden apartment two blocks from my parents' house. Though the notion of marriage was scary to me, little had changed. I was working steady, six at night to two in the morning. Gina would leave the apartment early, take a bus to a train to her job in Manhattan, and we barely saw each other. Disagreements between my father and me were growing, so there were fewer breakfasts.

Usually around four-thirty, Pete Schmidt and another TPF cop whose name was Henry Schroder picked me up for another night of combat in one of the ghetto precincts. When the tour ended we would have liked nothing better than to stop, unwind, and have a few beers. But we traveled in uniform and the tour ended too late for us to hit a bar or club. We found our relaxation in the middle of the night—driving home, pulling off the road, and shooting at rats that ran in hordes among the sawgrass and cattails along the Cross Island Parkway.

"Oh, you know, we're heading into nut country today."
— PRESIDENT JACK KENNEDY TO HIS WIFE, JACKIE,
NOVEMBER 22, 1963

I remember it was a payday, sunny. I was driving along the West Side Highway to the TPF office in the 4th Precinct. The music stopped and the announcer broke in, "There have been shots fired in Dallas. President Kennedy's motorcade has been shot at."

When I got to the office everyone was standing still, staring out windows, staring at each other. Somebody said, "Fucking rebel cocksuckers."

"What happened?"

"They killed Kennedy."

I got my check, left the office, and got back into my car. I was working in East Harlem that night, in the 23rd Precinct. I pulled over somewhere near the UN Plaza. A few months back I had watched him step from his limousine on his way to address the United Nations. To me he was golden—young, proud, and as handsome as any movie star. On that day I thought he had waved at me. He did, I'm sure he did.

I was so full of rage and agony and grief that all I could do was weep. I was positive it was those smug right-wing assholes who were responsible. The same buffed, thin-lipped characters who had been coming around at demonstrations handing out John Birch Society literature to any cop dumb enough to take it. I had never felt such pain, such a sense of loss. They had killed my president, those bastards. They murdered the Catholic golden boy.

THROUGH THE REMAINING part of that year and most of the next, I worked brutal precincts in Manhattan North and the South Bronx, dealing with an avalanche of street crime, seeing the human condition at its worst. What I remember of those times is a series of arrests, basements and rear yards and rooftops, an ever-increasing number of demonstrations and mini-riots. I was self-absorbed, collars were all that mattered, you looked at me crooked I'd come down like the hammers of hell. With Pete Schmidt and Dave Jackel to back me up, I led the squad in arrests.

Jerry Schremph was working Manhattan South and Brooklyn, and our paths rarely crossed. One night in late April, after I'd made a minor drug collar on a rooftop in the South Bronx, I picked up my assignment for the following week. We were going to Brooklyn, where I'd work with Jerry again. I telephoned him at home and we laughed, talked about routine stuff, collars and fights and women. Getting away from the beach and into the action had been worth it. Yes, sure it had. We were both proud of the fact that we were doing genuine work because it meant we were involved, doing all the things good cops should do. He was getting married to a Latin lady. He said she was intelligent and gorgeous. His parents were giving him a bit of a hard time, but he was sure it would pass. In time it would pass.

I told Jerry I'd see him the day after tomorrow because the next day I was going to court. I told him to try and get along without me.

Pete telephoned me sometime around ten o'clock the following night and told me to sit down. Along with everyone else in our squad, Pete had gone to Brooklyn.

"I'm sitting. What's going on?"

"You're sitting?"

"Yeah, what the hell is going on?"

Jerry had come out of a diner. A cop had stopped a car and was preparing to write a summons. The driver was racing his engine.

Jerry walked to the driver's window and reached into the car to turn off the ignition key. The driver dropped the car into gear and sped off. You know Jerry, an athlete, a strong, hardy guy, he grabbed and held on to something inside the car and rode it. The driver didn't believe it; no one believed Jerry could ride that car at high speed down Pennsylvania Avenue in Brooklyn. But he did. He rode it two, three blocks, the driver swerving, speeding, trying to throw him off. Jerry's arms were hard and strong, much stronger than they looked. It was seven o'clock at night and all kinds of people were watching from the sidewalk, saw the speeding car with the cop hanging on its side like some sort of circus stunt. The driver pulled that car into the path of an oncoming bus, slammed the side of the car off the bus. He crushed Jerry.

Noooooooooo.

Gina grabbed me. She was weeping too.

I knew Jerry's mind, and I knew he saw that bus coming, the impending doom. I wondered if he had the time to think, *Isn't this incredible, this is where it ends.* I don't think so, at least I hope not. Jerry Schremph was a hero. I wished then, as I do now, that he had been something else, anything but a hero. I remember thinking that if I had been there . . . if only I were there. I sat on the edge of the bed, weeping uncontrollable sobs full of rage and agony. I remember thinking, *What could I have done?* What could anyone have done?

God's will.

Thanks, Lord, thanks again.

COMBAT

junkie on a mission, flying to the cooker—drug addict walking quickly along the street carrying drugs.

cooker—a bottle cap or spoon in which powdered heroin mixed with water is heated before it is injected.

car booster—someone who breaks in and steals from parked cars.

Into the heat of the summer of 1964, we continued to work in East Harlem and the South Bronx. Spurred on by Jerry's death and a firm belief that we were at war in the streets, we charged through neighborhoods, over rooftops, through backyards, raising hell. I made scores of arrests.

There was a change in the air, growing tensions in the street. We could feel it and see it on the faces of the people in the neighborhoods, but none of us could have imagined how violent those changes would be.

Some of us were brutal and intolerant—of course we were; I

don't know how anyone could expect us to be otherwise. Brutality was all around us—it absorbed us, inhabited us, and made us feel a kinship that is unknown to outsiders. If you learned anything, you'd learn just this much: you'd never be quite as happy or feel quite as safe as you were during the hours that you spent with your partners.

I had taken the police test when I was nineteen, became a policeman when I was twenty-one. I was a cop, not a great cop but a cop, united by that fact to other cops, even those in other cities.

The changes in the street came on gradually at first, then more quickly. Smiles that had once been on the faces of people you'd see walking or hanging on corners had morphed into sneers and outright confrontation over the most minor incident. You'd walk past a group of kids sitting on a stoop in East Harlem, smile, say howyadoin', and get "Who is he fucking smiling at?" I'd stand there looking at them, wondering what the hell was going on. Diana Ross and the Supremes were singing, "Where Did Our Love Go?" and I was staring at rooftops wondering when the bottles and bricks were coming.

> gypsy gun—a nonissued or unregistered gun, a
> Saturday night special. Such a gun could be used, or
> simply dropped at a crime scene.

It was a Thursday in July when off-duty police lieutenant Thomas Gilligan became embroiled in a street dispute with a group of young blacks. One of them, a fifteen-year-old named James Powell, came at the lieutenant with a knife. Gilligan fired a warning shot, but Powell kept on coming, the great rage eating at him. Gilligan fired two more shots and killed the boy.

> On Saturday, demonstrators gathered in central Harlem outside
> the funeral home where Powell was being mourned. Then they

marched to the local precinct, though the shooting had occurred well beyond its boundaries. On their arrival they were met by barricades and a cordon of cops. A delegation entered the station in order to demand Lieutenant Gilligan's suspension from the force. The Inspector in charge replied that the D.A. was investigating the case. He gave the leaders a bullhorn to address the crowd and calm the tension. But as they spoke, bricks rained down from the roofs of nearby buildings. Some policemen rushed up to the rooftops while other cops struggled with demonstrators and made fourteen arrests. The inspector ordered his men to move the crowd back. Two blocks away, at 125th Street and Seventh Avenue, black nationalists were holding their usual Saturday night rally. The marchers and the rally-goers merged; by 10:00 P.M., a thousand people were milling about, many shouting insults at police and whites in general. A compact car with a white couple in it was surrounded and damaged by demonstrators before the driver managed to zoom off.

—JAMES LARDNER AND THOMAS REPPETTO, *NYPD*

to pop someone—to shoot someone.

When all of this started happening, I was on a rooftop on 124th Street near Lenox Avenue. It was sometime around 10:00 P.M., and new TPF cop Ronnie Heffernan and I were clearing bottles and bricks. It was an ugly night, hot and muggy. For the first moment or two I thought the sound was firecrackers; it couldn't be gunshots, there were so many. "Firecrackers?" I said.

Ronnie shook his head.

And then for maybe five seconds, we stood there looking at each other. Popping noises, not deafening but not soft either. There had been days of demonstrations and threats, and now on a sweltering Saturday night, the meltdown had come.

Thus began two days and nights of running, street fighting, ducking, and dodging bottles and bricks.

Once we came off the roof, Heffernan and I separated. A continuous roar rose from the crowds, an ocean of sound that just kept coming. There were wailing sirens, flashing red lights that reflected off the windshields of cars and storefront glass. Traffic had been diverted from 125th Street into the side streets; 125th Street was a battleground, with cops and looters in hand-to-hand combat. Someone said a tow truck was flying along 125th Street, stopping to attach its hook to the metal gates of liquor stores, appliance stores, and pawnshops, where guns were sold. The side streets were far more treacherous.

Traffic was backing up and stopping dead in the side streets. I was on the corner of 124th Street and Seventh Avenue when I spotted a white convertible with an even whiter couple in it. They were stuck in traffic in the middle of the block.

Cops from Lenox Avenue ran down into the block, and I came up from Seventh Avenue. All of us were shouting to keep the traffic moving along. Bottles and bricks were exploding everywhere. Some cops were hit, some went down, some of us shot above the car into the night.

When traffic finally began to move, the couple and their car were free, but the woman had been beaten badly. She was blond, a passenger in a convertible caught center stage in a riot in Harlem. I asked her if she was all right. Her voice was weak and trembling. I remember the way she turned away, wiping her eyes and her face with her forearm. Her hair was a bloody mess and it hung across her face. I had never seen such wide-eyed fear on the face of anyone, nothing like the fear on that woman's face.

I bumped into another TPF cop, Dave Christian, who was driving a sergeant when two of his car's four tires had been blown out. I told Dave I could swear I saw tracer rounds ricocheting off a building on the avenue. I remember how wide his eyes got and the way he smiled.

Cops were fighting in doorways and along the sidewalk. They stalked bottle throwers in the center of the avenue, and you could see obscure figures running along the rooftops.

A young man, barefoot, muscular, stripped to the waist, was jumping up and down on the roof of a car, his face gleaming, his eyes wide with unspeakable rage. Theatrical and dramatic, he held a bottle in each hand and was throwing karate kicks at the cops who were trying to grab him. He stretched his neck and thrust his jaw forward as he screamed out, "White motherfuckers." Half the cops who were trying to take hold of him were black, but to him they were all white motherfuckers.

He threw a circular kick and I reached up to snatch his ankle and missed. I swung at him with my stick, went for his leg, missed again, and he swiftly kicked me in the shoulder. He was dancing, spinning around, throwing kicks like a ninja warrior in a Kung Fu movie. I scrambled up onto the hood of the car, thinking that maybe I could find an opening and tackle him; it was then that I saw a motorcycle cop ride up. I couldn't figure what he was up to, shouting for me to get out of the way.

Then the guy on the roof of the car changed everything. He threw a bottle at the motorcycle cop. The cop drew his pistol, fired a shot, and blew the guy off the roof of that car.

Everyone froze.

Then everyone ran.

A cop in civilian clothes wearing a helmet started shouting about stupidity, saying, "That fucker had better have had a gypsy gun."

I ran and ran, repeating over and over, "Holy shit, holy shit." It's astonishing when you actually see how the human body reacts, you know, after being shot, the way it flies back. It's like a marionette whose strings have been jerked. The shooting affected me in an exceedingly strange way. It didn't cause me anguish so much as a kind of amazement. I couldn't push out of my head the picture of that motorcycle cop leveling his gun, the gunshot, then the guy flying in the air. Someone said, "Did you see that?" I said I didn't see anything.

INSPECTOR MICHAEL CODD, the commanding officer of TPF, had been an army major during the war. He was tall, lean, and gray-haired, with precise military bearing. A hard-nosed and fair man, the kind of commanding officer who did and said things that stuck to your psyche, to your heart and soul. In the frenzied midst of the riot, I remember the way he smiled, the way he gave commands, and little bits of reassurance.

"You don't fire those guns unless yours or someone else's life is in danger. In this country we don't shoot people for crimes against property."

—INSPECTOR MICHAEL CODD,
THE NIGHT OF THE HARLEM RIOTS

Forty-eight hours of the wildest, most colossal gang fight you could imagine. Pete or Dave Christian, one of them, told me that there was a photo of me in the *Amsterdam News* or *Mohammed Speaks*. I'm supposedly standing in the center of Lenox Avenue and 125th Street, my arms in the air, a gun in one hand, my nightstick in the other; the caption: Cops Riot in Harlem.

During the riot I saw cops do any number of heroic things, protecting the law-abiding citizens of Harlem, the elderly, and children caught in the middle of all that madness. That's true. Then there was something else, something quite different from that which we had thought ourselves to be; there was a deep sea of racism and bitterness, poison and untamed cruelty in our souls. It was a boiling cauldron, and it didn't take a whole lot to push it over into the streets, onto the rooftops, or into the alleyways of Harlem on that night in July of 1964.

THE WONDERFUL THING about TPF was that one night you could be doing battle in Harlem, then the next be in Times Square, Yankee Stadium, or in and around the Waldorf—sometimes guarding the president.

A week or two after the riots, about ten of us were standing behind the stage at Forest Hills Stadium, while thousands of teenyboppers did their thing at a rock and roll show. We were told to just stay put, not to move until we were asked for help. If these kids charge the stage, we want you out there, quick.

"Pete, who are these guys?"

"The Beatles, something like that. They're from England."

"Who?"

"I dunno; what the hell do I know? They're singers."

It was louder than anything I'd ever heard. Loud beyond belief. Suddenly the stage manager, a tall, thin, panic-stricken man with a handkerchief tied around his neck, started screaming. "Now! Now! Now! Get out there!"

I ran to the front of the stage, jumped over a police barricade, and went right on my ass, doing a picturesque and quite athletic forward roll. Pete Schmidt stood there looking at me; his mouth was moving, but I couldn't hear what he was saying.

Out front the noise was like an express train coming straight at you. The lights were powerful and disorienting, and all sorts of dark possibilities slid through my mind. How do you protect someone if you can't see or hear? The band members were young men my age, but they looked like kids. One turned to me. "The bloke's bleeding," he yelled. "This officer is hurt."

I'd cut my arm when I fell.

"I'm fine," I said, "I'm okay. But why are these kids going nuts?"

One of the band took my hand and shook it. "You tell me," he said. "This stuff is crazy, it's all a mystery."

It was George Harrison, and "My Sweet Lord" remains one of my all-time favorite songs. But back then, George Harrison was just some underweight kid with floppy hair, singing his ass off, having a night on the town.

The revved-up audience decided to make a charge up onto the stage. They weren't getting past the TPF cops, but they were trying.

"No sticks," someone yelled.

Someone else said, "Fuck that."

Thousands of kids in the audience were screaming, "Paul, John, George, Ringo." Ringo?

Pete pointed at me and shouted, "He touched George." A good-sized group followed us back to the TPF bus, pointing at me, yelling, "He touched George, he touched George." They were some dippy kids.

Another day we were in Washington Square Park when a bearded folksinger went up on a platform. I was standing right below him, and Pete, Dave Jackel, and some other TPF cops were nearby. I enjoyed all this, loved the music.

The folksinger was Theodore Bikel. He was in a fury, explaining, or trying to, why he considered himself at war with the government. After the speech he began an upbeat version of "This Land Is Your Land." I smiled at him and he threw me an annoyed look. I smiled some more and he spit at me. Then he stopped singing and spoke loudly about his family and Europe and Nazis, things I hardly heard and didn't understand. I told Pete, I said, "Shit happens, I'm gonna nail that fuck." Pete said, "After me."

When I think of those months in TPF, I remember a seemingly endless series of demonstrations, mini-riots, street fights, and arrests. It was strange and thrilling and there was the illusion that you were part of something important, history in the making. But most of what I heard was intolerable to me; it was full of rage and dismissive of anyone who disagreed. The flower children and so-called peaceniks were an aggressive, mean-spirited bunch, and I found plenty of violence behind those peace and human rights signs.

For instance, we're again at the UN Plaza. A bright, sunny day, hundreds of people swinging peace signs, screaming "Fair play for Cuba" and "Jim Crow must go" and "Down with the pigs." I'm standing right at the barricade, Pete on one side of me, a cop named Joe Flynn on the other. Not long out of the marines, Joe was one impressive-looking cop, six-one or -two, in great shape, his striking good looks a recruitment poster. Gabe Pressman, a local NBC TV reporter, stuck a microphone in my face, saying, "Officer, what do you think?"

In a moment like that, any cop who is thinking knows that you should keep your mouth shut.

I said, "I think this is all misdirected."

Pressman turned and put the microphone into the face of a tall man carrying a sign. It was a drawing of a pig wearing a police hat; there was a Nazi symbol on the pig's chest. The sign carrier was in an all-white outfit and he wore a turban on his head. I remember a black stickpin in that turban.

"The officer said your demonstration is misdirected," Pressman said.

"Sez who? The pig? Pigs smell like and know shit."

Pressman was laughing, having a grand old time.

I stood still and waited. I remember the anxiousness, the grinding teeth, the bright sunny day, and the endless chatter. I had turned this guy on; now he was into one continuous, aggressively boring rant. Coming up to me, right in my face, his face a great sea of snarling insult. I tried to relax, curled and uncurled my fists.

"He wants to hit me," the turban said. "Well, c'mon pig, let's get it on."

Sergeant Burke, our squad leader and an old TPF hand, appeared out of nowhere saying, "Okay, enough of this, move these people; get them out of here." It was enough to make you believe in God or destiny or kismet or all three.

With a roar we went over and around and under the barricades. The crowd dispersed, running in every direction but up. I lost sight of Pressman, but I found the turban. When I grabbed him he screamed like a girl. I feel guilty sometimes, thinking about how much of it I enjoyed.

THE LEVEL OF anger focused on the police that summer was fierce, and there were demonstrations all over town. On the worst days, a kind of angry despair set in among the TPF cops. We saw criminals running wild, and the average citizen, it seemed to us, took pleasure in referring to us as pigs. We saw the politicians, all of them, as people with personal agendas that they pushed on a media that seemed to love the opinions of people who had way more sound than substance. On top of all that, heroin had become the street drug of choice and the epidemic was spreading like wildfire.

Violent crime began to rise at an unbelievable rate. The number of homicides alone had almost doubled, from 390 in 1961 to 637 in 1964, and would continue to rise into the thousands. Opposition to America's involvement in Vietnam was building, and the activists in the civil rights movement saw public attention being diverted from their cause to the war and they weren't happy. Cops would swear up and down that the same white people who were at all the civil rights demonstrations were also at the antiwar rallies. Those whites were vulnerable and came under physical attack by militant black demonstrators who detested all white people. There were times at demonstrations when the white hippies would run to us for help, a situation we found amusing.

One night I found myself completely cut off. It was a blistering hot night, the air bathed in blaring music and the shouts of overheated, inebriated, and angry people. As I turned the corner at 118th Street and Madison Avenue I spotted a man sitting on the curb, his hands wrapped around his throat. There was a crowd gathered around him, glaring at him, saying, "That nigger cut you, man. You gotta get to the hospital."

As I drew closer the crowd stepped back and I spotted a man

wearing a leopard-skin tunic, with a shaved head and a linoleum-cutting knife in his hand. I bent down and touched the seated man's shoulder.

"What happened?"

"My friend cut me."

"Let me see."

When he took his hands from his throat, the blood started flowing. I panicked. I'd never seen such a grisly wound. He was cut from ear to ear.

Kneeling down beside him I put my hands over the wound and pressed. His face was smooth and hairless, his blood leaked through my fingers. Someone shouted for me to get a taxi, to put the bleeding man in a cab. Then everyone joined in, cursing me. I was afraid to move my hands from his throat, terrified that he'd bleed to death. I wasn't going to call a cab, I wasn't going to move him. I was so startled that I could feel my entire body tremble and I could feel the crowd closing in on me, the bleeding man's voice a small terror, "My friend cut me. He killed me."

I shouted at the guy holding the knife, told him to use the pay phone and call the police, tell them an officer needs assistance and an ambulance on 118th and Madison.

"Hurry!"

I was nose to nose with the bleeding man, my hands under his jaw pushing. People in the street were getting louder, threatening me.

"Who did this?" I said.

"Don't let me die, please don't let me die."

"You're not going to die, an ambulance is on the way, you'll be all right."

"The nigger cut me," he said. "The motherfucker cut me. I'm gonna die."

"You're not dying."

The call went in as a 10-13 and in no time at all there were sirens. The size of the crowd had increased and they were all around me.

Tears ran down the bleeding man's cheeks. He let out a small whimper. Someone poked me in the ribs, put their hands on my back, and shoved me. I had a sudden fear that next time he would stab me. I didn't turn around, I couldn't move, I had the bleeding man's face in my hands. An anxiousness drained me. It was so overpowering that I could hardly move or speak.

I spotted a sector car, two wheels in the street, two on the curb, its blaring siren disbursing the crowd, heading straight for me. Right behind it, an ambulance.

We carried the bleeding man to the ambulance, and there was a doctor. He looked frightened and grubby and smoked a cigar. As the ambulance sped away a local precinct cop turned to me and said, "What the hell did you do? You got blood all over your uniform." He was laughing.

The sector car left. Now I was alone standing on the sidewalk. The crowd continued to shout at me, curse me. Some kid on a bicycle sped past blowing a whistle, his hand in the shape of a gun, shooting me. There was blood all over my arms, on my hands, and on my cheeks. I was shaking and I couldn't speak clearly. Many in the crowd stood around and stared at me. They looked like they were passing a death sentence.

My TPF side partner pushed his way through the crowd and told me that I should go to the hospital. "There's so much blood," he said. "Maybe you're hurt."

I was not hurt.

"Go to the hospital, get checked out, you look terrible."

I found a bathroom at Harlem Hospital and washed my hands, my arms, and my face. In the mirror my skin had this odd color, like cement. No matter what I did I couldn't stop shaking and couldn't get the blood out from under my fingernails. I took deep breaths, found a paper bag, and blew into it. Nothing helped.

When I left the bathroom and walked into the emergency room I spotted him. He was sitting on a wooden bench, his hands folded in his lap. He still wore the leopard-skin tunic, and for the first time I noticed that he was wearing a large crucifix around his neck.

I sat down alongside him and asked him why he was at the emergency room. He grinned and told me he'd cut his thumb. When I asked him if he still had the knife, he reached into his pocket and showed it to me. It was an evil weapon, sharp as a razor and hooked like an eagle's beak. He handed it to me blade first, a silly smile locked in place. It was the kind of smile that showed neither glee nor tension. It was a little insane.

"Why did you cut your friend?" I asked him.

I remember his answer so clearly. I can't remember who my side partner was that night or how I got to the hospital or to the precinct later on. But I do remember that man with his shaved head, his leopard-skin tunic, his crazy eyes and weird-sounding voice telling me, "I couldn't have cut him. Ya know why?"

"Why?"

"Because I'm Catholic."

I cuffed him and brought him to the 25th Precinct. The on-duty detective was an older guy. He looked morose and fatalistic explaining that the ambulance doctor had attempted heart massage on the bleeding man. The ambulance had delivered a DOA to Harlem Hospital.

One of the sector car cops who had come to my aid was making the case that he should take the arrest. He told the room, now filled with cops, that he was on a list for the Detective Bureau and a homicide collar could help him. The detective was saying no way, "It's the TPF's collar or it's mine."

He had interrogated the perp, gotten him to admit cutting his friend. It turned out that they'd argued over the cost of a bottle of wine. The squabble grew into a fight, the linoleum knife flashed, and the bleeding man lost his life.

"He said he cut him over a bottle of wine?" I asked.

"Well," the detective said, "it happens."

"I guess so."

"It's not unusual."

I stared at the prisoner, who was walking in tight circles in the holding cage, glancing over his shoulder, staring at me. Every so often he'd shrug his shoulders. I wondered what sort of voices that man heard in his head, what sort of visions he had. They had to be horrible things that made dreadful sounds. The rest of that night is a total blur.

MY MEMORY OF those months is spotty. Certain incidents, high and low lights, moments of fear, more of laughter. I'm twenty-four years old, things at home and at work seem to be on track, and in most ways I was having a pretty good time. But I was learning that police work was a psychological minefield of dangerous and disturbing possibilities. It was easy to become darkened in both mind and spirit; you began muttering to yourself about the average citizen: ungrateful bunch of hypocritical assholes.

That's how I felt, and I wasn't alone. It was a dangerous feeling that died hard, if it ever really died at all. You wear a uniform, you carry a gun, and you rarely come into contact with people on pleasant or uplifting occasions. Sure you're there to protect and serve, but most people don't see you that way. They don't want to see you at all—I mean ever. You're a cop, and you do your best—that's what it was all about; trying to do your best. People, you would think, would appreciate it when you try and do your best. But this was the whirling, psychedelic, mind-blowing, skewed world of the sixties; most people didn't give a shit.

OUR APARTMENT WAS the street-level floor of a converted two-family house. A long narrow living room, a bedroom, and a kitchen that opened to a rear yard with a tiny patio. The apartment was small but sufficient for Gina and me. My parents' house was just around the corner, and my mother would stop by to bring food and sometimes pick up laundry. We didn't have a washer or dryer, but the apartment was brand-new, and although in those days we were like ships passing in the night, Gina and I were happy.

That fall Gina's mother arrived from Europe. She was an attractive, energetic, earthy and hardy woman. Born and raised in Italy, she had emigrated to Germany shortly before the war and spoke German with a heavy Italian accent. She had no English at all.

She dug a garden in the backyard; we barbecued on the patio and did the shopping together. I called her Oma and knew her by no other name. "So much meat," she'd say, "America has so much meat." Once I found her scrubbing the front steps of the house and washing the sidewalk. I told her that we don't do that in this country. She said, "Ja, okay, it's okay. I do it."

I stopped watching the news on television. I didn't believe journalists, didn't trust them. We had been in the same places at the same times, but the things I saw and heard were not what they reported. I read no newspapers or magazines. For current events I relied on other cops; it seemed like the thing to do.

I had three women in my life: my mother, my mother-in-law, and my wife. At home they did all things for me in a lovingly attentive way. I was experiencing the prosaic contentment that comes from always being the center of everyone's attention, and I grew accustomed to having my life made easy. I was absorbed in the world of me. On a trip to Italy, Oma would climb twelve hundred steps on her knees, to a holy place where she had a medal blessed for me, to protect me.

THAT WINTER, DURING the holiday season, TPF was assigned to work with officers from the motorcycle units in something called "Operation Checkpoint."

The idea was to stop cars and make certain the driver was sober. If you set aside cops and firemen and members of the clergy, there were still plenty of drunks out there. We took the keys of the cops and firemen and clergy members and telephoned either friends or family to come and get them. All others were arrested.

That winter was particularly bitter, and Pete and I took turns freezing our butts off while the pair of motorcycle cops stayed warm and cozy in the car.

As cars approached the checkpoint, we profiled the drivers. That one looks like he's been drinking, that one doesn't. It's not rocket science.

After an hour or so, we took a break and sat in the car, and the two motorcycle cops, striking in their leather coats and thirty mission hats, decided to play with our heads. One of them told a painful story, a tale that was every cop's worst nightmare.

Arnold, the driver, was in his late thirties, maybe early forties. He had deep creases in his cheeks and a hard, leathery face from all those hours of riding a motorcycle in the sun. He was sucking on an unlit cigar. I'll call the other cop the recorder. He was also in his late thirties, fair-skinned, blond hair spilling out from under his cap.

"Tell them," Arnold said. "You can tell them the story. They're cops like us, they'll understand."

Pete: "What story?"

Me: "What?"

The recorder: "Naw, I feel lousy telling people, ya know, Arnold. It's nothing to be proud of."

Me: "What?"

"C'mon, you tell people all the time, I mean that's what you did, right? You told people."

"I guess you could say that."

Me: "What?"

Pete: "Quiet, let him tell it."

"It was weird the way it happened. I mean I come home from work, it was a day tour, a seven to three; soon as I get in the house she tells me the bathroom bowl backed up, water ran down the stairs, the place was a mess."

Pete: "You got kids? Kids are always throwing stuff in the toilet bowls. You gotta watch 'em."

"No, no kids, we've been trying for years. No kids. Anyway, she tells me she called the plumber, and he fixed it. The guy cleared the clog, left his card, and told my wife to have me call him."

He lowered his head and began to massage his leg. "My leg was swollen that day from riding the bike. Sometimes it gets that way. This leg of mine can give me trouble."

Me: "From riding the bike?"

"Oh yeah, it hurts, that motorcycle. Ya know, you go eighty, ninety miles an hour chasing some asshole, you get that front-end wobble, scares the shit outtaya. Squeeze the bike with your legs, you can hurt yourself. It happens."

Pete: "That front end wobble at high speed, it's scary."

Me: "So?"

"I was in a lot of pain that day, so I put off calling the plumber till the next morning. When I phoned the guy, he tells me, 'Look, there's no problem, I fixed it. Just make sure you throw those rubbers in the wastebasket, not down the toilet.' 'What rubbers?' I ask him. 'Whadaya mean rubbers?' "

Arnold, the driver, lit his cigar. "Man, wait'll ya hear this one. I mean it's heartbreaking."

I turned to look at Pete.

"Anyway, the plumber tells me he found two, three rubbers, ya know, Trojans stuck in the trap. Trouble is, I don't use rubbers, never did. I mean we were trying to have kids."

Pete: "Jesus Christ!"

Me: "Wow."

Arnold: "No. No. Wait, wait till you hear this."

"The next day I'm supposed to be doing another seven to three. I call the roll-call man and tell him I'm taking a day off. I dress, make it look like I'm leaving for work, get in the car and circle the block, and then park up the street. I've got my own house under surveillance."

Pete: "Oh man."

"I see the guy. It was nine, nine-thirty. He leaves his house—the guy lives right across the street from where I live—and cool as you like, I mean as cool as you like, he cruises over to my house. Doesn't even knock and goes in my front door."

Pete: "Jesus Christ."

Me: "What?"

Pete: "I'm ready to kill somebody. I hope you had your fucking off duty."

Arnold: "You ain't heard anything yet. I mean wait till you hear this, what this poor man had to endure. It'll make you cry."

"Ya know, I thought I'd give them some time, get the small talk out of the way. We got this guest room down on the first floor; I'm figuring that's the spot. I mean, she couldn't be fucking him in our own bed."

Pete Schmidt threw a forearm at the car door. The cruiser rocked.

"I creep into my house, go in the back door, into my own house like a fucking burglar. Sneak in, ya know, quiet like. I hear sounds, whimpering, almost crying sounds, my wife's voice. 'It's sooo good, so goddamn good. It's never been this good.'"

Pete shouts, "Oh, for Christ sake!"

"My wife, she's very religious, went to Stella Morris High School, Dominican nuns, the whole bit. To hear her take the Lord's name, I mean in that context, it was very disturbing."

Pete dropped his head into his hands. His cap fell off and hit the floor of the car. I reached down and picked it up. My hand was shaking when I handed him his cap.

"Well, anyway, I caught 'em, she was straddling him, going like hell. I mean she never got on top of me, ya know, it's always me on top. And the funny thing was, she was wearing this T-shirt I bought her, the one I got at the World's Fair."

Pete: "I'm going to throw up."

I begin to laugh.

Arnold: "This isn't funny."

Me: "I'm sorry." And I was.

"I got my gun in my hand, my off duty. They see me, they panic, she screams, 'Don't shoot,' he pushes her off and jumps to his feet. I aim at his prick; it was no big deal, same size as mine, maybe even a bit smaller. The guy's a fireman, a buddy of mine, we bowl together, an Italian guy, ya know those fucking wops."

Me: "Ey?"

Pete: "I'm going to vomit, really, I'm going to puke."

"I don't shoot him. Ya know what I do? This is what I do."

Pete: "You should have shot him, shot him right in the balls. You catch your wife fucking some guy in your house you can shoot him. They'd cut you loose in a heartbeat."

Me: "Bullshit, that's manslaughter."

Pete: "No fucking way, there's case law on it, I remember reading something about it, ya know, in your own house."

Me: "Bullshit, that's Texas, in Texas maybe, not in Queens."

"Well, I don't shoot him, not him, not her. What I do? Here's what I do. I tell him, I say, 'Joey,' his name's Joey. 'Give me five bucks.' He goes to his jeans, takes out a pound and gives it to me. His hands are shaking, I mean really shaking, trembling. I tell him to get the fuck outta my house. My wife, she's sitting cross-legged on the bed with her head down. I could tell she felt bad, I mean really shitty."

Me: "Yeah?"

Pete: "A fucking fireman. Geeze."

"I take the five bucks and iron it. Make it nice and neat, flat and smooth, and I put it in a picture frame and hang it in the kitchen."

Arnold: "Now, listen to this guy—he's a sick man—listen to him."

Me: "You hang the picture frame with the five dollar bill in it on the kitchen wall. What for?"

"People visit, ya know, friends, relatives, neighbors, they come in, maybe for coffee, something like that. They always ask, 'What's with the five-dollar bill in the picture frame?'"

Me: "And?"

"I tell em, I say, that's what Joey the fireman gave me to fuck my wife."

Doubt was dancing pinwheels in my head, but I ignored it because what I was feeling was stronger.

"You say what?" I said.

Arnold said, "Ya know what, it's time for a meal. Whadaya say? You guys like roast beef sandwiches? My partner, he's a sick man. You, partner, you're a sick man."

I looked at Pete and he looked at me. Arnold and the storyteller sat still and silent.

"Is it a joke?" Pete said.

I said, "I don't know."

Arnold said, "You TPF guys, man, you are one gullible bunch."

Pete: "So it's not true. You made the whole thing up. This is supposed to be some kind of joke? I got that right? Your wife is not fucking a fireman."

We all roared with laughter and that laughter brought us together. Four cops on a bitter cold night, strangers an hour before, now sitting as one in a police cruiser. It was like being drunk or high. Laughter so warm and friendly that I was convinced there was no other place on earth I would rather be and there were no other people I would rather be with.

We exchanged war stories all night long, talked about women, about politics and sports. We drove 100 miles per hour to a diner the motorcycle cops knew. Four coffees and sandwiches on the arm, something that never happened in TPF. In TPF we always paid full price. The sandwiches and coffee tasted wonderful. Pete and I agreed that they were the thickest, best-tasting roast beef sandwiches we'd ever had.

yellow sheet—history of prior arrests.

Sometime around midnight a late-model black Chrysler approached the checkpoint. The traffic signal was red, but when the driver spotted Pete and me, he punched the gas pedal and sped on through. We jumped into the cruiser, and I'm thinking of the absurdity, a butt-head thinking he could outrun a highway cruiser with a motorcycle cop behind the wheel. As Arnold threw the car into gear, I saw the look on his face, something like "Now here's an asshole just begging to get jammed up."

We chased the Chrysler at high speed down one avenue and up another, flew down narrow streets with cars parked on both sides of the road. I was getting off on the ride, loving it, hoping it would never end. The sound of the siren, Pete's heavy breathing, my nerves afire from the adrenaline rush. I was awestruck by Arnold's pure driving talent. The Chrysler made a turn at a cross street and we shot on through and lost him. Arnold jammed on the brakes, threw the cruiser into reverse. "There," I shouted, "there he is." The Chrysler was parked on the side street, a hairbreadth from a clean getaway.

"He's all yours," Arnold said.

That was the deal, motorcycle chased them and TPF collared them. I walked to the driver's door, Pete to the passenger's. I hit the window with the back of my hand. "Okay," I said, "c'mon, get out of the car."

He didn't move. Just sat there, his hands on the steering wheel, staring straight ahead, a little smirk on his face. The light from a streetlamp angled down and I could see his car seat. There was an empty bottle of beer. I was looking for a gun, narcotics, something, but there was nothing else.

I punched the window with the side of my fist. "Out," I said, "get out."

He opened the door and stepped into the street.

He was tall, a well-dressed man, the smell of alcohol rising from him like a sour purple haze. I was waiting for him to make a move, any kind of aggressive move. Pete was alongside me and he felt the same way. He didn't say so, but I knew he had it too, the urge to kick this character's ass. We had put our lives on the line for this jerkoff. Maybe he had an explanation, a story of some kind, but I didn't give a ratfuck what his excuse was. There were four men in that cruiser, each with a family, each with a valued life of his own. Years later, when I watched the video of the Rodney King whipping, it was easy to imagine how fear and anger and frustration could manifest themselves in one helluva beating.

I tested the driver in the street; he could hardly walk, much less touch the tip of his nose with the trembling tip of his finger. He couldn't remember the alphabet. In the precinct he refused the Breathalyzer test, and that should have been a clue that he'd been through this all before. He flunked every response test miserably, and although none of this was a perfect science, there was no doubt at all that Randolph Johnson was totally slammed, drunk, unable to function behind the wheel of a car.

His yellow sheet came back with three prior arrests and one conviction for drunk driving. The second arrest was a felony, and two convictions meant automatic revocation of his driver's license. Johnson had managed to beat two others; he wouldn't beat this one. He was going down and rightly so.

In the police department, where going along to get along governed, you learned over time to let certain things pass. I was a uniformed cop, the lowest rung on the ladder. This arrest would give me an education on how to make compromises to avoid complications.

Standing in the hallway of the Queens County Criminal Courts

Building, waiting for my drunk driving arrest to be called, the last thing I needed or wanted was trouble.

Randolph Johnson's arrest for DWI wasn't a simple drunk driving collar; it was his third, a felony. He could face jail time.

A reedy little man came out of the circle of bail bondsmen, lawyers, and private investigators, the gathered knot of courthouse sharpies. He came over to me and asked if I had made the arrest. He was Johnson's lawyer, and wanted to know how the arrest occurred. I told him it was simple. Johnson had jumped a light; we had chased but lost him. Then we found him parked on a side street. His client was slammed, stoned, and could hardly walk. I arrested him.

"You lost him?" "Yes, for about thirty seconds. He'd turned a corner and parked." The lawyer grinned. Then he walked off.

A detective who had been on the job awhile was giving me an amused look. "Why are you talking to that man?" he asked. "He's my defendant's lawyer," I told him. "He's a fixer," he said. "You watch yourself. He fixes things. He could fix you."

The grinning lawyer came back and stuck out his hand to me. "You testify like that," he said, "say you lost sight of my client even for a few seconds, and that will help us." I remember how frightened and humiliated I felt. I tried to bail myself out. "Your client was stoned drunk, and he couldn't drive. He ran from us, drove at high speed trying to get away. Finally he parked, trying to hide on a side street. That's the truth."

He went into his pocket and came out with a twenty-dollar bill that he folded neatly into the palm of his hand. He reached across to me. I closed his hand over the money and said, "You're under arrest."

He yelped, and said something insulting.

I marched through the courtroom doors, dragging mister fixer behind me. Seated on the bench was a judge named Manual Gomez. I remember him clearly; he was an attractive, solid-looking man, friendly to the police, friendly to everyone. When the judge saw me and saw the look on my face and the look on the face of the fixer, he hunched his shoulders and ran off the bench as if he had seen the approach of his own death.

Someone separated me from the fixer and led me into the judge's clerk's office. "You're a police officer," they shouted after closing the door. "You should know you can't make a bribery arrest without corroboration. Are you insane? What do you think you're doing?"

I knew I should say something, but I didn't know what. The man speaking was James Robinson, the son-in-law of Queens District Attorney Thomas Mackell. Then others came into the room, several other high-ranking assistants to the district attorney. At first they threatened and took the twenty-dollar bill from my hand, then they started bargaining with me. They asked me, if the fixer excluded himself from the case, would that be all right with me? Grim faces were staring at me; it wasn't anger so much as genuine concern.

Sure, I told them, give him back his twenty and let me get the hell out of here. I was out of my element. This place had a secret language. It was a world populated by politicos and lawyers in very expensive suits. Here language was everything and winks and smiles were ever-present. In time I would learn how cases went up in smoke in places like this, courtrooms where deals were made. You could accomplish almost anything in the courthouses of New York City. The buildings themselves were both a place of law and a marketplace, a place of physical substance and a place of illusion. A fistfull of dollars could turn into a wand and make bad become good and up become down, drunk become sober.

When I left the Queens courthouse that day, I had the sickening intuition that all that had happened was pure bullshit. Lawyers were lawyers and prosecutors were lawyers and judges were lawyers, and they treated each other with reverence. If you got in the way of something they wanted to accomplish, they would humiliate and crush you.

Randolph Johnson ended up with a third acquittal. They returned his driver's license and gave him the right to drive a car. I had seen enough drunk drivers and gruesome car wrecks to know that there was no permanent cure for a guy like Randolph Johnson, and sooner or later he'd turn his car into a killing missile. No one, on that day, in that courtroom, seemed to care.

ON ONE VERY cold night in the South Bronx, I was patrolling Fox Street near Southern Boulevard. It was a narrow street with four- and six-story tenements on either side. The avenue was lit with bars and clubs, but the side streets were desolate and dark. I was alone; just me and a wind that rode through the street with a howl and rage and bite the likes of which you would not believe. It was a little before 2:00 A.M. and I was taking my last turn, moving quick step, walking steady and hard, my head bent, one hand on my cap, the other buried deep in the pocket of my overcoat, my eyes on that cold hard sidewalk.

My high-collared overcoat, the same design that had been worn by New York cops for a hundred years, had slit pockets. You stick your hand into the pocket, and through the slit, you can feel the butt end of your pistol. Alone, on a blistering cold night, in a part of the city where people were killed with regularity, that gun butt felt thick and comforting in my hand.

I finished up at two and could head in. I was cold and miserable, my hands and feet and face were numb. All I wanted was to be done with this night. I moved with a feeling that was more near coma than exhaustion.

Most of the time, when on patrol, I'd feel like the good yeoman crime fighter for the city of New York, the designated lightning rod for all the madness that took place in ghetto people's lives. Still, I knew that along with the skels, there were hardworking, good people in these neighborhoods, people who counted on me.

As I moved, I eyed the alleyways, hallways, and storefronts. I wasn't stupid, or very brave, still I forced myself to go into the dark places, the long alleyways that ran between the tenements. At the end of those alleyways were doors that led to stairways that led to basements that were lit with candles, where mattresses were scattered on ice cold floors, where rags were blankets and buckets were toilet bowls, the tenement cellars where desperate street people slept.

Even on that cold night, I could see faces at windows, shapes in hallways, forms traveling in out of the darkness. Believe this when I tell you, the ghetto never sleeps.

I had been a visitor—sometimes invited, most times not—in many ghetto apartments. I knew that on a night such as this, ice formed inside the glass windows and on the sills of those apartments. I had seen ice on the floors and on bathroom mirrors. Slum landlords, who made concentration camp commanders look like humanitarians, regulated heat in this part of town so that none rose after 6:00 P.M. My father was right; it was small wonder these people wanted to burn these buildings, equipped as they were with rats the size of cats and leaky faucets that ran ice water and ceilings that dropped lead chips of paint into cribs where infants slept. I once saw a girl baby whose toes had been knawed to stumps by a rat. I saw that and wondered what in the hell country I was in anyway. Now, when I spoke to my father I'd say, "You were right. Were you ever. Jesus."

Most of the apartments had holes in the floors, ceilings, and walls. Many had paint on velvet renderings of Christ, Jack Kennedy, and Martin Luther King Jr. They were a sideshow of boundless misery understood only by the people forced to live there, cops on patrol, and firemen.

That night I wandered up one street and down another, the one ahead the same as the one behind. I found a street-level hallway and ducked in. I took off my cap, rubbed my head, trying to get some blood to move, put my cap back on, reached into the pocket of my coat, found a cigarette, lit up, and checked my watch. I had fifteen minutes before this tour would finally be over.

I heard them long before I saw them and what I heard went like this: "Leave me be," she said. "Just go, man, just scoot."

"I'm a marine," he said, "and marines don't leave till they wanna go. Marines," he shouted, "stay put when people want them to go."

I poked my head out of the doorway and stared up the street. They stood in the hallway of the building adjacent to where I was standing, and although the wind was strong and howled through the street, I could hear their conversation clearly. I could tell he was stoned and crazed, a typical street psycho.

She told him, "I'm gonna call the police you don't go. I'm gonna call the poooo-leece. Tell them you a marine, see where that gets ya." She sounded like she was talking to a child.

He said, "I'll fix it you can't call anybody, baby."

I lay back in the hallway and thought I'd let things slide for a minute or two. All the while I was praying that these two would somehow vanish. I'd seen it happen dozens of times, a flare-up and burnout like a supernova.

She told him, "You gonna scare me, honey? You can't scare me, with your jelly belly and big ol' wobbly ass. You don't scare me none."

I glanced at my watch; it was 2:00 A.M. and my tour was over. *Go away,* I thought, *disappear.* But this type never leaves. I could hear him hiss as if to illustrate just how serious he was.

"My ol' man usta whip me. Shiiiiit!" She shouted with no small conviction. "He could whip me with one hand tied behind his back better than an ol' jelly-belly, wobbly-ass country boy like you."

"Say what?" he said.

There's this old patrol cop bromide, a truism. "When you think you should make a move, go to it, don't wait." I could have walked over to them, listened to a scream from hell when she spotted me coming. "Lock him up," she'd yell, "bust his ass. He's harassing me and I'm pressing charges. I'm a citizen and I want him arrested."

But if I did what she asked and arrested him, she would never follow up. They never do. She wouldn't go to court. In a day, two at the very most, she'd have him back in her bed. I was way too tired to play that game. I decided to stay put and hope that they would get past all this. It was ghetto comedy.

So I made a decision, one that would wake me in the middle of the night for many years to come.

"You and your fat ass still here?"

He took awhile to answer her.

"You got a bad mouth, honey. I'll go to your funeral you keep talking trash like that."

"Easy," I whispered.

"Ah said you ain't shit," she told him. "My ol' man have me down screaming for Jesus by now. You talk, talk, talk."

"Here ya go," he said. "How ya like that?"

"Ow," she said. And that's all she said.

A patrol cop can boil his life down to ten or fifteen seconds of real choices made. I had seen time and again the futility of becoming involved in a lovers' dispute. You learn to wait. Wait and see where it goes. I was exhausted and cold, and I waited too long.

I stepped from the hallway out onto the sidewalk. She came from the adjoining doorway and slowly walked toward me as if to pay her respects. I saw it; it was an immediate thing, a total presence extending from her chest as though it belonged there. I was dumbstruck, amazed, bewildered.

"Officer," she said, smiling, panting a bit, "you see what that man did?"

"Lady," I said, "I see it, but I don't believe it."

I thought I had given no sign of the panic that had taken hold of me.

She asked, "Are you all right?"

Am I all right? Christ, I thought, there's a screwdriver in your chest. I looked at her face. For a moment I didn't talk and neither did she.

Her skin was the color of chestnut. She had fine features and gray eyes, deerlike eyes. She had brown freckles on her cheeks and they splashed across the bridge of her nose. But it was those eyes that hooked me. I mean the look of them, all the hopelessness right there. Her face, the soft sweetness of it moved into a part of my heart I never knew existed.

"Did he kill me?" she said, half sulking. Then she laid her head against my chest.

"Sit down," I said.

"Damn," she said as if it was finally reaching her. She sat on the curb of the street and dropped her head into her hands. I took off my overcoat and draped it across her shoulders. "Damn," she said again.

I asked, and she told me her name was Pauline.

I banged on a street-level apartment window and told a round-faced man to call the police, tell them I need an ambulance and assistance.

She had told me her boyfriend's name was Rodney and that after he'd stabbed her, he'd run to the basement. Her hand made a little gesture. "He's down there," she said. "It's the basement where he went to." She looked at me, gnawing her lip, and then she smiled. Smiled.

"You'll be okay," I told her. "They'll be here in a minute." All I could see was that screwdriver protruding from her sweater.

She shrugged.

I waited until I heard the sirens, then I went into the building. There were warnings spray-painted on the walls and glassine envelopes scattered on the floor. I went to the door that led to the basement and opened it.

"Come out of there," I shouted. "Put your hands on your head and come on out."

"I'm a marine," he answered, "and marines never surrender."

He sounded as though he meant it.

I pulled back on the hammer of my pistol and the cocking of that gun made a sound that exploded in the silence of the basement.

"I'm gonna count to three. If you don't come out, I'll come down there and blow your ass up. You hear me?"

Silence.

"One."

"You come down here, c'mon, I'm waitin'."

"Two." I'm wondering why it's taking so long for my backup to get here. Then I'm thinking, it's past 2:00 A.M. TPF are all back in the precinct.

I saw his form, a dark shadow, move to the foot of the stairway. I uncocked my gun and jumped him.

I remember hitting him real hard with my gun. I don't remember any sounds when I hit him. He was thick-necked, sturdy, a powerful man. He had been drinking and the smell of him made me queasy. The sirens were right out in front of the building, and then I heard the panicked shouts of cops in the hall and on the stairway. Flashlight beams were everywhere.

After I cuffed him, he jerked his head back. He was smiling like he'd just won the lottery. In the center of his mouth was a gold, silver-framed tooth with the initials RS scripted in the center.

I delivered him to the precinct, where I booked him for Assault One and resisting arrest. I telephoned the hospital to check on the woman. She was in the operating room.

All I can tell you about the rest of the night and the morning after is that it was a nightmare.

His name was Rodney, he was a bull of a man, and he refused to be fingerprinted. He ran his inked fingers across the fingerprint cards, smearing them. He tossed papers in the air and kicked desks. With the help of two enraged squad detectives, I handcuffed him to a chair and slid a two-by-four between the chair slats to hold him in place.

The woman in that hospital had a life as valuable as any other, and I had allowed Rodney to try and take it from her. I was as angry with myself as I was with Rodney, and when he smiled, flashing his fancy tooth, I hit him with my blackjack. I knocked the tooth loose and felt better for it.

The judge at the morning arraignment sighed. He rubbed his scalp, put his hands over his ears, and read my complaint. He stopped halfway through and asked, "Will she live?"

I told him it looked promising; chances were good that she'd survive.

"When setting bail," the Legal Aid lawyer said, "I'd like the court to consider this defendant's military record."

Rodney had received a serious face wound in Korea. His entire cheek had been replaced—sheepskin, he told me.

Serious assaults on women perpetrated by men, were a profoundly sensitive issue with that particular judge, and he impressed everyone standing around, myself included, when he announced, "I will adjourn this case for ninety days."

"And bail?" asked the lawyer.

"None," said the judge.

Rodney smiled.

"If this woman dies," the judge told him, "I promise you that smile of yours will fade."

I went to visit Pauline the following day at Lincoln Hospital; the doctors had just removed the drainage tube from her chest. I sat on the chair next to her bed, held her hand, and told her I was sorry.

"You didn't stab me," she said.

"I could have been faster," I said. "I could have spared you this."

She didn't answer me.

I visited her once more at the hospital and once at her apartment. During these visits I found myself staring at her, wanting to sooth her, to help make her life better. I brought her a steak and she cooked it for me with onions and mushrooms. She asked me why I was coming around; she asked me if I wanted to fuck her. She smiled and turned the full light of her street charm on me. I considered her offer for a moment. When I told her I didn't think it was a good idea, she smiled. Pauline had a great smile, a beautiful face.

Three months later, we returned to court. All three of us. Pauline was fully recovered.

I suppose I always knew what the outcome of the assault case would be. We were in the hallway, drinking coffee from Styrofoam containers. I asked Pauline if she was going to follow through and sign the complaint. She took my hand and squeezed it, telling me that her life was a hassle. She had no money and she had asthma, couldn't find work. She said that Rodney cared for her. He paid the bills and brought her food. They had lived together six months and he had been okay, not bad, when you considered the other men she'd known. She needed him to help her get by, she told me.

While she carried the hard look of a woman raised in the streets, her smile concealed endless fears. Rodney offered her protection from predators. They had lived together long enough to have had some good times. The night of the incident had been the only bad time, bad for both of them. She too, she felt, had been at fault. She went on to tell me the strange and improbable story of her life, the way it had swirled back and forth between the streets of fear and bedlam until Rodney came along. She laughed when she told it. Her laugh was full and clear, and her eyes, those gray deer eyes, shone bright when she said that she was a loner by nature. But a woman could not be alone on South Bronx streets and survive. A woman, she said, was always in need of a man to help her get by.

She wouldn't sign the complaint. She wanted to drop the charges, and no matter what I said, no matter how I said it, Pauline would not change her mind. The Legal Aid lawyer assured the judge that the couple were in love and planned on staying together. The judge shook his finger and warned Rodney to behave himself in the future.

He gave Rodney time served for the resistance charge. There were no objections from the assistant district attorney, just a small dead smile and a little nod of the head.

to be in the wind—to be running, hiding from the police.

Rodney and Pauline walked from the courtroom hand in hand. The cops standing around, the lawyers, assistant DAs, and clerks of the court all made jokes about this.

A month to the day later, I again was assigned the Fox Street post. I found myself searching out Pauline's apartment. When I rang the bell there was no answer. I spoke to the superintendent of the building, who told me that Pauline and Rodney were gone. "Wasted and gone," the super said. It was an offhand remark, a joke really. Rodney had wasted her and now he was gone. He had used a knife this time, one of those big old shiny things you can buy on 42nd Street. Gone, the super said. The super's wife told me that Rodney had finished the job this time and now he was in the wind. She'd bet to the Carolinas, back home to his family. That's what she had told the detectives.

Pauline was gone too. The world she inhabited was a savage place and it had aged her and taken her, the same way it was taking me. You grow old way before your time, way before you've grown up. For months I found myself thinking about Pauline, her cool detached view of the world, her stately air and puzzling smile. Pauline was dead and gone, stabbed to death in the wasteland. And I knew I'd be doomed to play it over and over again, her laugh in my head, the hopelessness in those beautiful gray eyes.

As for myself, there were things growing in me that, no matter how I tried, were impossible to ignore. Incomprehensible things that, in years to come, I would find impossible to forgive.

THERE IS A point of view that says that the moment of highest anxiety for a cop at a shooting is not the split second before, or while the action's happening, but the minutes immediately after. Then, completely drained, emotionally off kilter, you analyze and analyze your decision to fire that gun.

"I'd rather be judged by twelve than carried by six."

—A COP'S MAXIM

When it flashes in my head, watching a movie or being asked if it ever happened, I remember a rooftop in the South Bronx. It was a moonless night, impossible to make out forms or colors, and it was still, quiet; sounds carried. My partner that night was Mario Melita, a wiry, athletic, and energetic cop. Together we heard the invading footsteps that made the night resonate with the sound of someone climbing metal stairs.

We watched as they mounted the fire escape, two of them. Saw them go to a window, break and unlock it, and we kept an eye on them as they scrambled into the apartment.

Mario ran into the building; he'd call to me when he found his way into the backyard. It was a minute, maybe two before Mario yelled to me from the street, telling me he couldn't find his way into the yard.

I went to the gooseneck of the fire escape. The burglars were two floors below me, and one was standing on the fire escape stacking the loot. I shone my flashlight onto his face. "Stay right there," I said.

Sure. Okay.

He was tall and thin with a mustache and chin whiskers. There was a small television at his feet and what looked like a stereo and a stack of records. His partner joined him in a hurry, and both of them were now staring at me.

"Hold it."

Yeah, sure.

Two weeks earlier, a cop named Henry Weinstein in the 9th Precinct had gone onto a fire escape after a burglar and was shot and killed. The horror of that story resounded in my head.

They were moving, uncertain, a kind of dreamy smile on both their faces. I had my gun out. "Stay put, man, stay where you are."

Yeah, sure.

I grabbed the gooseneck of the fire escape and went over. My back was to them and I kept repeating, "Don't move, stay put."

Yeah, sure.

I hate heights; let me repeat that, I really hate heights. A great shudder ran up and down my spine as I realized that the fire escape ladder was loose and was pulling away from the building. Suddenly they're escaping down the steps. I shouted for them to stop and they yelled, "Fuck you!"

Absolute darkness. I don't know what or whom they left in that apartment and in what condition. I could no longer see them. I did not know then and I do now know now what to make of my decision to fire a warning shot.

Cops don't fire warning shots. There's no such thing as a warning shot.

I fired a shot off to the right, into the ground, in the opposite direction from where I thought they were running, and I heard, "Ow, the fuck shot me."

I was in a state of baffled anxiety, nervousness right at the edge of panic. It was dumb; firing that shot was incredibly stupid. In those days a cop could fire at a fleeing felon if he had reasonable grounds to believe that a felony had been committed and that felon was fleeing. He could shoot, but that didn't make it any less imprudent.

The patrol sergeant arrived with about a half a dozen other TPF cops. We found a stereo, some records, and a smashed TV set in the rear yard.

"I fired a shot," I said. "I think I hit one of them."

The sergeant laughed, but the laugh was halfhearted and listless. "There's no sign of blood, nothing in the yard."

I hit him.

I hope not.

Fifteen minutes later I walked into Lincoln Hospital and saw him at the end of a long hallway, sitting on a gurney, arms folded over his chest. He was smiling. It was near 1:00 A.M.

"It's you," he said. He looked younger, with a boy's smile. He was not quite as tall as I had thought, but he did have a mustache and slight beard. Still, he looked young.

"Why the hell did you run? Jesus," I said, "are you all right?"

"Yeah," he said, "I'm great, except where you shot me. Man, you're a helluva shot."

He said that, I remember that clearly. That's exactly what he said. I asked him how old he was, and when he told me fifteen, I said, "Oh Jesus, I'm sorry." I do remember that, how that felt. He showed me his wound. "Man," he said, "what a shot. How'd you learn that?"

The bullet was visible. It had torn a hole in his pants and lay just beneath the skin of his thigh. It must have ricocheted off a half a dozen things in that dark alleyway, everything except him.

"Shit, man, I'm in trouble," he said, "here comes my mom."

I didn't want to turn around, and when I did I saw them coming, about twenty of them, the whole Puerto Rican family, Mom out in front, her arms held out, and she was running at me. There were brothers and sisters and cousins and aunts and uncles, and suddenly they were all over me. His mother kissed me, his sister thanked me, and young boys patted my back, all of them saying and thinking it was intentional, the ricochet shot of the century, an extraordinary rodeo act and some sort of police benevolence.

I swore to myself that I'd never shoot again, never again, unless someone was coming at me, someone with a gun. It was a good and bad decision, but I stuck by it.

The boy and I went to Children's Court, where his guidance counselor, a delicate, exquisite black woman in a red dress and about my age was waiting for us. I thought she was bound to let me have it. She asked my name and told me hers. She took my hand, shook it, and said, "You know, you look like one of my students."

Police officers appeared at Children's Court out of uniform and in civilian clothes. I was in my standard out-of-uniform uniform—chinos, penny loafers, a shirt, and crew neck sweater.

tutsoon—Italian dialect pejorative for black person.

Her name was Marilyn and she seemed to be studying me. I tried my best to appear professional. She was smiling, saying, "You know, you should have killed the little bastard. He's a nightmare. He beats up teachers, two that I know of."

I told her he didn't seem like a bad kid; a bit wild maybe, but not a bad kid, I didn't think so.

"You want to see his record?"

Marilyn showed me a thick file, then took a seat, telling me she was going to do all she could to send this kid away.

We were waiting in the witness room, a comfortable place with sofas and chairs and attractive prints on the wall. I had been riddled with fear, thinking that functionaries at Children's Court would rip me for shooting a child. Not this woman. Marilyn treated me like a hero.

The room began to fill with guidance counselors, teachers, probation officers, and other cops. They all knew her, went to her and made small talk. She nodded her head and laughed; then she turned toward me, a sly smile on her face. At that time in my life, married or not, I was incapable of monogamy. I knew that before I married. I loved and respected my wife, in my own self-centered way, I suppose. Still, in those days I'm sure that I had no comprehension of the words *love, respect,* and *value.* Anyway, this woman was drop-dead gorgeous, and to be sure, far better educated than I was. Still, she was black, and in the world I came from back then, it did not happen, not ever.

The judge arrived late. He held hearings in an office, not a courtroom, and he wore no robe.

As lunchtime approached, the men in the room came over to Marilyn and asked if she'd like to go to lunch. She kept raising her eyes and glancing at me. She told everyone who asked that she had some work to do; she'd skip lunch. Finally, when everyone had left, she said, "C'mon, let's go."

We ran down the steps like a couple of kids cutting out of school. She was excited and giddy, suggesting that we find a place away from the courthouse. I knew of a street a couple of blocks over that had a few Italian restaurants and a coffee shop. As we walked she took my arm and held it. I felt a curious nudge of guilt and instinctively scanned the faces of people on the street. It was an old Italian neighborhood, and the looks I was getting were not at all friendly.

We found a tiny, narrow restaurant; it had four booths and a small round table. There were pictures of Joe DiMaggio and Frank Sinatra on the wall and a colorful map of Sicily. The booths were taken, so we sat at the table. There were Italian cooking smells, garlic and basil and tomato, sausage and onions, the perfume of home.

Marilyn told me that she lived alone in East Harlem, a building near the FDR Drive. It was middle-income city housing, a big apartment with a great view of the river. She said she collected African art. I looked around the restaurant, and I saw nothing but fixed, angry faces.

Marilyn had an ample mouth with lipstick the color of burgundy. Her eyes were focused on me and she seemed completely oblivious to the stiffness and resentment that surrounded us.

"You know," she said softly, "if I saw you somewhere, walking in the street or at a club, I would never think you were a cop," sounding as if she were somehow sorry for me.

"You wouldn't be the only one," I told her. It was the best I could do. I was trying to figure out what to say, how to act. I was unprepared for her openness; when she spoke she touched my arm. The other customers sitting nearby began coughing, hissing, and muttering "*Tutsoon.*"

We ordered sandwiches from a waitress who looked like my Aunt Louise; her eyes never rose from her pad, and when she delivered my sandwich, she slid it across the table. I wasn't at all surprised.

I sat frozen for a second.

Marilyn smiled and shook her head.

I excused myself, got up from the table, and walked to the kitchen door where the waitress was waiting. "What's the problem?" I said.

"What problem?" she said. "There's no problem."

"C'mon, you practically threw the sandwich at me."

"Why you come in here with the *tutsoon*?"

"What?"

"You heard me. They don't come in here."

"Look," I said, "I'm a police officer, that woman's a schoolteacher, we got business in the courthouse around the corner."

"Ach," she said, "you're no cop."

"Sure I am. So what's the problem?"

She shrugged. Her face grew gloomy and something changed in her eyes. She let out a taut, quick sort of laugh.

"You know, it's nice to be nice," I said. Weak, but that was all I could come up with. This was 1965 and there were many neighborhoods in New York where attitudes were not all that different from those in Biloxi, Mississippi.

I returned to the table and gulped down the sandwich; I was so uncomfortable and anxious that I could hardly sit still. I wanted out of that restaurant. I wanted to bring Marilyn back to the courthouse, to a place where we both belonged. Marilyn had written her phone numbers on a napkin and handed it to me when I sat back down.

"I hope you're not married," she said.

"No, but I'm engaged." The hair on my arms stood on end, it was so easy to lie and so silly.

"Will you call me?"

"Sure," I told her, "absolutely."

"I'd like to show you my apartment," she said.

It felt like a challenge, a dare, me going up to Harlem on a date. The thought was stimulating. The deed was utterly out of the question.

At the end of the day, I threw the napkin with her phone numbers into a trash can that stood on a corner near the courthouse. A few minutes later, I was driving along the Grand Concourse when I made a quick U-turn and headed back. I wanted that phone number and tore the trash can apart looking for it. I finally found the napkin. It was wet and soggy and the numbers were unreadable. I can find her, I thought. I'm a cop. I'll find her.

It occurred to me that I could take Marilyn out, go walking hand in hand in Greenwich Village. In the Village we'd be safe. I could see it, the two of us spending a night at a Greenwich Village jazz club. I pictured a bed surrounded by African wood carvings. I could imagine sleeping with her.

Absolutely.

I'll call her.

I never did.

BECAUSE I'D GONE to court a day before my two days off, it was three days before I returned to work. Mario and Pete Schmidt were waiting for me. Mario told me that the night after the shooting, Lieutenant Sullivan had addressed the outgoing platoon, telling everyone that my shooting had been bad—legal, maybe, but bad. He said it was obvious that I didn't want to close with the burglars.

The idea gave me a bit of a jolt, the thought of taking the two burglars on hand-to-hand.

"He wasn't there," I said. "How does he know what happened?"

"Sullivan's wrong and he knows it," Mario said, "insinuating you were a coward."

I tried to be casual about it, pretending I didn't care. But I felt sick that an important lieutenant had called me a coward. Maybe others felt that way; maybe Pete and Mario did too. I couldn't imagine going through life like that—with people thinking you were a coward.

Pete told me that I shouldn't have said I fired a warning shot. "Ya know," he said, "there's no such thing as a warning shot."

I know. I know.

THE FOLLOWING PAYDAY when I was in the TPF office, the commanding officer asked to see me. Inspector Michael Codd listened patiently while I explained, or tried to explain, the shooting. He said he knew I knew the shooting was bad. He said the notion that any police officer would take a life for a crime against property infuriated him. "It may be legal," he said, "but it's a law that needs changing. You understand what I'm saying?" he said.

I told him it would never happen again. Then he told me that on the night of the riot, I had made him proud, that everyone in TPF had made him proud. "I like being proud of my men," he told me.

I nodded.

"Are you following me?" he said.

"Yes I am."

He had my arrest record out and in front of him. "You do good work," he said. He went through some papers on his desk, his brow furrowing. He put in plain words that any good police officer in a combat situation will always use his brain first, then his stick, and when all else fails, his gun. It was a matter of deep pride in TPF that no one thought of you as a coward, or worse, stupid.

I told him, "I understand."

"Keep up the good work" was the last thing he said.

I began questioning myself, wondering if Sullivan was right.

Maybe I was afraid to close with the burglars. Maybe, when it really counted, I had behaved like a coward.

Lieutenant Sullivan, the very same guy who thought I was too short to be in TPF, now thought I was gutless. Maybe he wasn't the only one. I'd have to prove them wrong, and I took that on as if it were a sacred duty.

to break out the gym set—to give someone a beating.

"Fuckin' muggers, I hate 'em. We break out the gym set on those bastards."

—OFFICER PETE SCHMIDT, TPF

One day they announced that TPF would be the first patrol unit in the NYPD to utilize decoy cops. In those days there were no women on patrol, so some of us dressed as women and went into the streets as targets for muggers. Sometimes we'd dress as Orthodox Jews, sometimes as derelicts. When it came time for my platoon to set up a decoy operation, it didn't take Sergeant Burke long to pick the decoy. When all was said and done, everyone in the platoon was three inches taller than me.

THE NUMBER OF random muggings, street robberies, and assaults was increasing all over the city. It wasn't hard to find a high-incidence location, a dark place, and wait for the phantoms and predators of the night to make a visit. And when they did, it was "Surprise!"

Break out the gym set.

It was a strange feeling, setting myself up as a target, a victim. But immediately I found that I had a problem. No one, it seemed, was interested in mugging me. Everyone, it seemed, wanted to sell me dope. I would sit on a bench in Central Park or stand in a hapless way on a corner in the East Village with this dreamlike expression on my face. Probably I looked just too goofy to mug. I'd hang around and in no time at all there'd be a *pssst-pssst*, a voice pleasant-sounding and gloomy.

"Ey, you looking to do something?"

"Whadaya got?"

Handfuls of glassine envelopes of heroin. I'd nod and smile. We had a prearranged signal, nothing complicated—my hands through my hair. A little gesture to my backups, and bingo, a nifty piece of work. The drug dealers went down smooth and easy.

"You're supposed to get mugged," the sergeant told me.

"I know."

"You know."

"Sure, trouble is, as soon as I find a spot and get ready, a drug dealer comes along pushing stuff on me."

"Let them go by."

"Go by."

"That's what I said. We don't want drug arrests. Drugs are not what we do. Muggers are who we're after."

"But it's a direct narcotics sale to a police officer, a felony, an easy collar."

Silence.

"I'll try and get mugged."

"Good."

Back out on the street, the drug dealers continued to haunt me. I'd tell them to go away and sometimes they would. Other times they insisted and insisted, so I ran my hands through my hair and my backups charged in, firing up the dealer's night.

But nobody mugged me.

On a Friday night not that long after the shooting, I was working decoy on the Lower East Side of Manhattan when I joined up with a group of five or six street runners on the prowl. I figured that they were looking to either mug someone or score drugs, I wasn't sure which.

My backups that night were John Bray and Roger Peachy. John was a no-nonsense, tough street cop. He was six feet tall, blond, and about 170 pounds. John had a ferocious temper and he could hit like a bull. He would eventually rise to the rank of captain, raise nine children, and practice law. Back then he was a wild-ass Irishman who took absolutely no shit.

Roger, when he was off duty, did bodyguard work for Sammy Davis Jr. He was nearly six feet tall, 230 or so. He resembled the fighter Sonny Liston and was just as bad tempered.

I followed the crew into a tenement off Stanton and Forsyth Streets—eight to ten people in that hallway, I remember the anxious looks on their faces, the air filled with Spanish. The two dealers moved quickly collecting money. I gave one of them ten dollars.

I hoped that John and Roger hadn't lost me. I was seriously out-numbered and messing around in the playground of evil.

One of the two who had been leading the crew wore a sporty straw hat and he had the longest fingernails I'd ever seen on a man. He told us all to wait where we were and then he went through a door into the basement. In a few seconds he returned, his hands filled with bags of heroin.

"This is no big thing," I said. "I don't want anyone to lose their head, but I'm a cop."

I had my gun in my hand. My shield was on a chain around my neck and I pulled it out. Suddenly things began to whirl, and chaos ruled.

"Fuck you," Straw Hat shouted. "That gun ain't real. You're no cop. I can buy one of those badges too."

His partner was looking at me as if I were insane. "He's a fucking kid," he yelled. "He's no cop."

I stood waiting for Roger and John to come charging through the door, and when they didn't, I motioned for some of the group to leave. I told the two dealers to stay put.

As the others scurried out the door, the two dealers stared hard at me. I stood in that hallway holding my gun, thinking, *Well here we are, this is it, this is the place, the time when you can't fake it.* I was filled with self-doubt, but excitement was also tumbling inside me. There was no panic, I wasn't afraid, and for that I was grateful.

If I became involved in another shooting so close to the last one, I knew I would be in one hell of a mess. "Be cool," I said. "I am a cop. Don't do anything stupid."

"Yeah, yeah," Straw Hat said. "It's a'right man, I'm cool."

They were sizing me up, deciding.

It was when I reached behind my back for my handcuffs that they came at me. I told myself, *They're junkies, little guys, you can take these two.* I slid my gun into my coat pocket. I'd forgotten that there was a hole there. My pistol went through that hole, hit my knee, banged off the tile floor with a resounding clang, and slid under a radiator. For a moment the three of us stood there staring at each other. Then, as if on signal, all three of us lunged for the gun. I dove between them and the radiator, punching, kicking, and screaming.

Straw Hat somehow got to his feet and began to kick me. He kicked me two or three times, then he ran out the door into the night. My eye was half closed and my nose was bleeding but I had my hands full with Straw Hat's partner. I pounded and pounded him; he was doubled over trying to pull a butcher knife from his belt. Somehow I grabbed the knife and threw it. Then I pounded him some more, until finally I managed to handcuff him.

John and Roger stood in the middle of the street holding Straw Hat and two others. "Let those two guys go," I yelled. "Kick the shit out of the asshole with the hat."

And they did.

You know, when there's action, when you've been frightened and hurt, you lose your sense of civility. Savagery sucks you in. You don't dwell on right and wrong. The only certainty is anger and survival and then, finally, retribution.

We broke out the gym set on Straw Hat and his partner.
Boy, did we ever.

"You remember, if they're not other cops, they're out to screw
you. Don't trust anyone."

—PATROLMAN JOHN BRAY, TPF

The following morning I delivered Straw Hat and his partner to
court for arraignment. The Legal Aid attorney and the judge were
distressed at the physical condition of the defendants and they let
me know it. Soon the judge, the Legal Aid, and the ADA, a prissy,
buttoned-down recent law school graduate, joined forces and all three
told me they were unconvinced by my description of how the arrest
had gone down. The mix was amazing. Obviously, what they were
trying to tell me was that they didn't like cops, especially TPF cops.

"Why is it," the ADA said, "that whenever you TPF cops come in
here, your prisoners always look like hell? Like they've been
knocked around. You know, we're hearing stories that you guys are
pretty abusive out there."

I didn't say anything. What could I say? But I was thinking, *You
little blond prick, I'd like to see what you would have done in that hallway.*
I couldn't understand why an assistant district attorney, a man who
was supposed to be on my side, would say such things and then join
forces against me.

It was true that while on patrol most TPF cops had little patience with anyone who gave them a ration of shit, and it was also
true that we didn't think of ourselves as social workers as some
precinct cops did. Even so, I felt that these courtroom characters
were idiotic, like their brains had shadows in them. What the hell
where they thinking?

It seemed to me, as it did to most cops back then, that all these
bureaucrats and functionaries, in their drive to appear enlightened

and humanistic, were turning those courtrooms into genuine loony bins with built-in escape hatches. All of us believed instinctively, if not consciously, that they would rather see us in bandages than the bad guys.

Such experiences and thoughts are the mortar and the stone, the very building blocks, of the blue wall of silence.

I REMEMBER IT was on a Friday, a day before I was to start a week's vacation, that I received a late morning telephone call from the TPF's clerical man, Joe Borelli. "You've been transferred. Feel good. It's a promotion. You've been sought after. You're going to PMD [Public Morals Division]. It's a great job, you'll love it."

He seemed thrilled for me.

But I knew better. PMD was a lateral move. Yes, you worked only in civilian clothes, and you were in a special operations unit, but you were still under the command of the chief of patrol, a part of the uniformed force. Most of the work was gambling enforcement, prostitution, and all the various violations of the public morals code. You could get a bellyful of that jazz real quick.

And that wasn't the worst of it. You hated to bring it up, no one ever did, but all the units of PMD were up to their necks in institutionalized, systematized corruption. You went to work in PMD knowing that. It was no secret. PMD worked the same way it had worked since Prohibition. It was an outfit where you'd be assigned from four to six years, then be transferred back to patrol, wait to retire, get out, and buy yourself a saloon or a motel. Assuming, of course, that you didn't get jammed up and go to jail.

"Once you're assigned to PMD you get yourself a little safe deposit box. Make sure you save the first five thousand because you just might need it one day to retain a lawyer."

— SERGEANT PETE BURKE, TPF

PMD was a large unit, thirty-six-hundred cops enforcing the public morality. A moneymaking machine. A Harlem captain once told me that there were forty policy number drops in one Harlem division alone. To operate, they paid one hundred dollars a day, 365 days a year. Do the math. And that was only one of seventeen divisions citywide. The money was major, the backbone and heart of corruption in New York City. The pad went all the way up, right through police headquarters into the mayor's office.

To keep everything flowing free and easy, PMD cases were prosecuted in their own courtroom. It was called the "Gamblers Part" and no one went to jail from that courtroom. The cops, the judges, the ADAs, the defense bar, all who operated from the Gamblers Part had their own sneaky little tricks to turn a dollar.

"No way," I told Joe, "not me. I'm not going to PMD. I'm not chasing bookmakers, pimps, and prostitutes. It's not what I want to do."

"You've already been transferred, you're on the list. Sullivan told me you have no choice but to go."

"I want a meeting with the CO; I want an interview with Chief Codd."

"I'll see if I can arrange it."

"Please."

"I'll try."

I jumped into my car and flew down to the office. Inspector Codd was expecting me.

He took me into his inner office, and I sat beside his spotless desk. While I talked, he crossed his arms, sat back in his chair, and stared at me. The chief was a great field commander, I'd seen him in action. On a personal level, he had always been kind to me, and I knew that I would follow him through the gates of hell. But on that day he sat still and quiet, his hard blue eyes drilling holes in me.

I got into a rant, and there were times I thought I'd gone over the edge, stating my case, making the arguments, taking a stand.

"It's a promotion," he said.

"Yeah, sure, I know, but . . ."

"What?"

"Inspector, this is purely hypothetical, but let's say you had a son and he was assigned to TPF and then transferred to PMD, and say this son of yours came to you for advice, what would you say?"

I remember the way he tightened his lips and arranged his shoulders. The way he gave me this curt little nod. The way he shrugged and said, "You can't stay here forever. TPF is a three- or four-year assignment."

"I've been in TPF for only two years. Inspector, I'm just an ordinary guy with ordinary dreams and ambitions, and none of those dreams or ambitions have anything to do with PMD."

Silence from him.

"I really don't want anything to do with PMD. There are problems there that I couldn't deal with. We both know PMD's reputation."

He narrowed his eyes and stared at me. He almost nodded, but didn't.

"You'll stay in TPF," he said finally. "I'll find a place for you."

"Listen, if I have to, I'll drive the TPF bus," I told him.

"Sure," he told me and smiled. Inspector Codd almost never smiled.

The chief understood. In my mind and in my heart, Inspector Michael Codd remains to this day one of my heroes. Years later, they appointed him police commissioner, and he should have turned that job down. Mike Codd was a thoughtful and skillful field commander. He had an uncanny sensitivity for the working cop. But he was a terrible politician.

They said that Inspector Codd reread my file that afternoon;

then he made a few telephone calls. This facility of mine for passing as anything but a cop must have caught his eye.

Two weeks later I was walking a foot post on Central Park West when I spotted the TPF sergeant's car turning the corner and coming onto the avenue. The driver threw on the overhead lights for a second and gave the siren a short blast. Dave Christian was driving Sergeant Burke. They called me to the car.

I leaned into the car window, and between intermittent static and radio calls Burke told me that I had been transferred. The orders had just come down.

"Into the Detective Division," Dave said.

"Really?"

"That's what I said."

"Where?"

"You've been transferred to the Narcotics Bureau."

The Narcotics Bureau truly was a promotion; it came within the scope and under the command of the chief of detectives. The Narcotics Bureau was a part of the Detective Division and had a reputation for being a unit untouched by corruption.

"No cop in his right mind would take drug money."
— A WORKING COP'S PRINCIPLE

I had never been more excited. A little more than three years in the department, and I was going to be a detective—a New York City police detective. My life would be changed forever.

DOPE
STREET

He was sitting on a wooden bench outside the administrative offices of the Narcotics Bureau. He was wearing a shirt and tie, a spiffy camel hair jacket, and dark chocolate–colored slacks. I figured that his tassel-topped loafers must have cost as much as my entire wardrobe.

He knew me immediately, but I couldn't place his face. He looked like the singer Dean Martin—Dean Martin after he and Jerry split, the time when Dino became a star in his own right. His name was Joe Nunziata and he'd come to the Narcotics Bureau from the Mounted Division. He told me that we had met one hot afternoon in front of the 15th Precinct in the midst of a mini-riot. He was riding a horse back then and wearing a helmet. I was without my cap and under a lot of stress. I certainly remembered the incident if not the face. We had been transferred to the Narcotics Bureau the very same day and our lives would intersect again.

I joined him on the bench and we talked for a while about the job and riots and collars and friends.

"So you were the guy with the horse."

"Right, cuz, and you were the goofy TPF cop at the front door of the Alamo."

"That was me. You saved my ass."

People kept coming by welcoming him, saying, "Hey Joe, it's gonna be great to have you here." Ten, fifteen people—sergeants, lieutenants, detectives—all of them thrilled to have Joe Nunziata working in their command.

He stood and began to groom himself a little. He chitchatted with the clerical men, sent great big his and hellos to people who were clearly strangers. He exchanged greetings with three men in fedoras, topcoats, and with very serious expressions on their faces. "SIU," Joe said. "Those guys made the French Connection case."

I'd never heard of it.

People talked to him about his days playing pro ball, his days as a prizefighter, his days on patrol, and his days in Mounted. "Let him tell you about the time he chased a purse snatcher down subway steps on his horse. Let him tell you that story. And the one when he caught the skel who stuck his dick in a baby's crib. If I had the time I'd tell you what he did to that shit-bird."

Saga after saga, all of them told with myth-making force. I looked at Joe Nunziata and realized that this guy was a genuine cop legend.

The commanding officer's secretary appeared from the inner office and called Joe in. At the sight of him, she touched her hair and straightened her dress. The woman was all aflutter as Joe put his arm around her shoulder and told her to lead the way. She smiled and nodded. A whole lot of women smiled and nodded around Joe.

Left alone on the bench, I closed my eyes and went into a semi-sleep, a trick I'd picked up in the army—a place where I was half asleep for most of the time. Anxiety or boredom always made me sleepy. I must have dozed off for about fifteen or twenty minutes.

Joe came by, grabbed my shoulder, and shook me. "Ey, cuz, what the hell you doing? Are you sleeping?"

"Just resting my eyes."

"I don't believe it. You were sleeping."

"Was not."

"Oh," he said, "I think I'm gonna like you. I mean that is something. All this shit going on, our first day and all, you fall asleep."

I told him I was resting my eyes.

He had a strange laugh—a great big hiss and a huge smile, teeth clamped together. "Where'd they assign you?" I asked.

"Brooklyn, Group Five. I live in Brooklyn. It's gonna work out."

"Joe," I said, "we should team up, work together."

He said, "Well-l-l. . . ."

I was insulted. This guy didn't know how good I was. "Why not?"

"Well-l-l-l, I already have a partner."

"We just got here."

"Amazing, isn't it."

"I'll say."

"WE'RE ASSIGNING YOU to the undercover group."

"I'd prefer not."

"What? Why?"

"For one thing, undercovers in narcotics don't make arrests. You spend all your time pretending you're not a cop. I don't like that."

"We brought you here to work undercover."

"Really?"

"Yes."

"I would not like that. Honestly, I don't think I'd do a good job."

A long, long silence.

"Okay, we'll assign you to an enforcement group. That's Group Five—Brooklyn."

"Great. Thank you."

"We have a job for you."

"Okay."

"You're going into East New York Vocational High School. You'll go in undercover, as a student, and buy drugs."

"Will I make the arrests?"

"No."

"I see."

"Good."

SO MINDFUL AM I of those experiences that nothing goes away. I can see myself as I was then. None of it was real—like I was in a movie, some dodo up on the screen, some character in my skin making his way through a world he didn't begin to understand.

I'm sitting in homeroom at East New York Vocational High School. A bright Brooklyn spring day and the teacher walks into the room. He looks at me and looks again. I smile.

His name was Veltri. I called him Red when I was the pitcher and he was the great glove and light-hitting shortstop of our own high school baseball team. A fierce competitor and a dynamite guy, Red had been the center of more than one slugfest in the middle of a baseball field.

Later, in the boys room, he asked how life had been treating me. I told him that I was fine. I explained that I was a cop and I was at the school to do something that had to be done. He said he figured.

"Shit," he said, "I knew you weren't the best student. But hell, you couldn't have been that bad." He laughed, I laughed, he told me to be careful; there were some bad kids in the school.

"Couldn't be much worse than some of the guys we grew up with," I told him.

"Another world," he said.

"Really?"

"You'll see."

I bought drugs every day—pot, pills, and heroin. Red was right, there were some tough kids knocking around that school. Some had beards and some wore mustaches; many looked to be older than me. I'd worked East Harlem and the South Bronx and the Lower East Side of Manhattan. When it came to selling dope, these kids were amateurs.

It was my last day at the school. I had been there two weeks. I walked into the principal's office full of confidence and sure that I would be praised for the work I had done.

I remember how the principal came at me, how livid he was. Fourteen students—I'd bought drugs from fourteen different students. Suddenly he was horrified that an undercover cop had crossed the inviolable threshold of his school. He walked in circles—muttering, glancing at me, and muttering some more—then he rubbed furiously at his head.

"Who gave you the right?" he said. "This is outrageous."

I thought I had accomplished something good, something worthwhile, and something that needed to be done. Not by this guy's lights, not at all. The strange part, of course, was that he had asked for the police to help him. But the sudden clearing of the blurry line between suspecting and knowing had ruined his day, and he took his frustration out on me.

I felt a swell of hopelessness, a claustrophobic sensation. I thought I'd suffocate if I didn't get out of his office. He berated me, not unlike the district attorneys in Queens, asking me who I thought I was, telling me I must have taken advantage of his students—his kids, he called them. This the very same man who only a couple of weeks earlier was so happy to see me, so pleased that I would check and see if there truly was a drug problem at his school.

As he was into his rage, I had a picture in my head of a fifteen-year-old boy in jeans and a sweatshirt, a knowing smirk on his face, this kid telling me he could get all the drugs I wanted, whatever I wanted, as long as I had the cash. Guns? He could get me a gun too. This little shit tough guy, his hair long, flowing over his shoulders, a good-looking boy, looked a lot like one of my high school buddies from a few years back. But they weren't selling drugs. He was.

Walking out the front door of that high school, I had no sense that the principal was just one more milestone marking my way. There would be others, many others who would come later: judges, prosecutors, politicians, chiefs of police, some of my family, my friends, journalists, television commentators, cops, so many cops, scores of good citizens, my unborn children, all asking me about similar and different cases, wondering why I didn't mind my own business. I did try; you'll see how I tried. It just wasn't possible.

deontology—a theory in ethics in which duty is seen as the basis of moral behavior.

The Narcotics Bureau was divided into the enforcement groups of the Bronx, Queens, Brooklyn and Staten Island, Manhattan North and South, Undercover, and the Special Investigating Unit, with 135 detectives in all. It didn't take me long to realize that one hundred times that number could not have slowed the flow of drugs into the city.

It was the mid-sixties and that hedonistic culture was all around us. Paul Simon was doing the exquisite "Sounds of Silence." At the far end of the world our young men were dying, and we had another war blazing in our own backyard. At the time, even the most pessimistic observer could not have imagined that we could lose both.

Then as now, politicians and police brass were telling us how we could win the war on drugs and wipe out this plague. Their weekly memos and bulletins were quite inspiring. But when you went out into the street, up against that ocean of drugs, you'd see things differently. Even if you didn't pay attention, you'd have to be deaf, dumb, and blind not to see that somebody was bullshitting somebody.

"It's a war of attrition, we wear 'em the fuck out."
—A narcotics detective known as the Argentine

"Hey, this has nothing to do with causes or reasons, this is our job and we do it."
—A narcotics detective known as Viejo (old man)

"They're animals; all of them skel welfare cheats and filthy swine."
—A narcotics detective known as Slapperstein

After my gig at East New York Vocational High School, I began working the Brooklyn streets with a series of old-time narco cops. These men had been fighting skirmishes in the drug war for years and holding their own. Then the explosion hit, the great heroin epidemic, bringing with it hordes of addicts and unleashing rampaging street crime. The dark night of the heroin plague was on us.

The bosses told me that finding a steady partner was essential. So that summer and fall they continued to partner me up with various detectives. I spent weeks with this or that one, hopelessly trying to find a good fit.

In September Gina gave birth to our first child, Anthony. I borrowed down-payment money from my father and bought a four-bedroom house in one of the faceless housing developments out east on Long Island. It was a time of seeming abundance and prosperity. Fifteen hundred dollars down, a thirty-year mortgage, and you had four bedrooms and two baths, a colonial house on a quarter acre of land.

There were ten identical houses on the street, owned mostly by cops and firemen. And even though it was an hour and a half commute from Brooklyn, I didn't mind at all. I had seen enough of big city violence to know that I wanted my family as far from that city as possible. This growing fear of New York City was a weird emotion; to be frightened of the people of a city of whom, after all, I was one.

On one level, the job was easy. Arrest numbers were all that seemed to matter. Make your felonies and misdemeanors and the bosses will leave you alone, they said. Don't overdo, you make too many collars and you make the others look bad. I knew that the standard by which everyone got through the job was not to make waves of any kind, and I'd always thought it was a good one.

They told me it would take time for me to be accepted, to be judged by my competence, my willingness to be a team player. They wanted four misdemeanor and eight felony collars a month per team, and that was a cinch. I could do that in an afternoon. Considering the gangs of addicts and dealers overflowing the city, such numbers were absurd. On the other hand, I had no stomach to break with tradition so I didn't push. I watched the way more experienced detectives worked, and studied the activity chart on the wall.

All the detectives kept their numbers about the same and no one worked weekends. It should have been effortless to keep up and unproblematic to fit in. It was anything but. It became apparent that none of what you would call the regular guys were interested in having me for a steady partner.

Why not? I was never sure. Maybe they felt I was too young and inexperienced to be in the Detective Division. There were other men who were far more senior and who had good arrest records and had been working in war zones for years. Most of them were still stuck in uniform.

I didn't go to cop bars, didn't hang out, didn't like to drink, and maybe the old-timers took that as a sign of disrespect.

Maybe my young looks rubbed them wrong; it could have been that. Or it could have been that I didn't know the words—whatever those words were—that proved you were a knock-around guy, a stand-up guy.

Then again, there may have been no particular reason. It could have been simply a matter of luck. But I didn't believe that. It was something else. Maybe I was being paranoid, but I didn't believe that either. I figured it was the cops in the Narcotics Bureau who were peculiar, not me.

In TPF we worked, we laughed, we cried and hung out together. The muster room was always a riotous and joyful gathering of cops.

Everyone in Narcotics whispered, small cliques of bosses and cops bickering and snickering and scheming together in corners or at the Hanover Bar, a cop hangout across the street from our office. I'd come into the office and they would shoot me the strangest glances. I'd wonder what would become of me there. What did I have to prove?

On the days when I went to court it was only Joe Nunziata who would join me for lunch. On paydays, nobody invited me to the Hanover for a drink. On weekends when someone was having a barbecue or a party at his home, I was never asked. I was clearly an outsider—I felt invisible.

One day at lunch I tried to explain some of this to Joe—how much I yearned to belong, how hard I was willing to work, how I couldn't understand why none of the regular detectives seemed to like me. I sounded pretty stupid. Then Joe came right out with it.

"Nobody here knows you, it's gonna take time."

"Me and you, Joe, we got here the same day."

"They knew me, people here knew me. I don't know exactly what to say to you," he said. "It's something about your coming from TPF I guess."

"What?"

"There was nothing there. Why would anyone want to work where there's nothing but chickenshit."

"Chickenshit?"

"You know what I mean."

"No I don't."

"See," he said, "there it is." He smiled, "Well anyway, you'll do fine, just give it time."

"Nobody wants to work with me."

"You'll find a steady partner, and when you do, go out there and knock 'em dead."

"Sure."

I remember the way he got up from the table. How he walked out of the coffee shop, slowly, with a beat, relaxed with a special kind of self-confidence, treating everyone who crossed his path like a customer, smiling as he moved with hello and howyadoin', cuz, to everyone in the place. From where I sat I watched him go out into the street, light a cigarette, and head off to the courthouse.

I sat for a long time in that coffee shop, more confused than ever; asking myself, *What the hell was he talking about?*

Then one sunny afternoon, on a payday, after I'd gone through two more partners, my lieutenant called me into his office. I was nervous. I knew that I was still on trial.

"I'm assigning you a new partner," he said.

"Good."

"We like this guy. He's been around awhile and he'll work, but he needs direction. Look," he said, "Jim Bryan is going to be either flopped back to uniform, transferred, or promoted. He's been in grade way too many years and he's not making collars. Maybe you're just the guy to charge him up."

"You think so?"

"Nunziata thinks you're going to be one of the top guys here."

"Really?"

"Yeah."

"How the hell does he know, he's never worked with me?"

"Nunziata knows people."

the set—a particular street location where things are hot, where people are buying drugs.

It was in late summer that I began to work with Detective Jim Bryan. I wasn't so sure that this arrangement was going to work out. Sure, he was experienced, knew the job, knew the streets, and knew all the players. I'd work undercover, buy the drugs, and he'd arrest the dealers, but was he willing to put in the time? I wanted to work as many days and hours as it took, but not Sundays—on Sunday I wanted to be home. "Okay," he said, "sounds good."

Half Irish and half Cherokee Indian, Jim got an A+ in the tell-it-like-it-is game. Born and raised somewhere in the Southwest, he loved country music, a thermos of coffee, and Camel cigarettes. He was spotlessly neat, and he could fix anything from an automobile engine to a refrigerator to a pair of eyeglasses. When he was discharged from the navy in New York City, he had looked around, studied the hills and valleys, and told himself, This is where I stay; this is where I want to live my life.

He had age freckles on his hands and was old enough to be my father. We had practically nothing in common.

Jim was married to a woman twenty years his junior. He constantly worried that sooner or later, he'd lose her to a younger man. The street people called him Viejo, and long before we began working together, Jim's get-up-and-go had taken a hike.

I liked him immediately. I called him JB and knew that I could rekindle his slow-moving fires. He told me to do it—take charge, pick the spots, pick the targets, and he'd back me up. A bodybuilder, the years may have slowed him, but he had a helluva physique and he was strong as a bull.

"You have any idea where you'd like to work?" he said.

"Oh, yeah," I said. "Everywhere."

> gofer—a strung-out addict working for dealers and getting paid in dope. Although they did sell drugs, gofers were not truly drug dealers.

I felt confident in the mixed neighborhood of whites, blacks, and Hispanics in South Brooklyn. I passed easily; people rarely gave me a second look. It was as though I were invisible.

And so we started right in.

I bought from anyone who sold drugs; I made no distinctions between dealers and gofers. I gave you money, you brought me drugs, you went down. On the activity chart, JB's red line began to soar.

THE INTERSECTIONS OF Fourth Avenue, Atlantic Avenue, and Flatbush Avenue were a drug bazaar that never shut down. An island stood at the heart of where those avenues came together, and on that island was a brightly lit stand where you could buy coffee, sodas, pizza, and soft-serve ice cream. There was an outsized Bickford's Cafeteria across the street, and a block south on Fourth Avenue was a doughnut shop. The stand, the cafeteria, and the doughnut shop were drug addict gathering places that went strong twenty-four hours a day, seven days a week.

A short five-minute walk from Bickford's was the Long Island Rail Road terminal, the tracks running under the streets of Brooklyn. Commuters heading home to Massapequa and Hicksville could stop for the lurid thrill of a quick ten-dollar blow job or ten-minute fuck from one of the dozens of hookers who roamed that neighborhood. And plenty of them did.

At the foot of Atlantic Avenue, a few blocks from 4th Avenue, was the Brooklyn waterfront. Columbia Street, a gloomy, bleak, and treacherous set of blocks lined with tenements, social clubs, and bars, was home to all sorts of criminal activity.

I'd leave JB in the car and hit the set to buy drugs. He'd watch, my backup, my protection. When I returned to the car, I'd give Jim a name, a description, and the drugs that I had bought. A week or two later, Jim, with the help of one or two other detectives, would snap the dealer up. That was the idea, and it was easy. I'd find more pushers than you could shake a stick at. Within a couple of months Jim Bryan led the Brooklyn group in arrests, which pleased the bosses no end. They liked him. Everyone did.

I could see that the essential thing about the street was that one part was like any other part. But right and wrong, good and evil were not as clearly defined as I had once thought. I was learning to distinguish between the victims and the predators, and soon discovered that there were mostly victims out there.

I could buy drugs all day and all night long. There were hordes of addicts and pushers everywhere. But mostly I was buying dope from people who were so stoned that once they sold me the drugs, they were just as likely to turn around and walk into an oncoming bus. People who literally couldn't find their hands and feet. It was no challenge at all. Theses dealers were ghosts that aimlessly walked the street; fire your pistol alongside their ear, and they wouldn't blink.

If we were doing anything to even slow the flow of drugs I certainly didn't see it. Arrest after arrest, we just went through the motions. Jim didn't seem to care at all, or even pretend that we were doing anything of value.

> cure—just enough heroin to stem the onset of withdrawal.

> gorilla—a drug addict predator who robs from other, weaker addicts.

> to be taken off—to be robbed.

"Man, don't you know God is dead, got his ass taken off by a gorilla at Atlantic and Fourth."
—A junkie street whore named Chocolate

There were men and women out on those streets hopelessly addicted to the most powerful drug the world has ever known. They scratched along to get along, doing whatever they had to in order to feed the beast of their habit. Mostly it was small-time dealing, thievery, and prostitution. They spent their lives always alert to the dangers of patrolling cops and street gorillas—cold-hearted and brutal take-off artists who would beat them and cut them and steal their cure. The closer I looked, the more I found the drug world a dark, painful, and unforgiving place, a world where only the strong and quick-witted survived. And when they survived, it was never for long.

In no time at all, I became convinced that I was serving no purpose at all, buying drugs from morons. It was all a horrible fake, a joke.

Early on, I didn't unload my concerns on Jim. I buried them and went along. The more the arrest numbers built up, the more Jim and I were praised by the bosses, the less such thoughts troubled me. Since I was doing undercover work, Jim took most of the arrests— his red line now flying off the chart. The bosses acknowledged me, they knew I had consented to be made use of, and my ability to buy dope was becoming legend.

One late night when the street was quiet, sitting in Jim's car, drinking coffee and smoking cigarettes, talking quietly about the plague, what I was doing, talking seriously about this job of narcotics detective, trying to make it a dialogue, not an argument, I said, "Jim this is nuts, they're all victims out here. I'm buying dope from zombies."

"What?"

"I'm doing nothing out here. It's a joke."

"We led the borough six months running. You're knocking 'em dead."

"I'm buying drugs from drug addicts, sick people out doing their thing just to get their cure. I stand on a street corner and these schmucks trip over each other running to sell me dope."

"I'm going to tell you all you'll ever need to know about this business. You hear me? Are you listening?"

"Go on."

"Nobody, and I mean nobody, gives a shit. Arrest numbers are arrest numbers. Who you buy from doesn't matter at all. Numbers are what counts. Bust 'em, get 'em off the street, put those numbers on the wall. It doesn't matter what or who they are."

"It matters to me."

Then he embarrassed me—letting me know that it was pretty obvious I didn't have enough experience or patience to buy from the real drug dealers.

Silence from me.

"If you're serious," he told me, "and you want to learn what is really going on out there, you're going to need help. You need someone who can teach you, guide you, move you along." I told him that I spent a lot of time out on those streets.

"It doesn't matter," he said. He waved pensively. "You're good, but not as good as you think you are."

Well now, I thought. *Well now.*

That's when Jim told me he'd get me an informant, someone to walk with me, someone who could introduce me around and teach me.

I never wanted to work with an informant, didn't want anyone to know who I was. Didn't trust them; the breed gave me the creeps. Then again, all the old-timers maintained that you're only as good as your best informant. I told Jim that maybe he was right; he told me that there were no maybes about it

beeazag—a bag of heroin.

to get off—to inject heroin.

I knew him, had seen him many times hanging in the street. I had been drawn to the way he carried himself, the almost ghostlike way he moved through the set.

He walked toward the car wearing his customary Sherlock Holmes hat, his coat off his shoulders and buttoned at the collar so that it flowed behind him like a cape. As he moved, his head bobbed up and down like a horse's. When he got into the car, Jim greeted him with a great big "Junior, howyabeen?"

I looked at Junior and Junior stared at me, then all at once we both smiled. I had no idea then, but I am convinced today that meeting Junior was the beginning of the end of whatever innocence I still possessed.

"Hey, Junior," I said.

"Well, lookit you, you a cop?"

"Hey, Junior," I said again.

A strange, short, mean little laugh. "You do look good. Fuck, I'da sold you dope."

"You almost did."

Junior played the gofer role on the set, and he had hit on me on more than one occasion, offering, for the price of half the bag, to go and find me a cure. I had never been hard up enough or cold-blooded enough to lay a sale on him. On the set I had stayed clear of Junior. Even for me, he was way too easy.

JB made something like official introductions: Junior, Detective Leuci, Bob, Junior.

Junior kept staring at me.

We discussed how we would work in the street. Jim spoke, I spoke, and Junior continued to stare me down.

Jim outlined certain cautions:

> Buy from people you know.
> Stay away from gofers; you run into one have him bring you to the connection.

Make sure I know exactly where you are.

Don't go into shooting galleries.

I offered, "Junior, introduce me however you like, just don't say we were in jail together. I don't know anything about jail and don't want to have to answer any questions."

I told Junior that his job was to make the introductions and then back off. "I give up the money, the dope comes directly to me. Do not get between the dealer and me, and don't touch the drugs. Ever."

Junior frowned. Jim sighed.

"What?" I said.

"You two guys aren't bullshitting me, are ya?" Junior said. "I mean, Bobby, you're really a cop?"

I wore my badge on a chain around my neck. I popped it out and Junior smiled, not showing any teeth.

"All right, Junior," I said. "Let's get going."

On the outside he looked like every other junkie—raggedy, his hands and arms swollen, fingers like loaves of bread. As we walked to the set, he explained that he worked for the police because he had no other way to earn. He seemed self-conscious, a bit embarrassed, humiliated by his role as informant. He told me he had an outrageous heroin habit, and long ago he'd lost the will to steal. He couldn't run, could never fight, it was exhausting for him to get by. Junior was my first informant. He was black, born and raised in a South Bronx ghetto, and he would teach me all I ever needed to know about what it was like to live the harrowing life of a heroin addict.

At first he repulsed me; I hated what he represented. To me, Junior epitomized hopelessness and weakness, a kind of frailty that I had little sympathy for, the total collapse of the human spirit.

His eyes were the darkest brown, the whites highlighted by a slight yellow tinge. Bloated with water, Junior's skin had this silky, almost transparent look to it. My rule: Don't touch me, I won't touch you.

to make your cure—to get your hands on enough
drugs to feed your addiction.

Two brothers, both named Cubano, ran a bodega and a thriving
drug business at the corner of Pacific and Nevins Streets. I had tried
several times to buy heroin from them, and got turned away each
time. I'd walk in trying to do business, and they'd look at me, mutter
something in Spanish, and tell me to go away. With Junior at my
side, I walked into the store and was greeted like an old friend.

Junior's job was to bring me in, introduce me, and then to back
away. It was vital that the drugs went from the dealer directly to me.
When I testified in court, no mention could be made of Junior's
presence. If he got involved directly in the sale, giving the money or
taking the drugs, he would then have to appear as a witness, either
before the grand jury or, worse yet, in open court. Junior, an old
hand at this informant business, understood all that. At least I
thought he did.

I handed one of the brothers twelve dollars and put up two fingers. From a cigar box he kept under the counter, Cubano slid two
bags from his bundle. When he reached out to hand them to me, Junior stretched between us and grabbed the dope. Those two bags
were my evidence, and the chain had been broken. I was furious.

As soon as we left the bodega, I pulled Junior into a hallway.
"What in the hell are you doing? Give me my dope."

"What?"

"You heard me, give me the dope."

"What?"

I spun him up against the hallway wall and began going through
his pockets. I found bags of dope everywhere. In every pocket Junior had bags of dope. I took him by the elbow and dragged him the
two blocks back to JB's car. Jim was smoking his Camels, drinking
his coffee, lost somewhere in his own head.

I began hollering and carrying on, telling Jim that his boy had stolen my dope. "The son of a bitch has bags in every pocket, I can't tell which ones I bought. What the hell is he up to?"

"Get out of the car," JB told me. "Get out of the car. We don't talk in the car, so get out."

We went for a short walk to the corner and back, JB telling me that we never talk business in front of the informant and never, ever in the car. I nodded, even though I had no idea what the hell business he was talking about.

Jim explained that Junior had been an informant for years and that he'd made hundreds of buys. I told him that I knew that.

"Why do you think he works for us? I mean there are other ways he can spend his time," he said.

I figured that Jim kept Junior out of jail and maybe gave him a few bucks now and then.

"A few bucks?" Jim said. "The man has a hundred-dollar-a-day habit, and we get a hundred dollars a month expenses. You want to tell me how the hell we're going to pay him?"

"You keep him out of jail."

No response.

Jim was embarrassed; he looked at me as though he thought I was putting him on. I asked him to explain, to be clear and stop talking in circles. Jim thought about this for a second. He put his hands in his pockets, bent his head, and then explained that on the day Junior was going to work for us, he went into the street and bought a bag of dope. He took that bag home and cut it five or six times, making five or six bags. The stuff was no longer usable, far too weak to do an addict any good. But there was a trace of heroin in every bag. Just a trace, but it was there.

"Yeah. So?"

A long, long moment of silence.

"Jim?"

"When you two go out and make buys, Junior keeps what you bought and gives you the stuff he's made."

"You're kidding me."

"Wait, wait a minute," he said. "You turn your buys into the lab, it will always come back heroin present. And that's all that matters, heroin present."

Jim smiled in a matter-of-fact way.

220.20 New York State Penal Law—heroin, a felony to give, barter, or sell.

hot shot—heroin mixed with battery acid, kills you quickly and painfully.

"Bobby," he said finally, "you'll have your buys, and Junior is able to make his cure. Everybody's happy."

"No way," I said. "You're out of your mind. That's a felony."

Jim Bryan had thick, graying blond hair, the wide, broad shoulders of a weight lifter, and a great smile. He was a very soft-spoken man, almost shy. Everything about JB said here is a decent man.

"Bob, c'mon. Do you think you can get informants to work because they have some sort of civic pride? If Junior gets caught bringing an undercover cop around, somebody will lay a hot shot on him. I think he deserves some consideration. C'mon, man, think about it, what's the big deal? Say we had enough money to give him, say we gave Junior a hundred dollars, what do you think he would do? Buy himself a meal, pay his rent? Fuck no, he'd buy drugs, because that's what junkies do."

"I don't believe this," I said. "This is nuts."

Jim told me that he'd be willing to stand out in the street and debate me all night long. But the truth was, he'd been doing this job a lot longer than I had, and maybe there were some things about me that he'd taken for granted. Clearly, I didn't know my ass from my elbow about being a narcotics detective.

"You're not going to change my mind," I told him. "I'm not about to commit a crime to make some simple arrest. It's not worth it."

He nodded gravely. "Nobody cares," he said. "All they want are numbers, arrest numbers. How we get them is our business."

"Not me," I said. "No way. I'll do it on my own. I've done it on my own."

"Frankly," he said, "I think you need to grow up. You're naive, very naive. Not stupid, I don't mean that."

"Thank you."

"You spent too much time in TPF. You're in narcotics now, and you'll either make it here or you won't. It's up to you."

"Maybe I don't belong here."

"You belong here. If I've ever met anyone that belongs in narcotics, it's you. You just might have to change the way you think is all."

"That's nonsense. I've been buying drugs on my own. I don't need to give someone dope to buy dope."

He told me that there was a war going on out here. No way you can play by the rules in a war. "No way," he said, "no fucking way."

I told him to convince Junior to hang with me a week, maybe two. I said that I'd pay Junior, give him whatever money I could, if he'd just hang with me and teach me a few things. There was only silence from Jim, just a slow shaking of his head.

Junior agreed to two weeks, but no more. In two weeks he'd find another team to work with. We promised him two hundred dollars, the total amount of both our expense accounts.

"Agreed?"

"Okay."

"No drugs."

"Okay. When do I get my money?"

to skin pop—to inject heroin beneath the skin without using a vein, usually into the upper arm.

white lady—heroin.

OD—overdose.

to get off, to mainline—to inject heroin directly into a vein.

jones—a habit.

set of works—a hypodermic needle attached to an eye dropper, a bottle cap, and a tiny ball of cotton. Powdered heroin is put into the bottle cap, a few drops of water are added, the bottle cap is heated, liquefying the heroin. To filter impurities, the heated liquid is drawn through the cotton ball and into the eyedropper. Now you're ready to go.

booting—after an injection, the hypodermic needle remains in the vein, the user draws blood from his vein, and then passes the hypodermic to someone else. The next user injects his heroin, now mixed with blood. It increases the heroin's potency.

Do you want to talk about hepatitis and AIDS?
I had made a rule. Junior should not touch me.
Most days he looked old, diseased, weary, and consumed. During our first few days together, we'd sit on the curb hardly talking, just watching the parade of junkies, whores, and dealers go by. The dealers would cruise us, hit on us, asking if we wanted to score. Junior would pull me aside, whispering. "Not him, not her, they're gofers. That one, that one's for real, look how he's dressed—he's clean, he's smiling, and his nose ain't running. The others, man, lookit 'em, they're all fucking dying."

We'd spend eight or nine hours a day together, Junior teaching and me learning. Halfway through that first week, I forgot about the no touching rule. We'd sit shoulder to shoulder, making jokes and laughing, rolling into each other, and together watch the insane street world go by.

To my utter amazement, I discovered that Junior was a very bright guy and talented. He had a beautiful singing voice. He read three newspapers a day and always carried a paperback novel. His heroin addiction was brutal. He explained that his habit forced him to inject five to seven bags of heroin a day, and that was just to avoid the agony of withdrawal. Five to seven bags simply to be normal, whatever the word *normal* meant for Junior.

Junior explained how I should dress, how I should walk and talk. He told me when I should be aggressive and when I should lay back. In other words, he taught me how to look and act like a heroin addict.

Heroin was much more than his temptress; it was his master. He'd been addicted since the age of twelve. Forget getting high—getting high was a thing of the past. Nowadays he needed the drug simply to avoid being sick. And the sickness was horrible, worse than anything I could imagine.

"So why don't you just put it down? Quit?" I asked him.

"So why don't you just quit smoking? G'head; let me see you do it. Think about a habit that's about a hundred times more powerful. A jones that makes you physically ill, makes your bones ache, your nose run, and your stomach turn to knots of steel spikes ripping you apart until you feed the beast of your habit. Think about that, smartass."

"Jesus."

"Yeah."

We were the same age. He had a wife and child, and someday soon he was going to kick. Someday soon he was going to clean up— get in a program and clean up his act. Someday soon.

He loved jazz, and always talked about Billie Holiday. "The woman OD'd," he said, "you believe that shit? The white lady, she took Lady Day away.

"Babyface, if you pay attention to what I'm telling you, you'll learn these streets. Watch me and learn."

Junior had a sweet smile, and he called me Babyface. I should have put an end to that, right then and there, but I didn't. I sort of liked it. Babyface; cute. That nickname, like an evil spirit, would come out of the grave and haunt me for years.

One morning, at the corner of Columbia and Kane Streets, just across from the Brooklyn docks, Junior brought me into the basement of an abandoned tenement. It was a shooting gallery run by a dealer named Bee-Eye.

I walked behind Junior into the basement. There were drug addicts everywhere, zoned out on soiled mattresses, huddled in corners of the room. Bee-Eye sat on a chair behind a pink Formica table. He was young, dark-skinned, and Hispanic, and he wore netting over his hair. He sat hunched over the table. His eyes were huge and they glistened, and seemed as though they could do funny things, look around at impossible angles. There were bags of heroin on that table and sets of works. And there was a gun.

"Give us three bags," Junior said.

Bee-Eye slid three bags across the table, then he pushed across a set of works.

"What's this?" I asked him.

"This is my place," he said. "You buy here, you use here. Two dollars to rent the works." He spoke as if by rote. Then he picked up the gun and slammed it on the table. He looked serious. I turned to Junior; he shrugged.

I took the three bags and put them in my pocket. I told Bee-Eye that the drugs were not all mine. I had a girlfriend; she was sick and waiting for me. Bee-Eye reached for his gun.

All my experience and undercover skills, the entire cool I thought I had, vanished.

Junior looked at me and saw the panic in my face. I carried my gun in the small of my back. When I started to reach for it, Junior shouted, "No!" and kicked over the table. I turned and ran out the door, scrambled up the basement steps two at a time, ran out of the tenement and into the street. I ran and ran, along Columbia Street down to Union Street. Five minutes later, Junior came strolling and waving his hand in the air, his cap pushed to the back of his head, his coat flowing behind him. He was laughing.

"Babyface, you crazy brother. You gone. The hell you do that for?"

"That sonofabitch was going to make me shoot up," I told him. "He had a gun, that fucker."

Junior pinched my cheek, telling me that Bee-Eye's gun didn't work. The firing pin had been busted for years.

"You got to stand up to dealers like that," he said. "Look him in the eye and say, 'Fuck you, man.' Run out the way you did, people think you're a Section Eight. But that's awright, that's good, now everybody thinks you ain't nothing but another crazy junkie."

I had panicked; I'd totally lost it. I knew it and Junior knew it too.

"I ain't gonna take you where you can get hurt," he said. "Worse comes to worse, I'll tell you when to grab your gun. You got one, right?"

I did have a badge and gun and figured, rightly or wrongly, that I could take care of myself. I was worried about him. Junior had brought me around, and he had been telling people we were buddies and crime partners. "These people find out I'm a cop," I told him, "you're history."

"Don't worry about that," he said. "Comes the time we got no out, grab your gun and badge, don't worry about me."

But I did worry about him.

"Well don't," he said. "I'll worry about me."

Suddenly I felt tired and worn—but happy to be alive, lucky to be away from that shooting gallery, Bee-Eye, and his broken pistol. Junior put his arm around me and hugged me. We walked up the street, a pair of happy street junkies.

"What about the dope?" Junior said.

"What dope?"

"The man's dope, Bee-Eye's dope, you stole it."

"Whadaya mean, stole it?"

"You didn't pay him, Babyface. That's stealing."

to get busted—to get arrested.

bombita (Spanish for "little bomb")—liquid digitoxin, dispensed in a glass vial with a narrow neck. Digitoxin is normally used for heart attack victims. When mixed with heroin it catapults the drug at high speed through the bloodstream.

speedball—heroin mixed with cocaine or digitoxin, a killing combination.

to get ripped off, to get offed—to be robbed.

trick bag—serious trouble.

"You can give 'em junk or money. You give 'em money, they buy junk, so tell me, what the hell's the difference."

— DETECTIVE JIM BRYAN, NARCOTICS BUREAU

It was about a week later when I saw Junior waiting for me at Butler Street and 3rd Avenue; he looked awful. He was standing under a streetlight and looked as though he'd been crying.

He put his hand on me, saying, "Babyface, please, Babyface, you got to help me out. I'm so sick."

Before I had time to think about it, not even realizing it warranted thinking about, I turned away. His hand fell off my shoulder as if he thought less of me.

"I'm so sick," he said. "I don't ever remember being this sick."

I wanted to tell him he was a heroin addict, and heroin addicts were always sick. I didn't say anything.

"Shit, man, we've been together awhile now, been through a lot. Have a heart, will ya. Why do you give a shit? What does a beeazag or two mean to you?" He was angry. He'd confused my hesitation for a lack of concern.

He seemed so pathetic and helpless. Although I'd seen plenty of sick addicts before, seeing Junior in such pain broke my heart.

A month earlier I would have walked away from him and left him standing alone on the street. "Don't bring me your problems," I would have said. "You're the junkie, not me."

I stood looking at him. I don't know how long we stood like that, but it seemed like a long time.

He slapped the light pole with his hand. "You think I'm lying. I'm not bullshitting. You don't believe me? Look," he said, "I told you I'd work with you for two weeks, it's been three months and I'm still here."

He was right, of course he was right. I put my arm around him and pulled him in close. "I believe you," I said. "I know you're not lying."

"Man," he said, "if you knew how sick I was, you wouldn't hesitate. Babyface," he said, "it don't cost you nothing."

"It's not the cost I'm worried about," I told him. I'd had this conversation with other, more experienced detectives. Giving drugs to informants was a widespread practice, but not everyone did it. Some did, some didn't. Most did.

I felt pity for Junior, and a certain kind of admiration. He hadn't asked me for drugs for some time, and I had kept a list in my head of all the times he had stepped up for me in the street. I was never careful enough, and he was always concerned about my safety. I certainly owed him.

I was completely unprepared for this. No one had warned me that working with the same informant day in, day out—listening to the incredible story of his life, getting in tight spots and relying on him to get me out, seeing how fearless and bold he could be, laughing with him—was like no other experience in police work. I was confused and angry.

These feelings I had for Junior were, I thought, like having some kind of congenital weakness, or punishment for not paying attention to the principle of keeping it all business.

"I didn't have to stay with you," Junior said. "I could have cut you loose weeks ago, and nobody would have said anything. I stayed because I like you. I think you're a good guy."

Junior gave me a look as if he was disappointed in me. I didn't know what to say. When I did speak, I said something that surprised even me. "Okay," I said, "let's go find you a cure."

Courage and moral conviction, I had always thought, were clearly defined, bright as the midday sun. An ethical emergency presents itself, and you have little doubt as to how you should behave. It's a comforting theory. It dispenses with all those bothersome little questions about right and wrong, and all that gray area in between. It steels your backbone and eases your conscience. It had always been my view that you don't break the law to enforce the law. No one with any common sense could be divided on that. Or so I thought. But back in that summer, fall, and winter of 1966, I had come to believe that such thoughts were entirely an intellectual and abstract pastime. The war in the streets made such feelings seem foolish.

The sight of someone injecting drugs had always made me sick. I couldn't tolerate being around anyone who was high. I hated the way they spoke, the way they looked. By nature, I hated bullies, burglars, car thieves, muggers, and drug dealers most of all. But when Junior and I found a dealer that day, I bought four bags of heroin instead of two. When I handed those two bags to Junior, the way he looked at me, the way he smiled, the fervent way he thanked me—I felt guilty, sure I did, but seeing Junior's pain vanish, watching him come alive, hearing him say, "Okay, Babyface, let's go and make some cases"— this whole business became far too complicated. It required some serious thought, and I didn't have the time. I can't explain it, but looking at Junior I felt a kind of acceptance growing inside of me. It was real, and it was physical—the incredible irony of it all, a kind of schizophrenia, to have to break the law to enforce the law.

Such feelings gave birth to a kind of moral and ethical erosion that would carry me to greater depths then I ever could have imagined.

to pull his coat—to warn someone.

to burn someone—to expose an undercover or blow someone's case.

Junior was my first, and maybe my best street informant, but perseverance and self-control were not his strong suits. Maybe he got bored, maybe he got frightened, maybe I just never gave him enough drugs. In time he burned me, telling everyone that I had somehow fooled him and that I was a cop. The white lady fogged his brain. He had no answer when people said, "You brought him around, told people he was your crime partner; you're full of shit."

In time Junior fled the neighborhood and disappeared into the streets of the South Bronx.

Late one night, not long after Junior fled, I walked into Bickford's Cafeteria at Atlantic and Flatbush Avenues. There were fifty or sixty junkies sitting around, waiting for a dealer to show. When I came through the door, a cry rose from their ranks like a Greek chorus, putting an end to my days of undercover work in Brooklyn.

"Well look who's here, it's the narc, Babyface." Junkies were big believers in nicknames, and the virtues of clarity and immediacy and pulling coats.

FOR THE REMAINDER of that fall and all during the early winter I was fired up, keeping JB out in the streets all kinds of hours, kicking in doors and stopping people on a whim, searching and finding dope, playing hell with the Constitution. I still made an occasional drug buy, but it was a buy and bust. I'd make the drug buy and then collar the dealer on the spot. I took pleasure in the looks on their faces, the shock and disbelief.

We began turning the people we arrested into informants, and before long had more information than we could handle. In time, no dealers could operate or walk the streets of Red Hook without Babyface stepping out of a hallway, coming down from a roof, or jumping from a car to light up their night. We doubled and, for one or two months, tripled the number of arrests other Brooklyn detectives were making.

Having helped Jim Bryan to the head of the group, I could no longer be ignored. Our arrest numbers were going through the roof, and we were working hours that no one else in the Brooklyn group would even consider.

THAT NEW YEAR'S Eve, sometime around eight, eight-thirty, Jim telephoned me. He was sullen, quiet, and he spoke so softly that I had trouble hearing him. He explained that he'd had a terrible argument with his wife. She'd wanted to go out and spend the night at a club. Jim was exhausted and wanted to welcome in the New Year at home. She had called him an old man, said she was going to a club where there were young men.

"I didn't know what to do," he told me. "Who to call."

"I'll be right there."

We sat in his home office, a place where he kept a desk, a sofa, a set of barbells, and a workout bench. JB lifted weights every day, to unwind and to prove to himself that he was strong. Like the rest of the house, his room was tidy. But just like the rest of the house, it was a room without warmth. There was no feeling of affection in that house, and nowhere could you see a woman's touch.

For much of the night we drank Jack Daniel's and listened to country music—Merle Haggard, Buck Owens, Lynn Anderson, Tammy Wynette, Loretta Lynn, Eddie Arnold, Hank Williams, Patsy Cline, and Marty Robbins. Jim had hundreds of records, but when I asked if he had something by The Temptations, he smiled and shook his head.

Jim Bryan had lived with the fear that someday his young wife would bail out on him. He had done all he could and whatever he could to make her happy. He said he loved her so much that it made him ill.

That night he looked irreparably damaged, and I had the sense not to ask too many questions. We both lay back and listened to his music, both of us wondering where our lives were headed. To ease his pain was not possible. I did what I could, but I doubt it was enough.

At one point Jim went to his bench and pressed 250 pounds. I was suitably impressed. I watched the clock on his desk tick off the minutes to midnight. At the stroke of the New Year we drank champagne, and I telephoned Gina. Sometime around twelve-thirty his wife phoned and said she was on her way home.

He said, "I'm not very good at saying thanks," and I told him he didn't have to thank me, he was my partner. He smiled, sustaining the unspoken connection between partners.

A few weeks later Jim Bryan was promoted to second grade detective. He immediately put in for a month's vacation and told me he'd had enough.

"What does that mean?"

"When I get back, I'm only working days. I've had it with these hours. Maybe," he said, "you should think about finding another partner."

"C'mon," I said.

"My wife is fed up with my not being home. I mean she's really had enough."

"You can't just work days in this job, you know that."

I could feel my face going red. Working with Jim I had been able to keep at bay the idea that I couldn't keep a partner. But now thoughts of all my failings with the others began coming back to me.

"Guys like you have no home life," he said. "It's the job, the job, the job—and that's bullshit. I've seen it—and it's bullshit. Bobby," he said, "it's not worth it."

I told him that I'd find a new partner.

"We'll stay together until you do. Don't be pissed, okay. Don't be."

"I'm not," I told him, but I was furious at him. I was hurt and insulted, and another thought skimmed through my mind: maybe this cowboy was right.

house mouse—an inside or clerical cop.

stool (short for stool pigeon)—an informant.

By my lights, my home life was just fine. I was willing and able to abandon any and all responsibilities to Gina, and she showed no reluctance to take them on, all of them. Her devotion to her family and me was extreme, and since I was brought up to be a classic Italian American Prince, I took full advantage.

During the week, I'd leave Long Island sometime around ten in the morning and wouldn't get in until one or two o'clock the following morning. On the long rides into the city, and then back again from Brooklyn, I'd listen to talk radio. There was *Rambling with Gambling* in the morning, Barry Gray and Long John Nebel at night: Gambling the voice of no one I knew, Gray the voice of my father, and Nebel the voice of illusion and fantasy.

No matter what time I got in, Gina always had dinner waiting in one form or another. I'd eat watching my son as he slept, get to bed, and be up early the following day. A little more time with the baby, and then head off to work. On weekends, I did some work around the house, but like an inviting mistress, those Brooklyn streets were always on my mind.

I decided that what I needed to do was to spend more time at the office. Talk to the bosses, sniff around and see if I could find another partner. I began to go into the office every day, and kept asking myself, *What's wrong with you? You turn every partner off.*

It isn't easy to overcome that kind of insecurity, but I tried. In the office I'd sit at a desk sipping coffee, feeling sorry for myself, thinking that maybe I should have taken that assignment to PMD. Dumped that thought real quick. I kept on wondering if any of this BS would ever change.

The entire command was broken down into cliques and factions. That I had bounced from team to team, and now Jim Bryan wanted out, really preyed on my mind. My sergeant, Jack Cuddy, told me it was because I was young and hyper and too inexperienced. Nevertheless, my work with Jim had been outstanding. They were happy and I should be too. "Calm down," he said. "Jesus Christ," he said, "turn it down a notch, you're still new here."

"New, bullshit new."

I was there going on two years.

"Your head's too clear," he told me.

"Excuse me?"

"You got a clear head, ya know, clear."

A few years back, Cuddy had been a narcotics detective working Chinatown. After he made sergeant, he was able to get himself reassigned back to the unit. No easy stunt. The man was a charmer in the most positive sense, and he loved hanging out in Chinatown. Jack Cuddy was the kind of guy for whom everyone bought drinks.

Always exquisitely turned out, Cuddy must have owned about a hundred blazers. He was a scratch golfer who never used woods, only irons. An undemanding and even-handed boss, he began down-ing martinis—silver bullets he called them—around eleven o'clock in the morning, and never showed a sign of it. His best friend, the godfather for his son, was a man named Frank Waters. Waters had been a group leader in the New York office of the Federal Bureau of Narcotics and had been one of the agents who worked the famous French Connection case. In the film, the Eddie Egan character, Pop-eye Doyle, shoots and kills him—a major bit of dramatic license that would haunt Waters all his life.

Like Jack Cuddy, Joe Nunziata too was concerned about what he called my clear-headed view of the job. Someone with a clear head, it turned out, was someone viewed as empty-headed, immature. I wasn't serious enough. I talked too much, trusted too many people. "Stop trying to make everyone like you," Joe once told me. "And most important of all," he said, "put an end to that Babyface bull-shit. It's dangerous and it's disrespectful. I'd better never hear some junkie call you Babyface."

What else?

"Buy some decent clothes. You always look like you're going camping, for Christ sake."

I am by temperament impatient and insecure. It's not easy for me to admit that. But I was forced to acknowledge some major flaw in my personality that I was unable to identify. I could not hold on to a partner, and that was the reality.

Cuddy suggested that I hang out more, spend more time in the office and check records, read intelligence reports. "Make yourself known," he said.

For days I'd sit in the file room skimming old cases. I read through every case folder and learned nothing; there was nothing in them to learn. No one put anything in a file.

The Tuminaro case, also known as the French Connection case, was the most interesting. It had been, after all, the largest heroin seizure ever made by the NYPD. Robin Moore had written a book, and there was going to be a movie.

The detectives who worked the case, Sonny Grosso and Eddie Egan, along with federal agents and other SIU detectives, had put almost nothing in their files. Everything was marked Confidential— *confidential from whom?* I'd wonder. Weren't we all narcotics detectives, weren't we all on the same side? *How did they get away with this crap?* is what I thought.

The file room was near the stairway that led to the SIU office. I'd sit, drinking coffee, reading files, watching the SIU detectives come and go. They looked like the pictures you had in your head of old-time detectives: fine suits, expensive shoes, and fedoras. That's right, fedoras. Most of these men were in the Narcotics Bureau while I was still in grammar school.

Some things I remember clearly. Other things come and go. I remember Joe Nunziata coming into the office one payday, all spruced up and excited like a kid on his way to Disney World, too jazzed up even to sleep.

"Aren't you going?" he said. "Geeze, do you even own a jacket and tie? When are you going to do something about the way you dress?"

"What are you talking about?"

"The whole office is going to the set, we're all going to be in the movie."

"What movie?"

"*The French Connection* movie, that's what movie," he said, grinning and with a shrug. "I guess Sonny has enough guys."

Right before the final scene in *The French Connection*, there's a gathering of detectives and a shoot-out with the bad guys. All the extras in that scene are from the Narcotics Bureau. And there is Joe

Nunziata in his camel hair coat. You can see him firing his pistol, shooting from behind a barricade. Joe was left-handed, you can't miss him. He looked good, real, like a real cop, like an actor playing a real cop. "Mister Hollywood," I called him. He loved it, thought maybe he could find work as an extra someday, someday maybe even act in a movie.

Once he told me that he had an idea for a terrific book. He said he was going to meet with the writer, Robin Moore, and he was going to tell him this great story idea.

"Let's say a couple of detectives come up with a scheme to rip off the French Connection drugs from the police department property clerk's office. Let's say they do it, figure a way to pull that off. Wouldn't that make one helluva book and movie?"

"Run it by Sonny," I said. "See what Grosso thinks of that idea."

"I did. Sonny told me it's way too far-fetched, too over the top for anyone to believe."

I told him I agreed with Grosso; it was a wild idea, it couldn't be done.

"You're wrong. You're both wrong. I bet I can interest Robin Moore. Anyway I'm going to try."

"Good luck," I told him. "Who knows, maybe someday you'll be famous too. Just like Grosso and Egan, you'll be a star."

I remember the way he laughed. Joe Nunziata had a great, warm, wonderful laugh. He told everyone he knew about his book and movie idea. He told one or two too many.

ONE DAY, IT was a payday, everyone was in the office and everyone was ashen. I remember that now, certain things and certain images, detectives who had never said hello to me before giving me a sad smile, saying, "Howyadoin'? Did ya hear?" their faces going from self-pity to anger to sarcasm to blame. "Kelly, Imp, and Moskowitz. They've been indicted and arrested for selling drugs."

James Kelly, Ray Imp, and Marvin Moskowitz were a team of

SIU detectives. I knew that Kelly had worked on the French Connection case—I'd seen his name in the file—and Ray Imp and Marvin Moskowitz had worked in Chinatown with Jack Cuddy.

"How the hell did this happen?" I asked Joe later that day. We were drinking coffee in a shop across from the Brooklyn courthouse. He seemed dazed, and every so often he'd shake his head, puff his cheeks and blow. He said it was an informant.

to have a phone up—to install a wiretap.

The informant had been working with a team of federal narcotics agents in Nassau County. But there was more to it than that. He also worked with inspectors from the Drug Enforcement Administration (DEA), their internal affairs unit, and he told them that he could buy drugs from the federal agents.

And he did.

Joe thought that our office phones were up.

The DEA inspectors asked the informant if he knew any other agents who would sell him drugs. He didn't know how likely it was, but perhaps, it was possible. He set out to make a case against the SIU detectives.

And he did.

That's what Joe had heard.

When I asked him how well he knew the arrested detectives, he said that he knew them all to talk to.

"This is bad, this is really bad," he said. He took his left hand, and making it into a gun, pointed his trigger finger at his heart. "If it ever happened to me, that's my way out," he said.

I remember telling him that if an informant ever sucked me into a jam like that, if he pushed me into something I had never done before and would never do again, and I were arrested, I would probably shoot myself, but you'd better believe I'd pop his ass first.

I wondered briefly if I meant a word of what I had said.

Joe looked at me, and for the first time that day, I saw a smile, a little grin. "Yeah," he said, "right."

"It'll never happen to you, Joe, and it sure as shit ain't going to happen to me either. We don't sell drugs."

"They can nail you for other shit, you know. Plenty of other shit."

I remember thinking that maybe I should get myself out of narcotics. I remember thinking, "This is fucking nuts."

So much of my life I've forgotten, so some of my past ceases to exist. But sometimes the pieces come back to me, and sometimes I wish they wouldn't. Suicide is frightening—especially when men who are capable of it discuss in serious terms that final solution to a temporary problem.

People describe suicide as the act of a coward. I think not.

My suspicion is that people who describe it that way have never considered it—the whys and hows, that sort of thing. Historically, the police have always had an alarming rate of suicide, second only to that of psychiatrists.

There was a kind of panic in me that day, the kind of panic that comes from a terrible view of the future, a perception of dark possibilities.

WHEN THE TAPES of the conversation between the federal informant, Kelly, and Imp were played in court, Imp is heard to say, "Hey, watch what you say in front of Marvin. He doesn't know anything."

Marvin Moskowitz had not been in the car when the drugs and money were passed. The hard-ass internal affairs people heard that tape recording, as did the prosecutors, but it had zero effect. They indicted Marvin Moskowitz anyway, dragged him along with the others into court. At that point it doesn't matter if you're guilty or innocent: you're guilty. Marvin was acquitted, but his life and career were already awash in guilt. His neighbors, friends, and family saw the newspaper photograph of him in handcuffs, the TV film. And all those pompous, unfeeling internal affairs types and prosecutors, they couldn't care less.

You begin to hate the drug dealers in the street only a little more than you hate those heartless entities who roam the courthouse halls. With their prissy smiles and wrinkled suits, it seemed they were always ready to expound on police abuse and police corruption in an airy, detached, and theoretical way. They made the complexities of the street world seem simple. The very same characters, when they heard about a cop dying in the line of duty, would click their tongues, shake their heads, blink, and shrug.

You look at these people and wonder; man, hello, is anybody home? You want to say, Don't you know what it's like in those streets? Don't you know what we go through, day in, day out, and all night long? Why is it so tough to see things our way?

Okay, that was a rationalization. I rationalize because that's what cops who have bent and broken the law do. I am self-conscious because that's what people who should know the difference between right and wrong are. In retrospect, the arrests of Imp, Kelly, and Moskowitz were the end of one era in the New York Police Department's Narcotics Bureau and the beginning of another. Two different time periods, totally different types of detectives.

Most of the detectives and supervising officers of the SIU were transferred. The commanding officer of the Narcotics Bureau and his chief of staff were replaced. The arrests of Kelly, Imp, and Moskowitz rearranged the NYPD's Narcotics Bureau and set in motion a chain of events that would ultimately rattle the foundation of the entire police department.

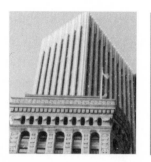 A PARTNER

watched them come in week after week and the merry-go-round began again. New narcotics detectives, mostly ex-plainclothesmen, smartly dressed and confident, they would team up and head out to those Brooklyn streets. The search for my partner went on. I tried out some of the new men. They were all good, and all with more time in the job than I had. They were street-smart and wise in ways that I certainly wasn't, but after a few weeks I'd be drinking coffee alone and dreaming about cases. Maybe a shrink would have told me that I was looking for my father, or an older brother. But that was too simple; I was looking for the perfect guy, someone who would fit with me—with me. My search was turning into something of a ritual and becoming tedious for everyone. Maybe my partner didn't exist, was a mirage, a figment of my imagination.

Along with the addition of new detectives, Chief Inspector Tom Renaghan took over as CO. I watched him operate, marveled at the way he moved, how he spoke, the way he dealt with subordinates. The chief had all the trappings of the great old Irish cop boss. He was larger than life, smoked foot-long cigars, and strutted around the Narcotics Bureau always holding center stage.

Whenever he saw me he'd call me "guinea bastard"; that is exactly what he'd say. "Hey, you guinea bastard, what are you up to?"

Chief Renaghan had been the commander of all Bronx detectives, and it was said that he personally had a hand in breaking over sixty homicides. The men called him Uncle Tom. He was a raconteur and a celebrated cop, one of the uncompromising old-line bosses, a mean son of a bitch. The stereotype comes to life.

Chief Renaghan believed that since we had taken former PMD cops into the Narcotics Bureau, the office should be making an occasional gambling arrest. He decided to make it office policy: one gambling arrest per month per team.

How's that for a horrible idea?

a monthly, the pad—money paid for protection to the police.

KG—a known gambler, a bookmaker or a numbers collector.

Until that time the Narcotics Bureau's only mandate was to enforce the drug laws. Gamblers were off-limits and it was sensible that they were. To send narcotics detectives out after gamblers was just looking for trouble, and there was trouble enough brewing throughout that ancient precinct on Old Slip and South Street.

In those days there was a KG list in each precinct, with photographs, frequented locations, and organized crime family affiliation. To arrest one of these characters was always a big deal. KGs were rarely arrested, and when one was collared, it gave the distorted impression that everyone was fair game. It was assumed that KGs were never arrested because they paid the police. Which, of course, they did. If you issued a traffic ticket to a KG, your boss would jump for joy. Back then I could never figure it, the department's singular obsession with bookmakers.

I could generate no enthusiasm to chase KGs, as I could generate no enthusiasm to chase hookers. Those weren't only my feelings, most detectives felt that their work was far more important and relevant than enforcing the public morals laws. Nevertheless, the new administration wanted gambling arrests, and there were certainly detectives in the Narcotics Bureau who could make them. Personally, I had drug dealers to hunt and search warrants to secure, and I could never get turned on chasing some character out taking sports bets.

to get on the sheet—to make an arrest. That arrest is recorded on a master sheet of the month's activity.

Bagging a KG presented certain challenges, so former PMD cops teamed up with narcotics detectives to get the job done. Then one day the order came down that the CO wanted two KGs arrested every month. Sergeant Cuddy wanted to impress the new chief, so he set the entire Brooklyn narcotics unit out to get them. But as the month drew to a close, no KG had been arrested. Cuddy took this as a reflection on his supervisory skills. He called a meeting and implored us to make a collar.

"Please, as a personal favor, can someone go out and arrest a bookmaker?"

"You," he said to me, "go get me a bookmaker."

I told him I had no talent for that, but I could probably locate all the bookmakers he needed, if that's what he wanted.

"Good," he said. "Get us the information, I'll give it to someone who can make the collar. C'mon," he said, "as a favor to me, get us on the sheet."

I contacted a few informants, got the location of two bookmakers, and gave the information to Cuddy. He passed it on to Joe Nunziata and a former PMD cop named Eddie.

Eddie was taller than Joe and older, and he smiled all the time. He reminded me of Larry from the 100th Precinct. It was the way he held himself, the way he spoke, as though he understood things. When I asked him if he had found a partner, he told me he had, one of the other new men. I was relieved and let down at the same time. I liked his style, I could have worked with him, but he was from PMD, carrying all that baggage.

"So quick, how did you get this information so fast?" Cuddy wanted to know.

"What's so hard?"

An informant of mine, Frankie Shay, a street-running junkie, house burglar, car booster, small as a bird with the eyes and ears of a hawk, gave me the information.

One bookmaker worked out of a candy store on 5th Avenue, off the corner of Saint Johns Place. He took horse and sports bets and kept his work in an old Coca-Cola cooler in the rear of the store.

The other bookmaker took his bets over the telephone. Every day, at precisely 1 P.M., he left an apartment on President Street. He carried a toolbox, and in that toolbox were about ten thousand dollars' worth of plays. These were not going to be tough guys to bring down.

A day or two later, Joe left a message for me to meet him and Eddie at the Hanover. We sat at a table drinking coffee while the daytime bartender set up the bar. I remember the jukebox playing Eddie Arnold singing "Let the World Go Away." I loved that song and that man's voice.

We sat in silence for a long time. Finally I said, "What?"

"With your sources and our brains, we could make a million bucks," Eddie said.

Joe lightly slapped my arm. Eddie was laughing. They were both giddy as hell, happy, enjoying this. They told me they had snapped up both the bookmakers, but they hadn't made an arrest. After the usual you-wouldn't-believe-what-happened BS, they got down to business. Eddie told me that both the bookmakers were "on the pad."

"Can you believe that shit? Two bookmakers and we nailed them, I mean we nailed them cold, all their work right there, and we couldn't make a collar," Joe said.

"You have got to be kidding me. The boss wanted those collars made."

"Hey, this is beyond us," Eddie said. "These guys are paying big-time pads. They can't be collared. That's the deal. That's the way it is."

I said, "Really?"

They told me I'd better believe it. But the information was terrific, right on the button. They both wondered how I was able to do that.

"I have informants that trust me, that like me."

"Yeah," Joe said. "They love Babyface."

"We all work differently," I said.

"No. Not we all—you do." I could tell it infuriated Joe that he couldn't get me to see what he saw.

I had more informants than anyone, many more. Partly it was because I had hung out in the street, and addicts remembered me from my undercover days. Maybe they thought of me as one of their own. I couldn't tell, but I treated addicts like they were human beings, and they appreciated that. There was my brother, rumors getting back to me, stories. I hadn't seen him in a while, my parents either, but family gossip was heated. Sometimes I'd look into addicts' faces and see Ritchie looking strained and frightened.

There was no more talk of finding other KGs, or making the boss happy. On that day with Joe and Eddie I was feeling good, sitting with two very sharp guys, sitting and talking like I'm one of them, one of the fellas, someone who knew what was going on. I sat, I relaxed, I was cool, one of the coolest people I knew.

"You couldn't make a collar," I said with one of those knowing nods, like—geeze, what a kick in the head. All that effort for nothing.

"That was why I had no use for PMD," I told them. "You bust your ass to snap up some bad guy, it turns out he's on the pad." I put together a sad smile, a knowing nod, and pretended that I was crushed.

"Well-l-l," Joe said, smiling, holding the tip of his nose with his thumb and forefinger, smiling like the cat that had caught, fried, and then eaten the canary.

Eddie stretched his arm under the table and tapped me on the knee. I reached down and felt a small stack of bills.

"What's this?"

"There's five there for you," Eddie said. "These guys can't be busted, but if you catch them with work, they have to pay. Bobby, it's a game, that's all it is, just a fucking game."

"You're giving me graft," I said. "Let's call it like it is, gambling money, you're giving me gambling money."

After a long moment of silence, I said, "Okay, why the fuck not. Sure," I said, "why not."

Joe exploded into laughter.

"I say something funny?" I said.

Joe bent over as though he were experiencing stomach cramps, the laughter coming harder now, tears falling.

Eddie said, "You are one weird fucker. Joe was right, you're one weird son of a bitch."

"Me weird? I'm not weird."

"Oh right, right, I'm sorry."

I took the money, five hundred dollars. It was the first time, and I was shocked that I felt no self-disgust, no regret. After a time I walked across the street to the office and handed Sergeant Cuddy two hundred and fifty dollars; always take care of the sergeant.

I said, "There's no way we can make gambling arrests, it's just not possible." He folded the bills and put them in his pocket saying, "You're probably right. But man, it sure is fun trying, ain't it?"

Later that day, we all went over to the Hanover to celebrate, everyone laughing, everyone excited. We hugged each other and drank vodka and tonics and played the jukebox, all of us giving thanks to a pair of bookmakers for the pleasurable afternoon.

We were wonderful and I was glad to be part of it, the camaraderie, the fun. Suddenly I was no longer dismissed as someone on the outside looking in. I was part of the group, one of the fellas, a stand-up guy, someone to be trusted. People began laughing at my stories, as I laughed at theirs. I felt something shift inside me. It was cockiness partly, but it was also a sense of change, actual change. I was never a big drinker, and after a few, a feeling of loss at what I had once been came over me. I set it aside and kept on drinking, smiling at people, implying that I had been through this kind of celebration many times before.

As the day wore on I felt both a sense of belonging and a sense of betrayal. Oddly, at the same time, I felt grown up and a certain pity for myself. Something had gone wrong. I'd come to police work as an ordinary, straight sort of guy, but after seven years out in those streets, all that I once believed in had been crushed under the weight of the daily routine of being a narcotics cop. It was a hard thing to admit, even to myself, but I knew that I was capable of doing whatever it took to belong.

What is honesty? What is duplicity? What is loyalty? And what does it mean to be accepted and acknowledged? I accepted, finally, that I valued that more than anything else, belonging just to belong. I noticed that Joe was watching me with an amused grin on his face. I winked at him and felt a melancholy ache in the pit of my stomach. I knew, even back then, that there had to be consequences for all this.

I remember one wild payday, an afternoon at the Hanover, a Bronx detective with red hair took me out to his car, opened the trunk, and showed me a brown, #9 paper bag. The bag was filled to the brim with cash. "The boss's money."

That was gambling money, of that I was sure.

If the Narcotics Bureau, all of a sudden, began to threaten city-wide gambling operations, started to make gambling arrests, think about it. We could have named our monthly number.

Eddie told me it would never happen, they wouldn't allow it.

"Who?" I asked him. "Who wouldn't allow it?"

He shrugged and smiled. "Who do you think?" he said. "The people downtown. They would never allow it."

"What people downtown?"

"Them, those people—the people that run the show."

"Oh," I said, "those people."

Eddie was right. It was a week or two after the first narcotics detective began hassling gamblers that word came down.

Cut it out.

And we did.

opium—a resinous sap extracted from the bulb of the opium poppy plant *(Papaver somniferum)* that contains numerous alkaloids, the most important of which is morphine. When smoked or eaten, the processed opium resin induces a state of dreamlike euphoria. Taken repeatedly, opium is highly addictive.

morphine—a granular alkaloid extracted from the sap of the opium poppy. Used medically to treat pain, coughing, or sleeplessness. Bonded with acetic acid through a complex five-stage chemical process, morphine becomes heroin.

heroin—a chemical compound of morphine and acetic acid, a fluffy white powder that is highly water soluble and thus easy to inject with a syringe.

key—2.2 pounds, a kilogram.

January of the year. Green Bay crushed Oakland 33–14. I was happy. A New York Giant and NFC fan, I remained a believer in the status quo. I was no admirer of rebels and had lost all patience for anarchists, Communists, socialists, pacifists, hippies, drug addicts, and university professors. Although I loved my father dearly, my years in the police department had washed away whatever small insights he had tried to instill in me.

It was Super Bowl Sunday, after lunch and over coffee at my parents' house. My mother and father both seemed more drained than I ever remembered seeing them. In memory, that afternoon carries all the darkness of the first accusation, all the guilt that somehow always finds a home in my head, and all the humiliation of an older son's inability to live up to his father's expectations.

"If it's not too much trouble, I want you to talk to your brother," my father told me. It was finger pointing, not a request.

I found Ritchie sprawled out in his old bedroom listening to his music. Seeing him, focusing on him, both surprised and moved me. He let me take his hand and when I looked at the back of it, I saw a tiny mark, a small track.

"What are you doing?" I said.

His voice climbed and quivered as he fought to get the words out.

"I'm not doing anything."

"If you're shooting drugs, that's crazy. Don't tell me you're doing that. Don't tell me that."

"I'm not," he told me. "Don't worry," he said, "I'm not crazy, no more than anybody else."

My brother had one of those very smooth faces, the kind that opposes any growth of a beard, but he was trying. Dressed all in black, sweater and slacks, he was wearing, as he always did, dark prescription sunglasses. Otis Redding, doing "Dock of the Bay," came from his tape deck.

"How do you stand being around screwed-up people day after shitty day?" he asked me.

"Because that's what I do."

"Locking them up, putting them in jail?"

"Yeah. Right."

"But ain't it depressing? It has to get to you after a while."

"I don't let it get to me," I lied. "Their lives are not mine, it's a job." Suddenly I felt trapped in my brother's bedroom, overwhelmed by the torrent of music and what I perceived as his unspoken rage.

"Look," I told him, "I don't think it's cute that you're doing drugs. If you don't care about yourself, what you're doing to yourself, think about your wife, your mother and father. You're going to hurt them all."

"People do what they do," he told me. "I don't tell anyone how to live their life. I don't want them telling me."

"Sure," I said, exasperated and fed up with it all.

I was as disappointed with myself as I was with Ritchie, at my inability to feel a real connection with him, my refusal to even try to understand my younger brother. In my mind and in my heart I judged him harshly, never trying to get to what he most profoundly felt. *Another junkie* is what I thought. *I don't believe it. My own brother.*

Ritchie looked at me as if he were feeling very sorry for me, and that angered me all the more. Then he broke my heart. "I do love you," he said.

I didn't say anything. After a long moment I told him to try and not fuck his life up.

"You too," he told me.

One day on my father's birthday, I asked him if he was happy. He told me that a father could only be as happy as his most unhappy child.

THE WORLD WAS wild with anger and pain.

American soldiers massacred 347 civilians in a place called My Lai, North Koreans seized the navy ship USS *Pueblo,* Russians invaded Czechoslovakia, President Johnson threw in the towel, telling us he would not run again, and in June Senator Robert Kennedy was assassinated. The show *60 Minutes* first aired on CBS, and if you wanted, sex was offered everywhere. Simon and Garfunkel were looking for Mrs. Robinson. Martin Luther King Jr. was murdered. Woody Guthrie died, and in the Dominican Republic, Sammy Sosa was born.

ON PURPOSE OR by happenstance, the police department sometimes did things right. They had sent us Chief Renaghan, but they also delivered to us a man who was his complete antithesis, a lieutenant by the name of Aaron Mazen.

His face was narrow, with a strong, prominent nose, and his eyes reflected the sort of decisiveness you'd expect to find in a confident military man. He was a man truly at ease with the world around him.

Sternly moralistic, Lieutenant Mazen was a stoic man with clear-cut rules of behavior, a strong, silent Gary Cooper type, with a huge disdain for lazy detectives and lazier bosses. Once a hardworking precinct detective, Mazen knew the job—how to do it, how not to.

He had no idea just how bad the Narcotics Bureau had gone. By the time he arrived, the horses were a long time out of the barn.

Early on, Mazen held meetings and spent time telling us that he understood how difficult the job of narcotics detective could be. I liked him immediately, his style, his manner, the way he communicated. I wanted very much to impress him, so I put some search warrants together and invited him to join me on raids. In the past this was something the bosses never did, but under this lieutenant, it became office policy.

Mazen told me that he never wanted any part of the Narcotics Bureau, but now that he was here, and a supervisor, he felt responsible. He reminded us time and again not to squander our most precious asset, our honesty. The men in the unit would stare at him in disbelief. The new lieutenant made everyone very edgy. "He'll never last," Cuddy said; "this guy won't be here very long."

Shortly before Mazen's arrival, I finally found a steady partner.

Near my own age, Frank Mandato was someone I could hang on to, someone who would teach me all those things that up until that time I was fortunate not to have learned. Lieutenant Mazen didn't know that, and to be honest, it would not have mattered. Right here, now, as I write this, I'm thinking of how far I had gone from my days in the precinct, my time in TPF, those first years in narcotics. By the time Mazen arrived, I had already gone over the edge and was fully involved in a corrosive process that had totally skewed my views of right and wrong.

There was no one but myself to blame. I didn't see it coming. I was still fairly young, and afraid to fail. Most importantly, I was bone tired of being an outsider, looking through a window at a party to which I had not been invited.

I had been working with Frank a week or two before Mazen's arrival. Frank was one of the new men, a patrol officer from the 77th Precinct. A hard worker and mature, he was strikingly handsome, always immaculately dressed, with a dense, perfectly trimmed beard.

It is difficult to try and type the people you meet in your life. But if my life were a football team, Frank would be the all-pro wide receiver, the troublemaking star who never came to practice, someone with world-class speed and talent, and the hero of every game.

We have all known people who become good friends and much more than that, people we know for years but in point of fact never truly know at all. That's the way it was with Frank and me. Over the years I'd grow to admire him and love him and would have given my life for him. I know he would have done the same for me; he almost did on more than one occasion. Still, as foolish as it sounds, I never truly knew Frank Mandato. A lot of cops talk about their partners, the bond there, the kind of affection that never goes away. That's how I felt about Frank. But Frank was an enigma, a puzzle, a riddle. He was indefinable. Capable of astonishing feats of courage, he was also a storyteller, a man with a lifetime of experiences that he never experienced at all. And although some of his stories would strike you as odd, you would not question him or call him on them. You'd look at him. That magnificent beard perfectly trimmed, a bright smile in an at all times tanned face, imported shoes and clothing, perfect hands, manicured fingernails, and a massive head of curly hair. You couldn't help but smile. Frank Mandato was quite a package, and my partner for close to four years.

Toward the end of our first week working together, we were patrolling in South Brooklyn and stopped in to see one of my informants, a diminutive mad man named Nicky Conforti. I had nicknamed Nicky "Little Cesar." He was slight, five feet three or four, and he wore a big gray fedora. On that occasion Nicky told us that there was a legendary gorilla prowling the street, a cold-blooded takeoff artist who hurt people. The gorilla wore a hooded red sweatshirt; the street people called him Red Riding Hood.

We were in Nicky's chicken and barbecue restaurant. The place was dark—hardly any light in Nicky's place. There was a jukebox, Eric Burden and the Animals, "The House of the Rising Sun" coming from that jukebox.

We found them all over the set—beat-up hookers—in hallways, standing on corners, sitting on the curbs. There are few things in this world sadder than the look of desperation on the face of a crying whore after she's been beaten and robbed.

I drove slowly, searching the streets for this Red Riding Hood character. I had heard of him, knew he was one nasty bastard. "What do you plan on doing when you find him?" Frank asked me. "I don't know," I said. And I didn't, but I knew I had to find him.

I spotted him standing in a hallway at the corner of Atlantic and Fourth Avenue. His shoulders were hunched, and he was throwing punches at shadows. This was a big guy, not tall, maybe five-ten or -eleven, but huge across the chest and shoulders. He had to weigh in at about 240 or 250 pounds. When I pulled to the curb Frank opened his window and yelled to him. The guy did not turn or look up; hidden beneath his hood his face was impossible to make out.

In the extraordinary landscape of South Brooklyn, this particular gorilla was famous. When I walked up to him, I'm thinking that maybe I made a mistake telling Frank to wait by the car. But there was nothing I could do, no way I was going to let this red-hooded freak think I was afraid of him, that I needed help. I remember having a hard time controlling the butterflies in my stomach. This was one big, mean-looking dude.

I showed him my shield and he said, "I know who you are. Baby-face." I asked for some ID and he didn't have any. I told him to turn around and put his hands on the wall. He said, "Make me," and he was smiling when he said it.

I heard Frank's voice right at my shoulder. "My partner said put your hands on the wall. Do it." It was at that precise moment I knew I had found a partner.

The gorilla sighed, and turned and put his hands up against the hallway wall. I went through his pockets and found nothing. I told him to take off his hood. He had curly blond hair. His eyes were blue, and maybe it was the light, I don't know, but they had an odd kind of glitter, a strange sapphire cast, a kind of coldness, some deep, dark, crazy shit there.

He told us his name was Vinny Ensulo, and he had been a prize-fighter. Now he was a junkie. He knew cops, all kinds of cops, knew their names, had done things for cops, said he was attracted to cops; he liked them, once thought about being a cop himself. He hated junkies, especially whore junkies, and dealers most of all. He said that the street was a jungle and he was a lion, the king of the jungle. He told us that he took what he wanted, and nobody was going to fuck with him, nobody.

I'm thinking, *This guy is an absolute psycho.* I told him that I was warning him, and he got but one warning. If I heard that he pulled that shit again, the shit of beating on the women in the street, I would find him, put ten bags of dope in his pocket, then I'd drag his ass to jail. Prick.

I remember the way Frank smiled, the way he said, "Well now, that's what I call good police work."

Vinny said he'd like to work for us, be our informant. I told him that the only business I'd ever have with a bad-ass like him was to put handcuffs on him.

I thought we had impressed Vinny, except he wasn't listening. He was staring hard up the avenue, at something or someone coming. I turned and looked, and saw Nicky Conforti's car rolling slowly down the street. I saw the window of Nicky's car roll down and saw Nicky's arm come out that window, a pistol in his hand. I shouted for Frank to get down. Vinny bellowed and pushed me and ran toward Nicky's car, screaming as he went, throwing an empty bottle of soda at the now speeding escaping Buick, running after that car with the blood-headed intensity of Hades.

> Hades—god of the underworld, keeper of dead souls,
> and the most relentless of the gods, the only one who
> would never give back what he had claimed for his own.

When we got to our feet, Frank said, "This Vinny, this asshole, he's going to make one helluva informant."

"Maybe," I said.

"Look at him."

"Yeah."

Vinny was running down 5th Avenue chasing a car, chasing the man driving that car, who had a gun.

Vinny Ensulo, "Kid Vinny" they called him, was the kind of human being I hated most, a cruel and vicious bully, someone in whose head and heart the word *mercy* had no meaning. In time I'd learn that most of it was an act, but not all of it.

During the next year or so, Frank and I would try and focus Kid Vinny's built-up energy and use him as an informant. There were times Vinny had the sensitivity of an injured child, and my heart would go out to him. Other times, he'd appear insane—dark, brooding, and dangerous, talking to himself under his breath.

You felt different about informants who were edgy and wild as opposed to all the time needy and almost insane. You felt it in your gut, that this one would always be serious trouble. That's how I felt about Kid Vinny, and in due course, I would cut him loose, knowing that he would never, ever be completely gone.

The next day, Frank invited me to his apartment in Brooklyn. He showed me around—the movie posters on the wall, the stacks of jazz albums, and the balcony that overlooked Ocean Parkway. He had a magnificent view of the Manhattan skyline, and a black Belgian sheepdog that he'd found abandoned in the precinct where he'd worked in uniform. He lived alone, just him and his dog.

I can't remember exactly how he phrased it, but it went something like this: "Bob, I spoke to Lieutenant Mazen. He'd like us to team up and be steady partners."

I looked at him in surprise. I'd been in the office for about three years, and he'd just arrived. I was a detective, the lead detective in our Brooklyn group, and he was a patrolman, new to the Detective Division.

He had spoken to the lieutenant.

"We've worked six days out of seven this week," he said, "twelve hours a day. I'm not complaining, I like it, love working with you. But man, you know narcotics is a special detail. In a detail you make time or money, and we aren't making either. What I'm trying to tell you, what I'm trying to say is, I mean you've got to learn how to enjoy yourself a little."

Then he excused himself and went into the next room. He came back carrying a bong and a bag of pot. "C'mon," he said, "take a hit and relax a little. We've got things to talk about."

A hippy, I thought, *I'm going to work with a hippy. Perfect.* I'd come to learn that Frank Mandato might have the soul of a hippy, but he had the heart of a warrior and the mind of a day trader. Yes indeed, Frank was the whole package.

ONE MORNING I was on my way to court when I noticed one of the nighttime hookers buying her morning cure on Pacific Street. Her name was Glenda Lopez. She was the sister of Maria Lopez; and the sisters had a brother named Dopey who tattooed his name, letter by letter, across the fingers of his left hand. Dopey was a teenage dealer, and both the sisters were hookers. In their early twenties, the Lopez sisters were stunningly beautiful, small, with dancer's legs, coffee-with-cream skin setting off huge black eyes, and dimples the size of a fingertip. Neither of them knew or understood how special they were. If they had they wouldn't have been selling themselves for twenty dollars a fuck.

I watched Glenda give money to the dealer when he handed her the dope, I stepped from the car and Glenda called out, "Shit, it's Babyface."

We were off to the races. He ran and I ran after him. As I passed Glenda, I told her to stay were she was. "Don't fucking go any-where" is what I told her. She stood there frowning and staring at her nails. I never expected that she would wait around.

Junkies could be quick, they could run like rabbits, but they had no staying power. Sprint for half a block, then they'd lose it. This man was small and thin and he ran like the wind. I chased him into a tenement, up two, three flights of stairs. On the top landing some-one had left a dresser. He stopped just long enough to push it down the stairs at me. Then he went out a window and up the fire escape, heading for the roof.

Screw this, I thought, *screw him*. I had gotten a good look at that clown, and figured I'd see him again.

the House of D—the Women's House of Detention.

Back at the corner Glenda was waiting. I was surprised. "You're going," I said. "I'm busting you."

"What? For two bags of dope?"

"Right. I'm tired of this Babyface bullshit."

"Please, I just got home. Those bull dykes in the House of D, you won't believe what they do to me."

"You're going."

I ran into Glenda a day or two after she was released. She was wearing a white topcoat and red high-heeled shoes. It was early evening at Bickford's Cafeteria when Frank and I spotted her. On that night junkies were out in alarming numbers, whores and pimps, tricks and various other street bon vivants. The world of the constantly sick or stoned sat at tables under fluorescent light drinking coffee and smoking, all of them looking wide-eyed and expectant.

A sign on the wall said No Loitering.

Glenda was sitting with her sister Maria, and when the sisters spotted me, Glenda spread her legs and opened her coat. Under the topcoat she wore a thong and was topless. She had tiny tits, and those tits were covered with hickeys, as were her neck and her thighs, all bestowed on her by the bull dykes of the House of D. Everyone in the place was watching us as we watched her.

"You do this, Babyface?" Maria said.

"Do what?"

"You give my sister all those love bites."

"Well," Frank said, "did you?"

"Are you nuts?"

"That's what my sister told me, that's what she told everybody," Maria said. " 'Babyface sucked me everywhere' is what she said." As we walked from the cafeteria amid the din of hoots, hollers, and laughter from the gathered crowd, Frank said, "You should do something about that Babyface bullshit."

"I do, I try."

"Try harder."

Deep into the night, like predatory birds, we swept through the neighborhood rounding up drug dealers, filling the cells at the 78th Precinct. We finished up near two o'clock in the morning. I suggested we stop at Bickford's for containers of coffee, a little boost for the ride home.

On the street in front of the cafeteria a gypsy cab sat doubleparked. I saw Maria and Glenda and a black prostitute whose name was Ronnie step briskly from the cab. Then I spotted him, the clown I had chased. He was wearing a white guayabera and a panama hat. He stood alongside the cab looking the street over.

"That's him," I told Frank, "that's the creep that ran from me."

"Are you sure?"

"It's him."

Frank was biting his lip, glaring in a bewildered way through the windshield. "So," he said, "what do you want to do?"

"Nail that fuck."

"Let's go get him."

I came up from behind and grabbed him, Frank took the women, and we headed into a hallway a few doors from Bickford's. The dealer turned his head and smiled at me as if we were friends. In the darkened hallway I got into his face. Our noses were an inch apart; I could feel his breath. I said, "You can't run now, can you, smartass?" I told him that I was going to lock his ass up, whispering all this, and then I heard one of the woman say, "No man, don't do that."

I heard a sound like *click*, then another *click*. I experienced a split second of horrifying recognition, then I hunched up and Frank shouted, "Gun!"

I froze, I couldn't move, Frank pushed me aside and dove between me and the dealer, the gun flying off. The three of us were rolling around in a tangled heap on the ground. The women screamed and ran out into the street.

That gun had misfired, and later at ballistics it would misfire again, but on the fourth try it went off, *pow!* My hands were shaking, and when I tried to use my handcuffs, I cut myself. To complicate matters, I must have rubbed my hands across my face because when we dragged the prisoner into the 78th Precinct, the desk officer freaked.

"What the hell happened to you?"

"Fine," I said, "I'm fine, I'm okay. But this guy here, this character, he tried to shoot me."

We marched the prisoner up a flight of stairs to the second floor and locked him in the detectives' holding cage. Then we went out to get that coffee, knowing we had many more hours ahead of us, at least five pounds of paperwork waiting.

Five minutes after Frank and I had left, four 78th squad detectives came into the precinct led by a detective named Ray Gallo. Gallo would later tell me that the desk lieutenant was frantic, telling Ray that when I came into the precinct I was covered in blood.

"His prisoner is upstairs," he said. "The son of a bitch tried to kill him."

When Frank and I returned to the precinct, we ran into Ray as he was leaving. Ray turned to me, his eyes wide and angry. Ray didn't use words like *nihilism* or *existentialism*, but he understood anarchy and lawlessness. "What the hell you doing?" he said. "You get the shit kicked out of you, and you walk your prisoner in here just like that?"

Yes, just like that, I thought, and since I hadn't been hurt, I was surprised at his reaction.

"Bullshit," he said. "You had blood all over you. A skel like that, he goes to the hospital. That's it. Have you got it?"

I nodded, thinking it best that I not get into any of this. The look on Ray's face, his smile, gave me this funny feeling. He was a friend, and recently I had helped him with a homicide investigation. Ray was old-school, a no-nonsense, uncompromising detective; the smile on his face was a bad omen.

He lectured me about something I had been told a thousand times, something I had been taught as far back as the police academy. Some skel takes you on in the street, you have a responsibility to send that shit to the hospital. Do something to protect the next cop he comes into contact with.

"You better call an ambulance," Ray said. "That bum is going to need one."

We should not have left the prisoner alone, I knew that, but we were tired, having already worked about twelve hours. I was happy to find our prisoner still locked in the holding cage. Not so happy to see his condition. He looked as though he'd been in a hammer fight, without a hammer.

What is cowardice? What is courage? Without giving it a thought, Frank dove between someone pulling a trigger and me. Gallo and the others beat a caged prisoner because they believed he'd tried to kill a cop and would probably try again if he weren't taught a lesson. In the growing chaos and violence of the street back then, every cop understood that you had no choice but to protect your own.

Throughout the country there had been an onslaught of police assassinations. "Kill the pig" was not simply a protest-march rallying cry, it was a national reality. To protect one another was the focus of all police passion, the one great link in the wall of blue and brass. I know I felt that way, and I'm sure Ray Gallo did too.

Lieutenant Mazen showed up around five in the morning to take a statement. When he saw the prisoner, his face swollen, black and blue around the eyes, his nose shattered, and bloodstains all over his pretty white guyabera, Mazen was horrified. "What the hell sense does this make?" he said. "Tell me, what purpose does it serve?" He understood the rage and frustration—who wouldn't understand?—but he called the beating unprofessional and stupid.

It was something he hadn't expected from us. He told us he was disappointed.

I got home late the following morning and Gina asked if I'd had a busy night.

"A little more than normal," I told her. I had something to eat and went to bed. I couldn't sleep; I tossed and turned in the curtained half light of my bedroom. That dealer's smile, the sound of the click of his gun, would not leave my head. When I finally fell asleep, I slept until the following day.

Gina woke me with a copy of the *Daily News*. There was a small piece, a paragraph about a gun misfiring, about Frank and me and a hallway in Brooklyn.

AS FOR FRANK Mandato and me, each of us, I think, fulfilled a need in the other. I had all sorts of energy and sources of information, but I was not directed. Frank, a seasoned cop, self-assured and politically astute, with absolutely steel balls, provided that direction.

Frank's father worked as a court stenographer at the Brooklyn Criminal Courts. Frank had been raised in and around the courthouse. He knew all the lawyers, the ADAs, the judges, and he had friends throughout the job. Frank had friends everywhere. Not long after we began working as steady partners, everyone became my friend too. Suddenly I was invited to people's homes, invited to lunch, invited to the Hanover for a drink every payday.

One cold winter night, the entire office assembled at the Hanover for a retirement party. The place was packed with detectives from throughout the city, along with defense lawyers and an assistant district attorney or two.

Eddie Egan was sitting alone at the end of the bar; Sonny Grosso was holding court at the other end. Frank walked over to Egan and bought him a drink, while I drank with Joe Nunziata. I asked him if he still thought our phones were up. He told me to treat all telephones as if they were tapped. "Your home phone too. Never say anything on a telephone you wouldn't want your worst enemy or best friend to know."

"No shit?"

"Right."

I told him I didn't have anything to hide. He smiled, saying, "It doesn't matter."

"Sure it does," I said. "Of course it does."

It was a festive scene, people giving each other hugs, the soon-to-retire detective with tears in his eyes. "I love this job," he said to everyone. "I don't know what I'll do without it."

For me it was a weird and wonderful gathering, evoking all sorts of unfamiliar emotions; the kind of convening that brought together all the canny observers of an elite netherworld. Everyone was drinking and matching stories.

I found myself standing in the midst of fifty ultracool detectives and felt this strange emotion building inside me. It was as if I were stepping into a mystifying bath. I'd find it was not warm and relaxing water I was moving into but something both affecting and razor-sharp.

In the center of that party, there was a real sense of danger. I could feel it, and it was exquisitely exciting. I tried to relax and simply go with the flow. *Well,* I thought, *so this is it, the brotherhood.* It scared the hell out of me, that kind of feeling.

I was smart enough to know that this was a trapdoor world of smoke and mirrors, a place where emotions ran very high, and paranoia was as common as guns and handcuffs. All of that would now be a part of my life too.

FRANK AND I searched for cases seriously, obsessively. We found drug dealers and we found laughs. The maddening caginess and slyness of the street dealers, the pimps, the prostitutes, all the yellow-eyed night people—it was a glorious show, and when the full moon was out, there was no better place to be. I knew that I was in a part of the forest where I didn't belong. I was using new language. I saw and did things I would someday pay for. But at the time, it was one helluva party.

The world seemed to explode around me. It gave me tremors and goose bumps, letting me know that I was dancing right at the edge. I knew that there was physical danger in those streets, but there were also women, money, and rock and roll.

The old longing to be selected, set apart, and wanted settled on me. I no longer felt that I was out on my own. No more was I fearful of not fitting in. It all came back to me on a solitary ray of recollection. In narcotics I'd been thought of as peculiar. Not anymore. Now I was, without question, one of the guys, and it was whoop-it-up time.

The neighborhoods and the streets where Frank and I worked had names that could raise the hair on the back of your neck: Van Brunt, Union, President, Columbia, Kane and Pacific, Sackett and Hoyt, Fourth and Atlantic, Flatbush and Atlantic, Sunset Park. Moving through those streets late at night, when the only people out and about were criminals and cops, everyone searching for the drug, hunting for the white lady, created in me intense feelings I had never experienced before.

We arrested scores of drug dealers; it was all we did. The number of dealers arrested meant nothing, changed nothing—there were always more. Nevertheless, I had found someone who enjoyed the chase as much as I did. Like me, Frank seemed to find downright joy in the work. There was a time when I used to feel guilty keeping partners out ten, twelve hours a day; like all their family problems were somehow my fault. It was a relief to have all that finished. After three years I'd found a true partner.

We'd finish work, and I'd drive the fifty miles out to Long Island to my home in Kings Park. I'd walk in the door, and the telephone would be ringing, Frank calling to see if I had made it home okay. Then we'd talk. Sometimes we'd gab for an hour. It was bizarre, but if Frank didn't phone me, if the telephone wasn't ringing when I came into the house, I'd call him.

"Hey Frank, how's it going? You know what we should do tomorrow? . . ." We'd talk and talk and talk, et cetera, ad weirdum.

FRANK STUNNED ME. He opened a door to a world that I had always suspected was there, but I had never been sure. Now, suddenly, I was sure.

What was truly remarkable was the fact that once you took it upon yourself to toss off your honor, and all restraint, money could be found everywhere.

One morning, over breakfast at our favorite coffee shop, Frank told me that if I directed someone I arrested to certain lawyers, those lawyers would split their fee with me.

"Are you serious?"

"Sure."

"Let's say some character jumps bail. You hunt him down, his bondsman will pay you a fee."

"You have got to be kidding."

"No, no kidding."

"I can find anyone in South Brooklyn."

"I know that."

"We execute a search warrant, and there's money laying around [there was always money lying around] we take a little. Not too much, never be greedy, just enough to cover expenses."

"Expenses?"

"Yeah."

I could feel the blood rushing to my face. My stomach tightened into knots. I was trying to think of what to say. Telling Frank how I felt was important. I didn't want to lose him and have him be another in the long list of failed partners.

"Look," I said, "I'm not opposed to making some money. I've crossed that bridge and I can deal with it."

"That's not what I heard," he said.

"I don't care what you've heard. I'm telling you how I feel."

"Okay."

"I'm going to tell you what I won't do."

Silence from Frank.

"I won't deal with lawyers or bondsmen."

He puffed his cheeks and blew. "Okay," he said, "I will."

"All right," I told him, "when the situation presents itself, we'll discuss it. But if I say no, it's no."

"Sure."

"I'll never shake anyone down. I'll never lean on anyone for money. I mean if we kick in a door and there's money laying around, we take a little off the top, I can live with that."

"Okay."

"I'm not cutting anyone loose for money."

"Whoa! Let's say we hit a place and there are two people there. Say one wants to take the weight, and he's willing to spring to cut the other one loose. You have a problem with that?"

"Yes. Listen, I think you know what I mean. I'm not asking, and I am not going to press anyone. I don't want people pissed off at me."

"I understand."

"I hope so."

"You have a hundred informants," he said. "I've never seen anything like it, it's amazing."

"Yeah. They trust me, they like me."

"That's bullshit."

"What are you talking about?"

"Half these characters are fucking dealers."

"Strung-out street dealers. They have no money. What they have are outrageous habits, that's what they have."

"They give you a little information and you let them operate."

"They give me plenty of information."

"No they don't; they give you what they want to give you, nothing more."

All at once, Frank seemed new to me; he was so sure of himself, so confident.

"Maybe you're right," I told him.

"I know I'm right. There's no reason why we can't hit on some of these characters every once in a while."

I didn't like that idea and told him so.

"You'll see," he said. "They'll be happy to give you a few bucks to get you off their back."

"That's a pad. You'd have to be fucking crazy to set up a drug pad. Not me, no way."

"No. No pad. No specific amount, no regular payments. But let's say we're short, we stop in on one of these guys and hit them up for a hundred or something."

"I don't know. I don't like it. They'll stop working."

Silence.

"By the way," I said. "If I ever caught a cop selling drugs I'd lock him up myself."

"Of course."

"Just so you understand. And no matter what we do, if money is made, we share it equally, and always take care of the boss."

How bizarre for police officers to have such conversations. All that talk led to the inevitable sleaze that was yet to come and began my descent into the night of full-blown corruption. All that was once my honor fell from me piece by piece. Later, I'd try to get it back. Later, when it was all but impossible.

> earner—Mafia term, someone who makes money for
> the group or crew.

> to do the right thing—Mafia term, to do whatever it
> takes to make a person in a position of power happy.

I don't mean to mislead and lay all this on Frank Mandato. Given the demoralizing standards of that time and place, Frank simply acted a role in the play of my life. He was a guidepost on the outlaw trail that I decided to take. It is as clear to me today as it was then; my own fingerprints were all over my downfall.

I knew it was wrong, seriously wrong, yet I did it willingly, knowing full well how asinine and outrageous such behavior was. And what is truly astonishing, I knew that it would harm me. Still I was prepared to do it.

During this time I affected a nonchalant, blasé attitude. I came up with countless reasons for my conduct and was able to weave into myself behavior that was alien to my nature and then accept it all as somehow a natural course of events. I was too jazzed up to look around and see the defeat, the hopelessness, and the consequences. No one did a better job on me than me when it came to rationalizing what I was doing.

With Frank at my side I made more arrests than I had ever made before. My red line went off the activity chart. Armed with some money in my pocket, I began spending more and more time in the street, and less and less at home.

> "[T]here was a message returned to us by our frontier that the outlaw is worth more than the sheriff."
>
> —NORMAN MAILER, *The Idol and the Octopus*

Before Frank, faced with grinding expenses, I'd go from payday to payday with maybe twenty, twenty-five dollars in my pocket. Now I walked around with a couple of hundred. We were not making a whole lot of money, but more than enough to take care of expenses. I had a mortgage that I could barely handle; I also had gas and insurance and phone bills that would choke a horse. Gina and I had decided she would not return to work until Anthony was old enough for school, and now she was pregnant again. I was being paid something like eighteen thousand dollars a year. Car repairs, clothing, food for the table—it had always been difficult—not impossible but difficult—to make ends meet. Along came Frank. He opened a window, and all that pressure eased.

Frank took me shopping. I bought slacks, shoes, Italian knit shirts, and a leather jacket. He suggested that I get the clothes I owned drycleaned and burned. He took me to his barber. I had my hair styled, my fingernails done. If we had a long night, the following day I'd get a shampoo and shave, look in the mirror and think, *Yo, look at you; you look like a mafioso.*

We still ate BLTs and drank bad coffee in Bickford's. Only now we could also go to Monty's on Carroll Street for gnocci, or drive over the bridge into Manhattan to Max's Kansas City Steak House for folk music and T-bones. Some nights we went to Puglia in Little Italy or to Chinatown or Sammy's Rumanian on the Lower East Side.

It was during those times that Frank was at his most cheerful and upbeat. We'd have what we thought of as serious talks about music and film, European travel, women and money.

Frank treated me pretty much as though I were his younger brother. He gave me advice on all things. I felt fine with it. He seemed so mature and worldly, and I believed he always had my best interests at heart. Frank convinced me that everyone was out looking to score. Everybody was on a hustle. "Look around," he'd say, "tell me, what do you see?"

We were continually in court, and during that time I met scores of lawyers and ADAs. I never met one, not one defense lawyer whose practice was made up mostly of narcotics defendants who didn't offer me some sort of dirty deal if I would help his clients. Frank had a point.

The ADAs were not all that much better. Sitting in their offices, with flags and law school diplomas and plaques on their walls, they'd give you that sly look, wink, smile, and say, "Are you sure you want to testify that way? If you do, we lose this case."

———

FRANK AND I spent the better part of the next year in and around South Brooklyn. During that time he was able to confirm to me all that I already knew. Just about everything in that Brooklyn courthouse was organized and coordinated by the DA's office and something known as the "Court Street bar." Kings County, it seemed to me, was thoroughly politicized and corrupt.

> Court Street bar—criminal defense lawyers with
> offices on Court Street in Brooklyn.

Say a lawyer wanted to become a judge in Brooklyn. First he joined one of the many Democratic political clubs, then he romanced the various politicos, and ultimately paid fifty thousand dollars to the club. Sooner or later he would be in a robe and on the bench. Once on the bench he could make make all that money back in no time.

Deals were made, cases sold—that courthouse was a marketplace, not a hall of justice. Democratic leader Meade Esposito, who dispensed all political patronage jobs in Brooklyn, ran the operation.

> to buy you a hat—to give a cop a small amount of
> money (e.g., "That was a nice thing you did for me. I'd
> like to buy you a hat").

Over the years there had been scandals. Major investigations and commissions had been put in place to investigate police corruption. There was never one to examine political corruption.

Frank explained all this to me; his father had explained it all to him. A defendant with money had a better than fifty-fifty chance of buying his way out of any kind of case. I saw it happening all around me. To the uninitiated and unconcerned, the system seemed to work. The court calendars moved, cases were solved, and poor people went to jail. It was better to turn away and go with the flow, far better than trying to struggle against it.

The system was so entrenched it didn't seem that anything could go wrong. Morale was high. The courthouse was an emporium, but no one seemed to care. It seemed that just about everyone, at all levels of the criminal justice system, was involved. Frank and I would have lunch with ten, twelve detectives at a time, talking over our cases, congratulating ourselves for being the best cops in the world. But every so often, late at night, two or three of us together, talking about all the things we saw and did, we'd quiet down, and one and all admitted it was crazy. That world out there was nuts.

Between what arresting strung-out junkies did to you, how depressed you got from collaring people who couldn't find their hands and feet; between the crazy shit you both did and saw in the street and what you lost as far as moral perspective was concerned, being there, seeing it all up close and personal, if you had any brains at all you could see that it all boiled down to a collective nervous breakdown of the system. You were part of it, your eye saw it, but your brain couldn't really take it in. Like this one:

It was late on a Friday night; I walked into the Brooklyn arraignment court. A busy night, the place was jammed to the rafters, and it turned the courtroom into a spectacle of craziness, a bazaar of victims and defendants, manipulators of all sorts.

I spotted Richard Smalls, an informant of mine. In the street, they called him Sweet Dick. He was standing with a bevy of his working girls.

Dick was a benevolent pimp. He processed his hair, wore sharkskin suits, and looked to all the world like Sugar Ray Robinson. Sweet Dick didn't bully or threaten his working girls so much as he charmed them. I guess he told them he loved them and made all sorts of ridiculous vows to protect them.

Most of these women didn't have much going for them in the way of self-reliance. Sweet Dick's women wore wigs and face paint and were street pretty. They all were heroin addicts.

I remember that night, the way Dick put his hands on his hips, turned to look around the courtroom, then turned back to me saying, "Man, you gotta help me out here. My brother, the kid got busted by some precinct cop. Bunch a bullshit. The kid didn't do nothing but ride in a car. The car was hot, he never knew it."

"And what would you like me to do?"

The five women standing behind Dick, as if on cue, gave me one of those perplexed, piercing looks. "You can go and talk to the DA. Have his bail lowered or something," one of them said.

"Please," said Dick. "Help me out here."

The assistant district attorney calling the arraignment calendar was Martin Light. Marty was a state's attorney, which was unbearable to him. He longed to be in private practice bringing down boxes of money.

Erudite and attractive in an Ocean Parkway, Brooklyn sort of way, Marty knew his way around the courthouse. He knew how to get things done. He favored navy blue pin-striped suits, off-blue shirts, and red ties. With his full head of curly black hair, you'd make him as someone who could work a lounge in Vegas.

"I have an informant whose brother is on the calendar. I'd like to get his bail lowered?"

Marty gave me a look, a kind of supercilious grin, an expression of both expectation and disbelief. It gave me a funny feeling, that look of his. "Does he have any money?" he said.

I went back to Sweet Dick and asked him. Dick raised his arms in the universal arbitrator sign and inquired of his ladies, "Does anyone have any cash?"

Standing in a ragged circle, the ladies went into their pocketbooks, their bras, and their panties. After much searching and shuffling about, they came out with about five hundred dollars in rolled-up fives, tens, and twenties.

I gave Marty what I thought was bail money—the rolled-up and scrounged-together hooker cash. He told me to go get the prisoner. I was stunned when the judge paroled the guy, paroled him into my custody. I said, "Whoa, wait a minute." Marty said, "Parole, better than low bail, no bail at all." The five hundred went south.

I left the courthouse that night and walked over to Court Street, to an Italian restaurant and bar called Villa Roma, a place we called Chick's. From what I could see, there was hardly anyone in the restaurant, just the owner, Charlie, behind the stick. There was one customer at the far end of the bar; he was sitting in semi-darkness sipping an espresso.

Charlie was the most urbane of bar owners. A New York guy, something of a philosopher, he understood the city, how it worked, what it took to own a bar and restaurant and survive. We were pretty good friends, and he was willing to take my word for it when I told him that the courthouse was a zoo.

"What happened?"

"Charlie, it's a bit complicated, but take my word for it, it wears you out."

He looked at me; then he turned to look down the bar, then turned back saying, "You should tell that man, he's a law professor."

Wearing a gray suit, the professor was hunched forward over the bar. He had the look of an athlete, with his broad shoulders. His whole posture and the way he sat there made quite a physical statement. This was my chance to say something indignant, a resounding irate speech. There were any number of strange stories I could have told him, some incredible, some beyond that, the absurd and the ordinary.

"I understand you're a law professor," I said. "Well, I'd like to know what the hell you're teaching these characters. Because I'll tell you what, you go into that courthouse and it's no different than the street. You need a scorecard to figure out just who the good and bad guys are."

The professor had a way of glaring back at you when you spoke to him. Like he was calculating the right moment to cut in. "Listen," I said, "lawyers run the whole show. They're the trendsetters, they're the role models. The prosecutors, the judges, the defense, all lawyers." I remember how upset he looked, telling me that the vast majority of people practicing law were decent people, dedicated, honest, and hardworking. He didn't know what I was alluding to. All this was said softly, as if talking to himself. He wasn't trying to persuade me, simply stating a fact. "Look to yourself," he said. "How have you been behaving?"

The way he smiled, the way he looked, made me think about all those priests back when I was a kid, how clean and innocent they all seemed, how they would not believe any of this. Try and tell them about it, they'd answer you with a question. "So how are you behaving?"

When I was leaving the restaurant Charlie said, "So you talked to him?" I nodded. He said, "Good, because that guy, you know, that guy is someone you should know. He's going to be an important man someday."

"He's a professor, Charlie, they're all naive."

"Not him. He was one helluva athlete, and smart as they come. You remember what I tell you, this guy, this Mario Cuomo, he'll be an important man someday."

"Sure, "I told him." I bet he will be."

Now and again at Chicks I would run into the man who would later be governor. We'd talk about the legal system, cops and lawyers, the courthouse and the streets. Blah-blah-blah—as if I could really say what it was that I did in those streets. Back then I believed that everyone knew what everyone did. Nevertheless, this man was a fresh voice, full of humanity, an old-fashioned incorruptible moralist. I remember wishing to God I could talk like that. Then wishing to God I could understand what the hell he was talking about. I would not meet his like again, not until I met Nicholas Scoppetta and then Rudy Giuliani, but that came later.

DURING THIS TIME, Frank and I ran roughshod over South Brooklyn; using our undercovers to knock over street dealers, turning those small-time dealers into informants, executing search warrants to move up the drug dealer ladder.

Often Lieutenant Mazen came along on these raids. There was always money, at times a lot of money lying around. With Mazen there we turned away.

One night, during the Christmas holidays, we hit a major heroin street dealer who worked out of a brownstone in Bedford-Stuyvesant. The guy had boxes and boxes of Christmas cards, all of them stuffed with hundreds of dollars. He had money hidden in books, bundles of cash wrapped in Christmas presents, every drawer in his apartment had money in stacks and bundles. There was so much money and clutter in that house, we were forced to contact the local precinct and ask for help with the search. Those precinct cops went from room to room repeating, "God bless America, God bless America."

Hidden in the oven door I found four or five ounces of pure heroin. Mazen was astounded.

"How did you find that? How did you know where to look?"

"The screws," I told him. "The screws on the oven door are worn. I could tell that they've been put in and removed many times."

"God, you're good."

Frank smiled.

Our informant had told us exactly where the drugs would be. He had been in the kitchen when the dealer had stashed them.

In the bedroom I found powder in a box hidden under the bed. I put on my supercool, experienced narcotics detective look, wet my finger, and reached down into the box. I licked the powder off my fingertip.

Mazen and Frank were standing in the doorway. "What is it, Bobby?" Frank said.

Mazen was startled; he asked why I had put the powder in my mouth.

Silence from me; it was horrible, harsh and revolting.

A kind smile from Frank. "What is it?" he said.

"Rat poison."

"I thought so. Don't swallow."

Mazen laughed, Frank laughed. I ran to the bathroom, and for the first time in many years, I heaved. Then it was my time to laugh, in humiliation and in relief.

Through all this time, my reputation and Frank's soared. We were heavy hitters. The bosses knew we were hard workers, big case makers, and earners.

Joe Nunziata and I were both promoted from third- to second-grade detective. He moved on to the special investigating unit. A short time later, Lieutenant Mazen recommended Frank and me. We were ecstatic; it was a major step, a walk to the very edge and one of the rewards.

THE
DARK SIDE
OF THE
MOON

There will never be a detective unit like the SIU
again. Each of its field detectives was handpicked
from throughout the department on the basis of
talent, experience, and accomplishment. Detectives
in the SIU were the best of the department's best.

— GREGORY WALLANCE, *Papa's Game*

S itting in on my first SIU meeting my senses blazed. It
was as though I'd taken a hit of cocaine. I was keyed up,
aroused, and thrilled. Each comment the CO made
sounded as though it was said expressly for my personal
instruction.

"We have major violator files here. Study them and then pick one
out and go and get him. In the SIU, numbers are not important,
quality cases are what count. You people are supposed to be the best.
Okay, show us what you can do."

I'm thinking, *No more chasing junkies across rooftops, no more basements and shooting galleries, no more giving dope to sick junkie informants*

with runny noses and lost souls. Now the targets would be sly and elusive men in expensive suits, driving El Dorados, smoking Cuban cigars, and living in Fort Lee, New Jersey.

The man sitting beside me was big and burly. I could feel the power in his shoulder and arm as he leaned in an affectionate way against me. The CO asked if there were any questions, and the man to my right said, "We know who these guys are. We know where they live. We know how much dope they're moving. We know that these shitheads have killed more of our young people than any war we've ever been involved in. I say we go out whack the fuckers, blow 'em all away. That's what I say."

Everyone laughed.

"I'm not kidding," he said. The look of profound bitterness on his face told everyone in the room that he was absolutely serious.

There was much murmuring and mean-spirited giggles, a consensus in the air. This was going to be, I thought, one helluvan outfit.

THE MAN ON my right, his name was Gene D'Arpe, Frank's new partner and mine. Gene was an amazingly thoughtful and quiet man, broad in the shoulders and neat as a pin. He was also an angry man, with practically no sense of humor.

Gene had a remarkable way of looking at the world. He was suspicious of everyone, and the expression that always seemed fixed on his face was as if he heard music off in the distance. Having been divorced for some time, he lived alone in Rockaway Beach, in an apartment that overlooked the ocean. Family Court had imposed a heavy lien on his salary, so he collected a paycheck of two hundred and twenty dollars every two weeks. I understood his quiet anger, anyone would. But it was his obsessive, controlling nature that drove me batty. "You talk to no one about our cases but me," he'd say. "We go to dinner and we socialize with no one but each other."

The guy was a space shot, but he was devoted to both the work and his partners.

As soon as Frank and I teamed up with Gene, we opened a case that would take us to the Bronx and Harlem. The target was a significant cocaine and marijuana dealer by the name of Major Cobb. The Major lived in Throgs Neck and ran his drug operation from an indoor parking garage, a building that he owned on St. Nicholas Avenue in Harlem.

The SIU worked almost entirely off wiretaps and bugs. Some were court authorized, some not. We put a legal one on the Major's home phone.

A horror to tail, the Major was relentlessly loaded on coke. He drove a red El Dorado at high speed all over the city and carried a .45 automatic. We learned quickly that Major Cobb was an absolute madman.

IT WAS A Friday night, and practically every detective in New York City was invited to pay court and attend a party at the Elks Club on Queens Boulevard. The affair was being held for Queens District Attorney Thomas Mackell.

The DA had been indicted and arrested; this gathering was to be a combination fund-raiser and retirement party. The entire SIU was going, everyone except Gene, Frank, and me.

They told us they wanted our team to set up on a motel in Riverdale. There were two Cuban brothers out of Miami, important cocaine dealers, staying at the motel. Three teams of SIU detectives had been working them for months.

"Get on them," they told us. "Watch them, tail them, but take no action. None. If anything out of the ordinary happens, call us at the affair."

We set up surveillance on two matching brown-on-brown El Dorados with Florida registration plates. Each of us was in his own car and in radio contact.

The brothers' room was on the first floor and opened to the parking lot. It was a good setup. Late that night, one brother came out of the room wearing jeans, a jean jacket, cowboy boots, and a cowboy hat. He went to one of the El Dorados and got in.

I fiddled with the radio, which wasn't working right. None of our department-issued radios ever worked right. "I'll tail this guy," I told the others. Within five minutes after leaving the parking lot, the radio went dead.

I followed that El Dorado all over the South Bronx and East Harlem. As I tracked him, I expected he'd look in the rearview, do something tricky on the road, run a light or two, pull a quick U-turn—but he didn't. The Cuban drove as though he had not a care in the world; his actions were orderly.

I tailed him to four or five bodegas in the Bronx and one social club in East Harlem. At each location the Cuban entered empty-handed and exited a short time later carrying a paper bag. When he walked out of the social club he was hanging on to an attaché case. The case and the paper bags he deposited in the trunk of his car.

Shadowing him I felt strong and confident and in collusion with absolute coolness. I was SIU. This may not have been the French Connection case—but it was a start.

Back at the motel, I found the others gone—the second El Dorado and Gene's and Frank's cars—all three gone. My guy parked his car and went into the motel. Lights went on; shades were drawn. Something was happening. I could feel it. I tried the radio. Nothing.

Five or ten minutes later, the cowboy was out and going to his car again. This time he was carrying clothing folded on hangers, and a suitcase. A short time later the second El Dorado arrived. I heard the radio and Gene's voice.

"Where did your guy go?" Gene asked.

"I followed him all over the Bronx and into East Harlem," I said. Suddenly the second brother was out of the room, struggling under a load of clothing and a suitcase. He went to the second El Dorado.

"These two characters are leaving," I said. "We'd better notify somebody."

I telephoned the Elks Club. Someone picked up and I heard laughter and singing. There was something that sounded like a carousel, and then the music of "Danny Boy." I asked to speak to one of our sergeants.

"Sorry you guys missed this show," Sergeant Scanlon said. "Renaghan is here and Mackell, they're both singing."

"The Cubans are leaving," I told him. "They're packing their cars and they're leaving. What do you want us to do?"

"Grab them, hold them, we'll be right there." Suddenly he sounded both drunk and somber. "Don't touch anything. Don't do anything until we get there. Just hold them."

We showed the Cuban brothers badges and guns. We handcuffed them, took their car keys, and sat them on the bed in the motel room. They gave us spacey smiles, told us they didn't speak English. Then they turned away and studied the bare wall. They never asked to see a warrant. Not that it would have done much good; we didn't have one.

They arrived in three cars, two sergeants and six detectives. Some went quickly into the motel. One of the sergeants took the car keys. I told him we hadn't searched, hadn't touched anything. I told him the brothers said they didn't speak English and he said, "Bullshit."

Frank, Gene, and I backed away. This was their case, their business.

They searched the brothers and found nothing. Searched the motel room, nothing again. When one of the detectives opened the El Dorado's trunk, I heard, "Geeze, look at this. Holy shit."

It was a cheery scene, no guns, no drugs, just money. Two car trunks filled with bags of money.

The Cubans were marched to the parking lot. They were both young, tall and thin and clean-shaven. Attractive men. They were made to stand near the cars' open trunks.

"Where did you get all this money?" Sergeant Scanlon asked.

"What money?"

"That money."

The Cuban said he didn't know how all that money got into his car. He'd parked the car in different places around the city, left it unattended all night long.

He said that someone must have stashed that money in his car. "It's probably counterfeit," is what he said. If it was his money, and it was real, he wouldn't be staying in this place. He'd be staying at the Waldorf-Astoria.

"Bullshit."

"No disrespect," one of the Cubans said, "but we've commited no crime; there's no drugs here, no guns, and that is not our money. Look," he told us, "whoever that money belongs to is not here to say it's his. So if I were you guys, I'd take half of that cash. You give us the rest, and we'll go back to Miami. I swear to God," he said, "we'll never come back to this city."

Spoken with sincerity, and just the slightest trace of an accent.

"You swear to God?"

"Absolutely."

The sergeant took us all to the side and explained, or tried to explain, that they had blown it. The teams that worked these two cowboys had somehow missed the drugs. Now there was no stopping the Cubans from returning to Miami. "The thing is," he said, "we have no crime here, no drugs, no guns. Screwed," he said, "there is no other word for it; we're screwed.

"Look," he told us with a sigh, "I don't know about you guys, but as far as I'm concerned, I've come to learn that these Cubans are incredibly religious people. If they say they swear to God, swear they'll never come back to New York, well, that's good enough for me."

Beg pardon?

"Let's say we seize this money," he said. "Let's say we confiscate all of it. We'll spend hours recording it, copying each and every serial number. Then we are obligated to turn it over to the city. The city will take this cash, and being the sensitive human beings that they are, they'll give it to the Department of Welfare. The Department of Welfare will take this cash and hand it to some asshole on welfare. That asshole will go out, buy a gun, and then shoot a cop. I'm not going to be responsible for the shooting of some poor unsuspecting cop."

There was a long moment of silence, and then he said, "Does anyone have anything to say, an objection, a suggestion maybe?"

Some rolled their eyes, but no one said anything. Everyone's head was down; some checked their fingers, some shuffled their feet. I stood there watching, thinking all kinds of things. I glanced over at Frank, who shrugged and smiled his best friendly grin. He mouthed the letters *SIU.*

Gene had a look of mild disgust on his face. "Look," he said, "you want to be criminals, let's be real criminals. Why don't we kill these two assholes, then there won't be any witnesses, and we get all the money."

"Jesus," I said. "What the fuck?" Frank's eyes got very wide.

"Are you nuts?" the sergeant said. "What are you, loony? Kill them? We're not criminals for Christ sake."

Everybody stood silent and still.

Wearily, the sergeant told us to leave. "All of you get lost. The leaders of the teams that worked the case, you guys stay put. I want the rest of you to go someplace and wait. In an hour, send one guy from each team back here."

Frank, Gene, and I found an all-night coffee shop and ordered breakfast. The place was empty except for a pair of uniformed cops who sat at the counter having coffee. They looked carefully at us, a glimmer of suspicion on their faces.

"Were you serious?" I asked Gene. "Back there, in the parking lot, did you mean what you said?"

He glared at me, then he smiled. "Put your mind at rest," he said. "I'm not a murderer."

Thank you Jesus, I thought.

After we had eaten, Gene left us and then returned in twenty minutes or so. He gave us the thumbs-up sign and handed each of us an envelope stuffed with cash.

And so it went, more or less.

To tell the story of this incident is like trying to diminish the sins of your life to a new friend. You go for amusing, a what-would-you-have-done-in-my-place kind of thing. You consider your truest self and search for some rationalization. At its heart, this kind of behavior might be described as mass insanity, but that too is a search for personal justification. After a time, you recognize what is the worst of you, and you hate it. Trouble is, first you must recognize just what you have lost, and that takes time. At least for me it did.

WE IMMEDIATELY GOT back onto Major Cobb. There were four of us now; a detective by the name of Jack Bergersen had joined the team.

The SIU was staffed with an extraordinary number of attractive men. Given that such observations are subjective, I'll ask that you take my word for it. Jack Bergersen was an unusually handsome man, the father of five, and deeply in love with his wife. He was strongly of the opinion that this job was not his life, and he made it perfectly clear that he'd be glad to put in hours, but he needed to spend time with his family.

We broke up in teams of two, Jack and Gene, Frank and me, to cover the wiretap, transcribe the incoming and outgoing calls, and maintain surveillance of the Major.

Major Cobb was constantly on his phone with women, customers, and friends, gabbing at all hours of the day and night. Blitzed on coke, the man never slept, and he was all the time boasting to friends that he was the cocaine connection for the New York Knickerbockers basketball team.

We needed to use all four of our cars to tail the Major. He drove like a madman and seemed to be always on guard. Nevertheless, late at night, when he returned home after a coke-filled mission on the town, he would lift the receiver and shout into the phone, "Sheriff, you there, Sheriff? I know you're there. I know you're listening. Peeping Tom motherfuckers! I got something for you, you hear me?"

We'd hear the sound of metal on metal, the smooth swish of a round being jacked into the chamber of an automatic.

"Ya hear that, Sheriff? That's what's waiting for you." Then he'd snort a line, telephone one of his friends or customers, and talk and talk about moving drugs. A lunatic.

Always dressed in a suit and tie, the Major was one spiffy guy, and man could he shop. The Major bought everything in sight. One time, before leaving for a weekend vacation in the Bahamas, the Major telephoned a local carpet store. He told the store manager he wanted his house carpeted.

"Carpet everything," he said, "the wine red carpet, the shag that I was looking at in the store."

"Everything?"

"You heard me. When I get back, I want to see my entire house covered with that carpet."

Five minutes after he left for the airport, a carpet company truck rolled up to his house. We watched as workers brought in roll upon roll of glittering red shag carpeting. The installer used the major's phone to telephone the carpet store, telling the manager that he was at the Major's house and ready to work.

"All of it," the store manager said. "Carpet the whole fucking house." A few days later, the Major returned from his vacation; as soon as he strolled through the door, he picked up the telephone.

The Major was laughing; it was a low growl, an insane sort of laugh. We could hear his wife hysterical with glee in the background. I figured that the Major was about to lose it. Any second, I thought, this guy is going to look around, shift gears, whip out that .45, and head on down to that store.

"You did the whole fucking house," he shouted at the salesman.

"Major, I did exactly what you told me to do."

A long, long moment of silence and then, "The ceilings and walls, inside the closets, the bathroom too?"

"Just what you told me to do."

"How much is this going to cost me?"

"Twenty-five thousand."

Another long moment of silence.

"We love it, man; my wife just loves it, and me too."

"I was sure you would. Listen, you got top-quality, very beautiful carpeting."

Frank said that maybe it didn't look so bad. "You know, red plush shag carpeting hanging from every ceiling in your fucking house, probably doesn't look too bad."

One afternoon, Frank and I in separate cars were tailing the Major along the West Side Highway. The road curls and wraps around the West Side of Manhattan, and traffic is always heavy. It is a treacherous road on which to speed.

We were doing a leapfrog tail. Frank would be on the Major's car, then he'd fall back and I would get on the car. I was clocking the Major at about 80 miles an hour. Frank radioed me, "Look at this," he said. "Pull up on this clown and take a look."

I pulled alongside the El Dorado. There was the Major doing a line of coke off the dashboard. He'd let go of the steering wheel and snort a line, and then he'd bang on the dash as though he were playing bongos.

The man was a floor show.

One night when Frank and I were alone in the wiretap plant a call came in. A heavily Spanish-accented male voice nervously told the Major that he was in Pennsylvania and expected to arrive in New York City sometime the following afternoon. The Major gave him directions to his parking garage, and then he told him to drive carefully. "Watch out for the cops," he said.

I telephoned Gene at home, woke him, and told him that we'd meet him in court in the morning. "We need to get search warrants."

The following afternoon, Gene and Jack set up on the Major at his house. Frank and I waited two blocks from the parking garage. This was it, the big event.

The trick was to get into the garage unnoticed. The place was always locked, and there was a sentinel at the door. The guard was a blown-away feral wino, an old-timer who spent endless hours with his bottle on a guano-spotted bench. The wino had a key to the garage and, in case of trouble, a buzzer to warn the people inside.

Linked by a pair of portable radios, Frank and I hid in the trunks of two limousines. A pair of very big and black detectives drove the limos. We got past the wino without difficulty.

The detectives parked the cars, turned off the engines, and left. We waited.

I heard the garage door open, then Gene's voice over the radio. He's pulling in; the Major is in the garage.

"Bobby, can you smell it?" Frank said. And I said, "What?"

"Pot. I smell pot. Even from inside the trunk of this car, I can smell it."

I smelled nothing but gasoline and exhaust fumes. Always a little claustrophobic, I hated small and dark closed spaces. The idea of a jail cell always terrified me. "I have to get out of here," I said. "Let's go."

We crawled out of the limos' trunks and spotted him. The Major's back was to us. He stood next to a full-sized, gold-colored camper with Mexican registration plates. He was holding a bulky cardboard box. Frank called out and the Major turned.

He was smiling.

"Sheriff's here," I said. "If you got your .45, you'd better go for it." For a moment we all three stood there, Frank and I with guns in our hands, the Major holding about 25 pounds of marijuana in a box.

Frank searched him, no .45. He put the cuffs on the Major and I opened the garage door for Gene and Jack. They had the wino in tow.

Inside that camper we found 1,000 pounds of marijuana. The fragrance of that pot spread throughout the parking garage. How, I wondered, did the driver of this camper make it across the border?

We notified the SIU office, and in no time Sergeant Scanlon arrived. He set up shop talking to the Major while we unloaded the truck.

"He wants to make a deal," Scanlon said. "The Major sees a way out of this for all of us."

No kidding.

"Major says he can come up with one hundred thousand dollars. If we cut him loose, the wino will take the collar."

Gene D'Arpe was a heavy man, big in a wholesome, muscular way, and there was always a peculiar kind of tension in him. He had fair, very smooth skin, and he also had an unusually large head. That head, that enormous light-skinned face, had gone beet red.

"What?" Gene said. "What did you say?"

"The Major says he'll either give us the money or give it to someone else, but he's not doing any time."

"Fuck him," I said.

"Right," said Frank.

Jack said, "Sarge, you've got to be kidding. Lay this kind of weight on the wino, the man will do a hundred years. I mean you're kidding, right?"

Without correcting himself or expanding on what he had said, Scanlon repeated, "Look, you'll have a collar, someone to take the weight, and a hundred grand."

I couldn't believe what I was hearing, none of us could. The sergeant, I was sure, had been drinking. Nobody could be that wacky sober. "Sarge," I said, "no way, it's not going to happen."

Then, as if he had been waiting for a signal, Major Cobb walked

THE DARK SIDE OF THE MOON | 195

toward us. The wino sat on the ground near the camper. Frank motioned the Major back with a flick of the back of his hand, saying, "You asshole, did you really think we'd go for that bullshit?"

"Your loss," the Major said.

Scanlon glanced at his watch; then said with an air of bonhomie that he had to leave. "Good job," he said, "good work."

Major Cobb spent exactly one night in jail. At his arraignment the following morning two federal drug enforcement agents appeared and bailed him out. He was an informant, they said, working an important federal case. The Manhattan DA went along with the Major's release and the judge too. We had taken 1,000 pounds of marijuana off the streets. Three months of fourteen-hour days had been productive. The judge and the ADA, they too said, "Good job, you SIU guys do good work."

As he was leaving the courtroom, Major Cobb smiled at us; he had a sort of dreamy expression on his face. That look, I understood, was something he wanted us to remember.

Although none of us believed that Major Cobb could possibly have been a federal informant (there was no indication of it during the investigation: no contacts, no telephone calls, no meetings), none of us were surprised at the outcome. All of us, by then, were well past any surprises.

I FELT BLESSED; I had loads of friends, and I knew all the right bosses. Nights at the Hanover, or farther uptown at Friar Tuck's phony English restaurant, hearing songs on the jukebox being played just for me—a number ten rush factor. All the good feelings—standing at the bar, telling and hearing stories with other detectives, laughing so hard that tears would run—confirmed for me the mental picture I'd always had of camaraderie.

Women everywhere.

Some of the money that had been taken in Riverdale had been brought to the office to be shared with other bosses. Everyone had gotten four thousand dollars, the most cash I ever had in my life. And Major Cobb's arrest, the largest marijuana seizure that had been made in the city in a long time, maybe the largest ever, had spotlighted me. Suddenly the desire to be accepted and the need to succeed had merged. Now there was a throbbing rhythm to my life, as though I were playing lead in a rock and roll band.

> wiseguy—someone linked to organized crime; an
> associate or an inducted member of the Mafia.

A short time after the Cobb arrest, I went to the office spruced up and ready for a big night on the town. It was one of those rare days when a meeting had been called; all the fifty-five SIU detectives would come together.

To catch up on paperwork I arrived early, got to typing, and found that the ink of the carbon paper had stained my fingers. The men's room was at the head of the stairs, and as I washed I could hear tramping feet arriving. I recognized Joe Nunziata's voice and the shouts and laughter of my partners. Keyed up, I left the bathroom quickly, leaving behind a gold Omega watch that had been a wedding present from Gina's parents.

Soon the office was filled with bighearted laughing men in leather jackets. Supervisors and detectives; rank was meaningless, we were all SIU, all of us partners and believing we were doing God's work, men who in the flower of our youth knew exactly who we were.

Eddie Codelia, half Italian and half Puerto Rican, a guy who grew up in East Harlem, grabbed my hand. Eddie was street-smart, and he was courageous, a classic undercover scrapper, another guy with movie star looks and a quick mouth. "Hey, Babyface," he said, "how you doing, got some pot?"

I smiled.

Eddie had come to the SIU from the undercover group. One

night, in East Harlem, while making a heroin buy, four street gorillas jumped him. They grabbed him, banged him around, blood
everywhere. They went through his pockets, took his dope, and then
went for the gun in his belt.

In a battle for his life, Eddie snatched that pistol and cut loose.
He shot all four gorillas, two in the head killing them instantly. One
he shot in the heart, and the fourth in the back as he was running out
the door. Eddie was not a big guy, five-eight or -nine, maybe 140
pounds, but it was all heart.

Jack McClean, a first grade detective and team leader, called out
to me. "Babyface," he said, "you, D'Arpe, and Mandato, a trio of
guineas, that's one helluva team."

Jack was always impeccably dressed. That day he wore a blue suit
and silver tie. A bit over six feet tall and blond, Jack was one handsome Irishman. He had been Gene D'Arpe's partner in the Brooklyn
narcotics group. Anything but a timid guy, Jack did his job without
any remorse or regret. The man was all swagger, and his enduring
string of big-time cases gave him the right.

"And Bergersen," I said.

"Hey," he said, "Bergersen loves gnocchi, make sure you get him
some gnocchi."

All of a sudden the office was wall-to-wall detectives, all filled
with a kind of exuberance that bordered on the fanatical. It was a
place hospitable to men in leather jackets and gold chains and tassel-
topped loafers. Everyone patting my back, tousling my hair; Joe
came through the crowd and grabbed me by the elbow and pulled
me into the hallway. He was being Joe, laughing, poking fun, but I
could see the anger there. Something had pissed him off.

"A good collar, you guys made one helluva collar," he said.

I was feeling very full of myself. I wondered how I looked to Joe
now—now that I too was a star, now that I had changed. I modeled
my new clothes. "Whadaya think?" I said. He nodded, and then he
wagged his head in a questioning way, toning down my excitement.

"Look," he said, "this is the last time I'm bringing this up."

"What is it?"

"Babyface."

"Oh for Christ sake. I've put an end to that. I come down on people when they call me that. That shit's over."

"Bullshit, over, it's never over. It hangs in the air around your head like poison gas."

"What are you talking about?"

"McClean called you Babyface, and Codelia too. You were laughing. I'm hearing stories about you all over the city."

"I don't work all over the city."

"Every young-looking guy on the job that's making collars is using that goofy nickname."

With inexplicable insistence he asked me to wait in the hallway. "I want you to meet somebody," he said.

He left and returned after a short time. He was accompanied by a balding, heavy-set, fair-skinned guy with an amiable expression on his face. "Bobby," he said, "say hello to Frank King."

"So you're Bobby Leuci?"

"Right."

For a man of his size he had a smallish hand.

"I don't know what Joe told you, but I'm telling you that I'm hearing that Babyface name being run all over the Upper West Side; and it's not good."

King stood up straight; he began to brush his hands and the front of his jacket. Suddenly I became brightly aware that I really did have a problem, a problem that I'd brought on myself, and the truth was there was not a thing I could do about it now. Now was too late.

"You need to put an end to that shit. If you want a hand, give me a call," King said. He smiled a warm, friendly grin, and with a certain amount of affection he pinched my cheek.

Frank King had all the trappings of a wiseguy; he looked, sounded, and acted like a wiseguy—an Irish wiseguy to be sure, but a wiseguy nonetheless. He was big, tough, and coldhearted—but he did have that Irish twinkle in the eye. I liked him, but knew I'd always give him plenty of room.

I glanced at my wrist to check the time and realized that I didn't have my watch. I went into the bathroom and looked around and found it gone. Back in the office, I called out to everyone. I explained that I had left my watch in the bathroom. It was a gold watch, a gift, and I'd like it back.

"For Christ sake," Jack McClean said, "who took the man's watch?"

Silence.

"What the hell is wrong with you guys? This is the SIU; everyone here knows that if you can't fold it, you don't take it," Jack said with real heat. "The rule here is that we trust each other completely."

For a long moment there was widespread murmuring, nodding heads, and shrugging shoulders. Then someone told a joke, and the laughter returned. I knew my watch was history.

When I think back on it, that SIU office was a theater of the ridiculous in a world gone insane. We were an arrogant, self-involved, self-important bunch, but I had convinced myself that we all loved each other. I was sure we did; and although I didn't see it, wasn't even looking, during that time so much had changed in me. The image I'd had of myself was gone. I felt confident and happy to be alive, but I was, if anything, falling even deeper into an abyss.

Sometimes, not often, I'd sit and think about what I was doing, what I had become, and then fight to rid myself of all such thoughts. Such thoughts would tighten and sour my stomach and make my head spin. My own unspoken rule: Don't think about it.

WHEN I WAS leaving the office that day I bumped into Aaron Mazen. He told me that he was on the list to be promoted to captain and had been transferred to the Harlem narcotics group as its commanding officer.

Mazen praised me on the marijuana arrest, and then asked if I knew a detective by the name of Vincent Albano. When he mentioned Albano's name it was not in a friendly or cordial way.

Sure, I told him, I knew Vinny. Not well, but I knew him well enough.

"Do you know him well enough to talk to him?"

In some secret way his asking made me feel pleased with myself. Albano was a big name in the office. He was different, a strange sort of man, detached and loud-mouthed. I never once heard him speak of cases or collars. With a thick city street accent, he was often charged with outlandish suggestions for the kind of activity even the worst of the SIU detectives would not consider.

"Sure," I told Mazen, "I can talk to him."

"Do me a favor. Go and tell him that if he doesn't quit trying to give me money, or theater tickets, or liquor, I'm going to lock his slick ass up."

"I'll tell him."

"Please, because he doesn't seem to want to listen to me." Then Mazen reached over and grabbed my shoulder. "Are you a friend of this guy?"

"No, no friend. I know him, everyone does."

"You don't belong with characters like that. He is bad news."

Suddenly I felt a terrible pang of guilt. If this good man, one helluva cop, could get through this job on the straight and narrow, why couldn't I? He knew what was worth it and what wasn't. That night in Bedford-Stuyvesant, the drug dealer and the Christmas cards filled with cash: "We can take some of this money," he'd said. "Hell, we could take all of it—this joker wouldn't know or care. But how could you spend it? It's evidence, it's drug money. Could you take drug money home and give it to your family? Could you?"

Listening to him that night I had thought, *So what if you're excluded and ostracized by the other men. Team up with guys like Mazen—*

they're around. You just have to find them. Except I knew that there were few if any like-minded men in narcotics and none in the SIU. I loved the SIU. Doing that job, a top-of-the-line narcotics cop, that was me. That was what I lived for.

Vinny Albano had become a cop to make money; it was no secret; he let everyone know. Another good-looking guy, he bore so strong a resemblance to the lounge singer Buddy Greco that he could have been his twin. He ran the Harlem narcotics group. His street behavior was so outrageous, the powers that be would not allow him in the SIU. Really now, it was possible to be that bad.

I found him, and I told him that he'd better back off Mazen. What he was doing, whatever he was doing, was pissing the lieutenant off.

"C'mon," he said, "I heard that you and Mandato took good care of him, and he looked out for you guys."

"A puppy."

"A dog?"

I explained that Frank and I had once given Mazen a puppy. I told Albano that the man was an absolute straight shooter—one of a kind. "Do not fuck with him," I said.

"I've never had a boss in this job that didn't want something from me," Albano said. "Not one."

"Well, you've met one now."

He stood still for a second, put his hands on his hips, and bit the inside of his cheek; then he shook his head with a what's-the-world-coming-to weariness. "Well, I guess I'd better go and get that case of liquor I put in his car."

"Yeah, I think you'd better."

"Are you sure about Mazen? I mean the guy's a Jew. You wanna tell me a Jew boss don't want theater tickets, a case of Scotch, nothing? Are you sure?"

"Positive."

"That's a shocker."

"Let me ask you something," I said. "Do you use that Babyface nickname in Harlem?"

"Me?"

"Vinny?"

"Ey, what do you give a shit? You think maybe you're the only Babyface in the fuckin' world?"

Apparently not.

Sometime later, in a Bronx bar, a wiseguy would shoot Vinny Albano six times in the chest. The wiseguy would shoot him because Albano was sleeping with the wiseguy's ex-wife and bragging about it. Burton Roberts, the Bronx DA, personally tried to get a statement from Albano. He told Vinny that he was dying, and he needed to say who had shot him. Vinny told the DA to go fuck himself.

Incredibly, Albano would survive that shooting.

Vinny Albano was an NYPD detective, never earning more than thirty thousand dollars a year. Nevertheless, the federal government would prosecute him for evading close to two hundred thousand dollars in taxes. He owned a liquor store, a candy shop, and a house on the ocean, apartment buildings, a condominium in Florida, and a yacht. He was no dope. He was a businessman, at his core a wiseguy. Vinny Albano carried a badge and gun, but the truth was he was like no cop I ever knew. He'd end his days shot in the head, rolled in a carpet, then stuffed into the trunk of his car. One more shooting, and that one he didn't survive.

Vinny, always laughing, saying "Howyadoin'," perfect teeth, and a head of hair the likes of which you would not believe.

IAD—the Internal Affairs Division, cops who investigate other cops.

made man—an inducted member of the Mafia.

On a roll now, I quickly fell into the swaggering beat of the SIU detective. It was all performance. You were a player; you were SIU, somebody to be respected and admired. In court, other narco cops carried their evidence in small property clerk bags. Their prisoners were strung-out junkies with runny noses and the shakes. We carried shopping bags of evidence, and our prisoners wore suits and ties.

Our team continued to make cases, nothing major but good solid-weight cases. I was having myself a time learning how to install wiretaps and bugs. I worked at developing informants who could point me in the direction of major suppliers. I read intelligence files all the time and was happy to spend hour after hour in the street. At the end of most days we'd all go to the Villa Roma to eat, drink, and party. I was hardly ever at home.

One Friday night after we had eaten and drunk too much wine, Frank, Gene, and I were discussing where to go next. I felt it was time to find an important target. Time to get serious, I said. We're ready for a long-term investigation, something worthwhile. Italians, I told them, time to go and hunt important guineas.

Gene D'Arpe was the connoisseur of supple doublespeak and perpetual obfuscation. Sometimes he spoke in codes. Most times he managed to drive me right out of my mind. I wanted to talk about the Mafia file, that it was the place to pick out a target. I couldn't get a word in. Gene was aboil with rage. I'm thinking it's the wine; it has to be the wine. Suddenly Frank nudged me, telling me to be quiet and listen. "I'm leaving this office," Gene said. "I hate this fucking place. Maybe I'll go work for IAD."

He looked at me in a suspicious, bleary way and pointed his finger. All of a sudden he began expounding on how simple and naive Frank and I were, how gullible.

"You can't work Italians," he said. "You can't work wiseguys. Most of those characters got caught up in the undertow of the French

Connection case. They have commitments and they're untouchable."

Frank gave him a what-the hell-are-you-talking about look. I said, "Gene, a commitment? What the hell's a commitment?"

"They owe money," he said. "It's hands-off till they pay up."

I had never heard of such a thing. On the face of it, it was absurd. I was learning from experience that Gene D'Arpe enjoyed his alienated status. He trusted no one in the SIU and was disapointed that Frank and I didn't share his revulsion. "They stole your watch," he said. "Those creeps would steal your shoes."

I was convinced that my watch had been taken by one of the cleaning people. I believed that in the SIU, we all looked out for each other. It was all for one and one for all is what I thought.

"Oh man," Gene kept saying. "When are you going to wake up?"

Jack McClean, Gene's former partner, had told me that it was the ex-wife and her father—they had ripped out Gene's heart and made him a bitter and angry man.

I'd found a case, I told them, one I believed we could work: a crew of wiseguys from Little Italy, made guys. The Indelicato family. There had been wiretaps and surveillances. The detectives that worked the case had been transferred leaving the file behind.

"What team?" Gene asked.

I told him.

Gene laughed. He laughed a long time.

"What's so funny?"

"Those two put a case together against a family of wiseguys. They had wiretaps and so on."

"Right," I said.

"They get transferred, and you think that they would leave that case behind?"

"Why not?"

Gene was shaking his head in disbelief. "They'd sell it is why. Those guys sold that case before they left. I guarantee you."

I told them I wanted to check it out and see if we could pick up where the other team left off. Frank agreed, and Gene shrugged his shoulders. "You know," he said, "you two guys don't need any partners; you two should work alone."

I was thinking precisely the same thing.

The bartender came over and told me there was a call for me. It was the office; Gina had telephoned and asked them to find me, or more precisely, pleaded with them to find me. Her water had broken and she was at that moment driving herself to the hospital to have the baby.

The man working the nighttime narcotics phones was Ciro Pastore. A religious family man, Ciro was incredulous that I would be out on the town while Gina was giving birth.

"What the hell are you doing?" he said. "Get home."

Feeling humiliated and guilty, I explained that Gina was already two weeks late. I told Ciro that there was no way to tell when she would give birth. "Yeah," he said, "yeah, yeah. Get the hell home."

I made it from downtown Brooklyn to St. John's hospital in Smithtown, Long Island, a distance of about sixty miles, in thirty minutes. Driving, I alternated between guilt and fear that something terrible would happen and I, as usual, would not be there. Twice on the Long Island Expressway I spotted spinning lights disappearing in my rearview. I kept right on going at more than 100 miles per hour.

Sometime during the middle of the night, my daughter, Santina, was born. I sat waiting, wondering how this had happened, that this life became my life. What the hell kind of man was I anyway? Leaving my pregnant wife to cope by herself, while I did what? Play at cops and robbers and then find my relaxation at a bar. I was a terrible father and a worse husband, and what the hell was Gene D'Arpe talking about? A commitment? Who was he kidding?

My parents arrived early in the morning. We visited Gina, then went to the viewing room and saw the baby, cooing at her through the glass. After a while my father took me aside. "You have two babies now," he said. "Gina is not working. How are things going for you?"

"Okay."

"You need some money, ask."

"It's all right."

"You look good," he said. "I don't think I've ever seen you look so, I don't know, good, I guess."

"I'm okay."

"The ring. I like the ring."

I was wearing a pinky ring, a gift from Frank; it was similar to the one he wore.

"You like it?"

"No."

"C'mon, Pop. You have your first granddaughter, go and check her out."

"Listen," he said, "I got a call from my sister Rose. Her son, your cousin John, he just came home from prison and she'd like you to go and see if he's doing okay. Check and see if I can be of any help. You know, see about a job, something like that."

"Sure, I'll go and see him."

"Your brother Ritchie has problems."

"I know."

"You know?"

"Of course I know."

"No matter what," he said, "family is number one. Everything else comes and goes, family is always there."

"I know that."

"I hope so."

La mala vita—a criminal life.

It's amazing, really, when you think about it, it's truly something, our fascination with wiseguys. We watch the evening news: a grainy

FBI surveillance video, John Gotti and Sam Gravano walking along Mulberry Street in New York's Little Italy. There's a storefront social club, bored-looking men in Italian knit shirts, sharkskin slacks, and forty-dollar haircuts standing out in front. A light rain is falling, Gravano is holding an umbrella above the head of his boss like a supplicant or a suitor. The two men begin wandering the neighborhood, walking and talking. You watch them move, gesturing with a certain tilt of the head. You can sense that something is in the air; something is coming for sure. On that rainy day, the dynamic duo of mayhem looked angry and spooky. Someone was going to die.

A few days later, on the street in front of Sparks Steak House, Paul Castellano, the powerful head of the Gambino crime family, was forced into retirement by a Mafia firing squad. Did John Gotti or Sam Gravano think or care about the consequences of such an act? Hard to say, but it's my guess that the Dapper Don and Sammy the Bull, paisans, wiseguys, connected guys, believed that they had the power to put on hold the normal workings of cause and effect. Rather than a concern, brutality was a condition of their lives. Violence stretched through the wiseguy world, way beyond the grasp of any normal person's imagination.

I don't know how the words *wise* and *guy* got linked. But I do remember when Gotti and Gravano, and others like them, were lords of the street. Like renaissance princes, such men followed no rules but those that were self-imposed. Wiseguys made no explanations or excuses for lives that were lived close to the fire. They scrounged for money any way they could get it, brazenly survived in a limited world made narrow by mistrust, jealousy, and a willingness to do serious harm in order to get what they wanted. In my experiences with wiseguys, I found them ballsy and wild. They were rarely wise. In fact, they were not unlike the detectives of the SIU.

YOU HAVE TO admit, simply for argument's sake, that many of us are beguiled by wiseguys. If you doubt it, look at the trillion dollars

The Godfather parts one, two, and three and *The Sopranos* have piled up. The point being, in terms of my life, I have always been one of the enchanted. So now, when I think about my life, peeling back the layers, older now and wiser, when I get to the part about wiseguys, there is very little I can tell myself about such a fascination, except maybe "Oy!"

WHAT I MOST remember about the three-story walkup on Hull Street in Brooklyn, the building where my father was raised, is the aroma. As soon as you walked up the brownstone steps and opened the front door, you caught it. It was the pungent fragrance of ancient wooden wine barrels. The heady scent of the maturing wine itself permeated the atmosphere and commingled with the moldy and stale layer of air in the hallways. The musty perfume seemed to rise up through the floors, seep through the walls, coming up out of the ancient cellar to enter through your nostrils and take up residence in your memory, never to leave.

At the very edge of my memory, I am seven or eight years old, and we are visiting my father's sisters. One, named Angelina, lived with her husband, Tony, on the third floor. They owned the building. My father's other sister, Rose, lived on the second floor with her husband, Marino. They had three daughters, Philamena, Frances, and Joann, and two sons, Salvatore and John.

It's summer, the Fourth of July, and that particular summer afternoon was hot—sweltering outside, hot and sticky inside.

My Aunt Angie had no children, but she had dolls everywhere, dolls that I was forbidden to touch, and uncomfortable overstuffed chairs and sofas. It seemed to me that every piece of furniture Aunt Angie owned was covered in heavy plastic. All her rooms burst with a kind of brilliant silvery radiance. I was wearing short pants that day, and every time I'd sit down, I'd catch my skin and jump up, embarrassed, rubbing the underside of my legs as though my butt were on fire.

In that house I saw myself as an alien. I felt different in every way from my cousins and their parents, different in the way I was dressed and the way I spoke. They were exotic and foreign and bore no resemblance to the people I grew up with.

One block from my Aunt Angie and Uncle Tony's house lived my father's older brother, Stanley, with his even larger family. Some of my relatives spoke English with heavy accents; others spoke no English at all. My mother and father were at all times happy to be among family. For them to be surrounded by their clan was always more rewarding than demanding.

I remember a huge table in the kitchen, and on that table big round loaves of crusty bread surrounded by cheeses and cold cuts and red peppers in dishes. This table was the place of my father's theater. With his family gathered round, his discussions went on forever.

In that remembered time, I'm looking out the window, down into the street, watching boys running along Hull Street, up toward Hopkinson Avenue, tossing firecrackers as they went. Wild boys, screaming, cursing, using words I heard only when the family traveled to Brooklyn.

Along the street the houses were all three-story attached brick and brownstone and very old. With cars parked nose to tail along the curb, the neighborhood kids played on the sidewalks and in the middle of the street. There were no lawns and no trees; the houses were all well kept, with freshly varnished oak front doors, cleanly swept stoops, and sturdy, black-painted wrought-iron railings. In the rear yards, high fences marked the property lines. There were small gardens where tomatoes and peppers grew. Some of the yards had gaunt fig trees, and benches where the old people sat.

One block to the south was Fulton Street. It was a line of demarcation, a border between the expanding neighborhoods of Brownsville and Bushwick. It was a frontier between the blacks and the whites. There were street gangs and violence, and each group stayed on its own side of Fulton Street. This noisy, frantic, abrasive, tree-less neighborhood was a twenty-minute car ride from the neighborhood where I lived in Tudor Village, Queens, but it might as well have been on the other side of the moon.

Suddenly he was there, my father's sister Rose's son John, coming through the door. I remember the smile, the blond hair and blue eyes. How tall he seemed then, how muscular. And my father, how shy he appeared when they greeted each other, grinning without any happiness.

Whenever I think about my cousin John Lusterino, "Johnny Tarzan" they called him, I wonder about the life he chose to live, a life that led to spending so many years in prison. What I remember most is that he looked so unlike any of us, with fair hair and skin and those blue eyes.

Cousin John pointed at me and then talked to my father. "Hey, Hooks," he said, "how come this kid of yours is wearing short pants? He looks goofy."

"What do you mean 'goofy'?"

"I mean goofy." Johnny turned his head and glanced at me. I remember how embarrassed I felt, pulling at my pants, telling myself, *I'll never wear these again, never.* Johnny stood still, his hands on his hips, smiling as if he'd told a great joke. "Why do ya wanna dress him like that? You know what I mean, right, kid?"

I knew my father was looking at me, and I didn't want to make eye contact with him.

I nodded.

"See," John said quickly, "Bobby knows what I mean. You hate wearing short pants, right kid?" He smiled, showing glistening teeth, and I wanted to throw up. "Bobby hates short pants, tell 'em, Bobby, gahead, tell your father."

This felt like a test. "Yeah," I said, "I hate 'em." The next thing I knew, Johnny leaned forward in a conspiratorial manner, a style of speech and body language that I would see him use often many years later. "You tell me what you wanna do?" he stage-whispered.

I told him that I wanted to play outside. I wanted to see the fire-crackers. "They have torpedoes and cherry bombs, Roman candles, all kinds of stuff down there" is what I said.

"So let's go," Johnny said.

"He's not going anywhere," my father said. I remember the way he said it, like that's it, no discussion.

My cousin Johnny could make things better with a smile and he smiled all the time. "What's the matter," he said, "you don't think I can protect him?"

The smile made my father shrug, and it helped ease the anxious look from my mother's face. My body tingled with an uncertain sense of excitement, the kind of feeling kids get when they believe they are about to set out on a wild adventure.

"I really would not like to see him go down into the street," my father said finally.

"Aright," Johnny said. "Fine, he won't go into the street, he'll come with me," those eyes of his squinting up toward the ceiling as if searching for some divine intervention. I knew that cousin Johnny, not my father, would decide my fate for that afternoon.

In all kinds of ways my father was a remarkable man. He could be strong and forceful, but he was always kind and he was bright. He had little formal education, but he read all the time, and man could he play baseball.

My father was always saddled with an astonishing amount of concern for the workingman. And I don't think anyone ever frightened him, except maybe cousin Johnny. What I remember more than anything was my father's deliberate shyness around him. My hunch is that he knew things about Johnny that no one else in that room did.

Ten or twelve years older than me, Johnny was already a man. He was a man who could not tolerate any authority, a man accustomed to getting his own way. His presence is strong in my memory in images that will last forever.

So many years ago. Johnny is standing at the very edge of a roof on that Fourth of July day. I don't remember how we got to the roof, or how long we stayed there. It's easy to challenge my memory on some of the particulars. Still, memory endures of the way he stood there. The solemn way he looked over at me and then down into the street.

It sounded as though there was a war going on in the street. There were fireworks everywhere, big ones, M80s and cherry bombs. Johnny began rambling on about his neighborhood—little things, like how important it was to protect it from trespassers.

The sun was bright and coming straight down, and there were vats of tar and garbage cans lined up at the edge of the roof.

I remember how he stooped over one of the garbage pails, searching through rags and towels. All of a sudden he came out with a gun. It was a pistol, a big one; to me it looked like it was a foot long. I felt this fluttery rush in the bottom of my stomach, half fear, half thrill. The gun was shiny, stainless steel or chrome. He stared at it a second and then he nodded.

"See," he said, "we have our own firecracker."

I remember that he did a little jig, a sort of dance in the middle of the roof. Then he cocked the hammer, pointed the gun at the sky, and let the hammer fall.

Kapow! is the sound I remember, I mean loud—a thunderous, monstrous blast, louder than anything I'd ever heard. The dazzling bright day, pigeons from a coop across the street exploding into the air, the great big crazy grin on Johnny's face, sensual and a bit loony; all of this conspired to terrify me out of my wits.

I climbed down a fire escape and jumped through an open window, excited and scared, a kid's game of hide-and-seek, getting away, afraid of being caught, running.

When I got back to my Aunt Angie's kitchen, Johnny was already there. He was sitting, taking a bite from a sandwich, and then staring at me. He was silent and still as a cat under a tree.

Now, nineteen years later, I was to see him again.

I DON'T KNOW how you judge the man I was then. I suspect that I was suspended in a link of emotional adolescence, with a constant need for attention, always hunting for new and even greater escapades and risks. I craved adventure and was too restless to settle down. My father's voice of proletarian concern and anger resonated not at all in me. There was no time to worry about the problems of others; I was far too self-involved for any of that. Immersed as I was in costly foolishness, I didn't grasp that, and sooner or later someone was bound to hand me a bill.

> the joint or upstate or inside—terms used to describe prison.

> good people—a wiseguy expression when speaking of other wiseguys, a term also used by police officers to describe someone who can be trusted.

> goodfellas—exclusively wiseguy term for inducted members of the Mafia.

> capo—a captain in a Mafia family.

I had not seen my Aunt Rose or my cousin Frances for years, and being in their house gave me a sense of warm elation. Having fled the old neighborhood, the Lusterinos now lived in a comfortable one-family house in Richmond Hill, Queens. Johnny was not at home, but Frances had telephoned him at his club, and he was on his way. My aunt offered me food. Whatever I liked, they would be delighted to make it for me. "Coffee," I said, "a cup of coffee would be great."

Frances brought me coffee, and I was taking my first sip when looking out the window, I saw Johnny step out of a brand-new blue Buick convertible. I left the coffee and went outside to meet him. When he saw me he brightened and put on his great big smile. I shook his hand and he said, "How've you been, cousin?"

After all those years in prison for hijacking and armed robbery, he didn't look all that different. Not as tall as I remembered, but still in great physical shape, and there were those eyes and that hair.

Home only a few months, John owned a real estate office on 101st Avenue across the street from Aqueduct Racetrack and a nightclub on Steinway Street in Astoria. I had seen intelligence reports that described him as a capo in the Colombo crime family. I doubted that he needed to find a job. He wagged his head, telling me to thank my father for the thought.

Johnny wore thick horn-rimmed glasses, a gray Italian knit shirt, black trousers, and black tassel-topped loafers. He looked like your average middle-aged guy; yet there was something faintly somber about him, a suggestion of don't fool with me. It was a look in the eyes.

"I'm glad you came to see me," he said. "Really, I get to meet Babyface."

"You're kidding me?"

"When I was upstate, I heard your name all the time. You filled half the joint."

I knew how many arrests I had made, how many people I'd sent to prison. A good-sized number, to be sure, but not nearly as many as I was getting credit for. When I tried to explain all this to Johnny, he nodded and smiled.

We passed the time that afternoon getting reacquainted. We took a ride in his new car to his real estate office. His sister Joann was managing the place, and after so many years, it was nice to see her too. Then we went to his nightclub.

It wasn't a very spacious place, but large enough to accommodate a small band and a stage for go-go dancers. Johnny had named it The Lock and Key. I was amazed; a few short months home from prison and the man owned a new car, a real estate office that employed ten or fifteen people, and a nightclub. Cousin Johnny Tarzan.

It finally dawned on me that I was not there to see if he was in need of any help. Johnny had asked his mother to call my father; it was he who wanted to see me.

It was early evening, I was sitting on a bar stool and Johnny was behind the bar.

"There was this guy," he said, "he worked the docks in Red Hook. Good people, a family man and hard worker with many friends. Anyway, a piece of machinery fell on him, killed him instantly."

Slowly then, without taking his eyes from me, Johnny told me that there had been insurance, but the money was slow in coming. So the goodfellas in and around the docks had taken up a collection for the dead man's family. He went on for a long time explaining how the money had come together. But on the day when all the wiseguys went to the wake to pay their respects, the dead man's wife threw a fit. The neighborhood guy who had volunteered to take up the collection had run away with the cash. Close to ten thousand dollars. They were all humiliated, dishonored, embarrassed, and to say the least, extremely pissed.

"Kid Vinny, they call him." Johnny said, "He's a junkie bum from Red Hook. I figure you've got to know him."

It was as if he knew that I knew Vinny. I was taken aback. "Never heard of the guy," I said.

"C'mon, that's your old stomping grounds, right? Red Hook is where you hung out."

"I don't know," I said. "I don't know every drug addict out there."

Johnny shrugged and began wiping the bar. He turned his back to me and rearranged liquor bottles on the shelves. When he turned back he said, "This guy is a piece of shit. You owe no loyalty to a piece of shit."

Looking at Johnny I saw a face without cheeriness, just anger there. His change of expression happened so quickly it was as if he were trying to frighten me.

"If I run across this Vinny, I'll let you know," I told him.

Johnny wagged his head sadly and glanced around the bar. His expression changed again. "You should have seen the way that woman was carrying on," he said. "I mean she was really hurt, heavy-duty crying and screaming at us. All because of this junkie prick."

I tried not to think about Vinny, but then I was thinking about what a lunatic he was. How the white lady had made him oblivious to the dangers of the world around him. Mostly I felt sad for him and afraid for him.

People began coming into the club. Some of them looked familiar, faces I thought I had seen before in intelligence files. Some smiled warmly at me, as though they knew me—it was probably my imagination, but maybe not. Johnny was quick to make introductions—his cousin the detective. Most of the smiles faded.

He called over a young, fine-looking blond, with a magnificent body. Her name was Bee, she was the club's star go-go dancer; Johnny told me he was planning to marry her.

As I was leaving he said, "Loyalty is good, cousin, I respect it, but loyalty to a scumbag is wrong."

Johnny was never to mention Vinny again, but the man knew, I was sure he knew.

I spent two days searching for Vinny. I knew that if he were caught by the wiseguys, the best he could hope for would be a three-month rest in a hospital. I finally tracked down his aunt; she told me that Vinny had gone to Florida. A vacation, she said.

"I don't know how he could afford such a thing. I just got a postcard from Miami. See," she said, "Vinny looks like he's having a big time."

The postcard was a photograph of Vinny standing at a tiki bar. There he was, holding up a drink with huge slivers of pineapple and tiny red umbrellas in it. His blond hair had been permed; he was tanned, wearing cut-off jeans and a sleeveless T-shirt. Kid Vinny looked very happy.

I WAS CONVINCED that the only people worth working were the wiseguys. I didn't like working blacks or Hispanics. I hated working Harlem or Bedford-Stuyvesant, places where I had no chance of passing unnoticed. I loathed listening to wiretaps when all the conversation was in Spanish and I needed interpreters to tell me what was going on. Wiseguys fascinated me, their mysterious and bizarre world was intriguing, and I could pass easily in all the neighborhoods where they hung out.

Gene D'Arpe protested, complaining that investigating wiseguys took a major effort. It was a twenty-four-hour-a-day deal, he said. They were all experienced and smart—just about impossible to bring down. Wiseguys had friends everywhere, and informants were rare or nonexistent. "I know, I know," I said. "Trust me, we can do it."

We opened a case on two members of the Bonanno crime family, Alphonse Indelicato, "Sonny Red"; and his brother, John Bruno.

It was late on a Sunday night. I was reading the Indelicato intelligence reports, going through the case file for about the hundredth time, trying to figure who the informant could be. The investigating detectives were a top-flight SIU team; their reports were concise, well written, and informative. I found a wealth of information in the file, intelligence that clearly had not come from the two wiretaps the detectives had monitored. There was nothing of a criminal nature on those wiretaps. It was no more than hours and hours of teenage chitchat and personal family business. These brothers did not talk business on their home telephones.

If there was drug dealing, and certainly the information in the file suggested that there was, that information was coming from somewhere else. It had to be an informant.

It was nearly eleven o'clock at night. Gina and the children were upstairs asleep when the telephone rang. It was Sergeant Jack Cuddy. Cuddy lived nearby. He sounded as though he were half in the bag and told me that he'd like to come over. He told me that he'd like to bring his friend Frank Waters—Frank Waters, he said, wanted to speak to me.

Frank Waters had been a group leader in the New York office of the Federal Bureau of Narcotics. He was Sergeant Cuddy's best friend, the godfather for his son, and a legendary federal agent. Waters had worked the French Connection case; everyone said that the case could not have been made without him. Publicly, Waters got little or no recognition. "Sure," I said, "why not, come over."

I met them at my front door. I could tell without being told that Jack Cuddy didn't like being there. They had both been drinking, and clearly Jack Cuddy was being forced to follow Waters' lead.

Waters came into my house acting as if he wanted to hit me. "Why are you so angry?" I said.

Frank Waters was so high he could barely walk. He pushed his way past me and made his way into the kitchen. Cuddy whispered that Waters was drunk and pissed off and that I should listen. "Just listen," he said, "don't set him off." He told me this while Waters made himself comfortable at my kitchen table, going through the Indelicato file.

Jack had told him that I was going to work the Indelicatos. He said he was here to tell me what I was not going to do. I looked at Cuddy and he shrugged.

"What's that?" I said.

"Work the Indelicatos, that's what."

Waters began to shout and I knew that his voice would carry

THE DARK SIDE OF THE MOON | 219

throughout the house. I motioned for him to keep it down. I told him my wife and children were asleep.

Waters read a bit more of the file, and then he tossed it aside. "You know that this is all bullshit, you know that, right?" he said.

Waters' voice was hard and strong, threatening. I couldn't stand the way he looked at me, partly like I was brain-dead, partly like he was some sly tough guy off the corner.

I asked him who he thought he was and what the hell he was doing using that tone of voice in my house. He apologized, quickly telling me that he was very angry, that the investigating detectives were full of shit, that they were a pair of shakedown artists.

He picked up a report, took one of the pages from the file, and tossed it at me. "I figure you don't know anything about these people, am I right?" he said.

"If you mean I don't know if they're moving drugs, you're right. I do know that they're connected guys, made guys, important wiseguys."

He kept on grinning at me and those grins made him look repulsive and menacing. I could not get it out of my head that my own sergeant had brought this character to my house.

"You know," he said, "these are good people, they've done the right thing before, they don't deserve to be screwed over like this."

He was shaking his head and his eyes looked wild, like they were trying to move in every direction at once. I was thinking that a drunken, pissed-off Irishman was a handful.

I said, "Thanks for the advice and the information. I appreciate it."

"What are you going to do," he said. "I mean about this case?"

"I don't know what I'm going to do. I'm not sure I'm going to do anything. I have a team. I'll talk to them, tell them what you said."

"You know, if it means we gotta go out and oil the guns, we'll do that, if that's what it means."

"What in the fuck are you talking about?"

"There is a stool pigeon in this case. He's bullshitting. I don't know why, but he's making all this shit up."

"Who is it, do you know?"

"The Baron, Richard Lawrence, that's who it is. He's lying. These guys are not in the drug business. I know it."

The Baron, I thought, *remember that name.*

"How can you be so sure?" I said.

"I'm sure. You'd better think about what you're doing. That's all I gotta say, you'd better think about it."

"I'll think about it."

"That's right," he said with a smile. "You do understand what I'm saying."

Suddenly I was very tired, my legs felt weak, I wanted these two jokers out of my house. I had liked Jack Cuddy, he'd always been a good boss and friend. I didn't like him anymore. He'd betrayed me to this character Waters. I felt that if these two characters didn't leave, I'd start screaming like a madman. *Be smart*, I told myself, *calm down.*

"Look," I said, "don't sweat it, I'll close this case down. Will that make you happy?"

A mean hard look came over Waters's face; it was as though he were judging me. "Good," he said. Cuddy smiled and patted my shoulder; he whispered that he'd call me in the morning. "Talk to you tomorrow, Sarge," I said as they went out the door.

This is not to be believed, I kept telling myself as I walked from the hallway back into the kitchen. Then I told myself, *You'd better believe it.* Waters had spelled it out. So what was there to doubt. This case was history.

I was fuming, wondering how Cuddy knew what I was working on in the first place. He worked Brooklyn, not the SIU. How could he possibly know what case I had opened.

All that had happened, all the conversation with Waters, had been filled with hidden menace, and maybe not so hidden. The case was a can of worms, but I still was not ready to let it go.

I found Gina sitting on the steps that led to the upstairs bedrooms. She was still and quiet and looked scared stiff.

"Who was that?" she said.

"My old sergeant, Jack Cuddy, and a friend of his."

"Police?"

"Yes."

"They didn't sound like policemen, they sounded mean, like criminals."

"Oh, come on, you know cops."

"This scares me. This job of yours—it frightens me and it scares your father too."

"What are you talking about?"

"Your father is worried. He says that you've changed, and he doesn't like the changes. That's what he said, that's exactly what he told me."

The last time I had spoken to my father, I recalled that he was restless. He walked around my house, went from room to room. He asked if I had spoken to Ritchie. I told him I hadn't, but I was going to. "He needs someone to look out for him," he told me. And I said, "Pop, don't worry about it, he'll be fine. He's just a kid, and kids sometimes do silly things."

"He's twenty-four, he's not a kid anymore."

I said, "Ritchie's a good guy, he has sense, and he's smart, he'll be fine."

"Sometimes it's the good ones and the smart ones that get lost," my father told me. He smiled at me that day, smiled in a way that made me feel he was extremely unhappy. It was the first time that I thought my father looked old.

I MET UP with Jack Cuddy at the office the following day. Embarrassed, he told me he was "damned sorry" for last night's scene. I figured that he had probably meant well; still, it bugged me that he knew I had opened that particular case. The two detectives, he said, they had told him. I telephoned one, and he reiterated that the case was worth working.

"These guys are big-time dealers," he said. "Read the case folder—it's all there." I had read it, and read it some more, and whatever was supposed to be there, I didn't see it. "It's there," he said, "it's in those reports."

I spoke to Gene and Frank. Gene was adamant: The detective was lying. "This case is history, forget it, it's been sold out," he said, probably louder than he meant to.

Frank, for his part, felt that we should stay with it for a while. "Maybe it hasn't been sold," he said.

I was thinking of speaking to my cousin, I told them. Maybe he could be of some help, but maybe not.

In spite of the fact that I had no idea how my cousin would respond, I wanted to run it past him. Gene thought it might do some good, Frank wasn't sure.

That night, on my way to The Lock and Key, I stopped at Joe Nunziata's house to have dinner with him and his wife, Ann. I wanted Joe's input; I wanted to see what he thought.

Ann was a very delicate, very Italian, very beautiful woman. She and Joe made a striking couple. That night she made us wonderful pasta, and all during dinner we had a lively three-way conversation. Although, for the life of me, I can't remember what it was about.

After dinner Joe and I sat on the stoop in front of his house, smoking and talking and drinking beer. When I told him about Waters and Cuddy, the business at my house the night before, his customary good humor disappeared.

"Sonny told me that Waters is a psycho," he said. "Grosso and Waters are at war, they hate each other." I talked some, but he talked more, telling me that when they made the *French Connection* movie, they planned on killing the Frank Waters character. A Grosso fantasy.

Suddenly he went still and stared at me, then he turned to see if anyone could eavesdrop. "Listen," he said, "you want to hear some strange shit, what if I told you that one hundred thousand dollars disappeared during the French Connection case?"

"I'd say wow, that's a lot of money. Is it true?"

He shrugged, smiled, and shook his head, "Who knows," he said. "I'm ready to believe anything."

Somewhere along the line, he'd become disgusted with the Narcotics Bureau, with the business of narcotics enforcement period. He told me that he had been reading a mind-blowing magazine piece. "You know, a few years ago there were only fifty-seven thousand heroin addicts in the entire country," he said. "Now there are three hundred and fifteen thousand—and during the next couple of years, they expect that number to double."

"Do me a favor," I told him, "don't leave the Narcotics Bureau until we have a chance to work together."

He smiled.

"Look," I said, "with all the craziness in this world people naturally just want to get high, and there's not much we can do about it."

"How's your brother?"

"Not good."

"You've got to help him."

"I know. You want to tell me how?"

Joe looked at me and shrugged. "You've got to try," he said.

"I know," I told him, "I know. It's all so crazy, you know, Joe—my own brother, its nutty." Then I told him I was on my way to see my cousin, to ask him about my case, to try and find out if it had been sold out.

"Now that is nutty," he said.

I FOUND JOHNNY sitting by himself at the far end of the bar. He was reading a newspaper and drinking coffee. At that moment he seemed to be very much alone.

He turned and put a thumb in the air, a Johnny Tarzan greeting.

He made me a drink of light rum and tonic, a drink I had come to enjoy. Smiling, he said that he had gotten a phone call from my father. My father, it seemed, was concerned about me.

"Why did he call you?"

Johnny pointed his finger at me, saying, "Are you being a good boy?"

I nodded to express my understanding, whatever might be called for. "He worries," I said.

"Your father has always been a worrier."

"Johnny, say I asked you something. Could you keep it confidential?"

"Depends."

"On what?"

"It just depends. If it's family, personal, anything like that, of course. I know you wouldn't try and make me a stool pigeon?"

"No. But listen, I do have a case I'd like to ask you about."

"Ask."

"I'm going to run a name past you. You tell me if the guy is in the drug business. Would you do that?"

"Italian guy?"

"Yes."

"With all the niggers and spicks out there, why the hell do you spend your time looking to put your own in jail?"

I didn't answer him.

"Who is it?"

"Alphonse Indelicato and his brother, JB."

I realized immediately that I'd made a mistake. I must have realized all along that it would be.

"Where the hell did you get that name?"

"I have it, that's all that matters."

"I know that guy, and I'm telling you that Sonny Red is not in the dope business. He can't be, it's forbidden. Whoever told you that he is, is a liar. Jesus Christ, where the hell do you guys get this shit?"

"Forget I ever mentioned his name, okay?"

"Okay," he said. "Ya know, the world is full of know-nothing rat bastards. You, cousin, you have a shitty job."

Johnny telephoned me the following day and asked me to come to the club; he had something important to tell me. It was early in the afternoon when I got to The Lock and Key.

"Bobby, they want to see you."

"Who wants to see me?"

"The Indelicatos."

In retrospect, my well-disguised need to please had somehow merged with my appetite for a kind of adventure that is hard to pin down. I clearly was not smart enough to realize that once I stepped out on that shaky road, my guiding principles, and the limits that I had placed on myself, would vanish like so much smoke.

"Johnny, I can't do that."

"Sure you can. You'll be doing me a favor, and you'll be as safe as though you were asleep in your mother's arms." He explained that it was a complicated situation that someone had to make clear to me—face-to-face. "Anyway," he said, "you're not going to shake anyone down; it's not some kind of scam situation. You'll gain insight, you'll learn something, and maybe you can help people that might just need it."

"Johnny, I know who these people are."

He exhaled slowly. "Look," he said, "what people don't understand is that these people you talk about—you know something?—people like Sonny, they get fucked over too."

"C'mon," I said. "Please, give me a break."

"When we were upstate," he said, "at Greenhaven, a guard sold Sonny a sandwich. Some other hacks found him eating it. They asked where he had gotten it. Of course Sonny wouldn't tell them. So they put handcuffs on him and hung him on the cell like Christ. He hung up there for twenty-four hours."

"Sounds like an interesting guy," I said.

"Exactly, interesting is a good way to put it. Look," he said, "go meet them. Listen to what they have to say. If they offer you money, don't take it. Take money, you're a whore like any other cop. You need some money, come and see me."

Finally he told me that I was to go to Little Italy, to a restaurant called Little Charlie's Oyster Bar on Kenmare Street. "They'll be expecting you."

A philosophical splintered carnival was going round in my head. There was no denying that I had been corrupted, but I also believed that I was basically a good person, and I thought of myself as a good cop. Incredibly, I had managed to convince myself that somehow I could be all three.

babanya (Sicilian word for garbage)—drugs, heroin.

Back then, I was firmly in the embrace of a kind of dark inquisitiveness, the kind of curiosity that drove Icarus to turn his back on all forewarning and constraint and fly way too close to the sun.

On the restaurant window a sign said Closed, but I found the door open. They were seated at a table waiting for me. Four of them, all faces I had seen in intelligence files.

Alphonse Indelicato, "Sonny Red"; his brother, John Bruno, "JB"; Louis LaFucia, "Louie Legs"; and Stanley Simmons. LaFucia and Simmons I knew to be major drug suppliers. Sonny Red and JB were made men and members of the Bonanno crime family.

As I walked toward them, I had this eerie feeling, part fear, part fascination. For a moment I was riddled with a strange kind of shame. Then they all stood and greeted me with smiles and handshakes and pats on the back, Sonny Red saying, "Look at him, man, look at him, this Bobby looks like a neighborhood guy. Look at him."

My stomach was in knots. A voice in my head said, *You don't belong here; this is their world, their campfire. You're a traitor.* They all knew Frank Waters; he was okay, just okay. They despised the investigating detective calling him the little Puerto Rican general. Sonny Red did most of the talking. He was about five-ten—in his cowboy boots, slacks, and zippered jacket, there was plenty of muscle. He was clean-shaven, with fair skin and light, intense eyes and he loved the word *motherfucker.*

His brother, JB, was somewhat shorter; he wore a brown suit and horn-rimmed glasses. JB was quiet and professorial and seemed to be nervously studying me, judging me.

Louie Legs was thin and tall, in silk slacks and a windbreaker, jovial, asking if I'd like something to eat, anything at all. Stanley Simmons looked like a lawyer in his pearl gray suit. His topcoat and fedora lay neatly on a chair beside the table.

"They want a hundred thousand dollars from us," Sonny Red told me. "A hundred for nothing; I've done nothing, my brother's done nothing; these thieving rat motherfuckers are trying to shake us down."

His face had gone burgundy red, his eyes wide in righteous anger. I told him to take it easy, calm down. His language frightened me, the way he delivered it. This was one scary guy.

Louie said, "Look, me and Stanley, okay, we've been in the business. We're not in the business anymore, but these other two gentlemen, no. It's wrong, not right—not fair. Stanley said the cops were trying to make money, that's what they do—try and make some money. But this way, no, it's not right."

Sonny pointed to Louie and Stanley, saying, "What these two fellas do is their business. Me, I don't go near *babanya*—never. My brother, it's the same for him."

I'd like to phone the detective, I told them, and have him come here. "Will you guys talk to him?"

"Sure, you get him to come here. We'll talk to him," Sonny said.

A half hour later the detective was sitting at the table, telling four very grim and unsmiling faces little family vignettes—tales he had overheard on the wiretap—Sonny's son talking about getting laid,

Louie's daughter's conversation with some uptown character—making jokes about it all, indicating how much of their family lives he was familiar with.

I was thinking there had better be more. Maybe a little something that showed he knew about a crime. How about the drug dealing? How about any goddamn thing other than personal family business? Apparently there wasn't. Sonny said, "You don't have shit. Everything you're saying is bullshit, and you know it. There's no crime here." That's when the detective said something that I figured could get us both killed.

"Hey look, you guinea fuck," he said, "all I gotta do is turn this case over to State Parole. They'll violate your ass in a heartbeat. I got you hanging out with these two drug dealers, spending time with them. I have photos; I have surveillances. I put you all together."

The detective was not a big man by any means. He was of average height, and thin—always neat as a new pin and always expensively turned out. He had a great head of thick black hair streaked with silver, another good-looking SIU guy who could have been a movie star. In his case, a Latin movie star. Another guy with dinosaur balls.

Sonny's eyes went wide with fury. "What?" he said.

"You heard me."

"I'll tell you what; you remember that badge of yours ain't no bulletproof vest."

"Ey, don't threaten me," the detective said. "I have a bigger gang than you. I'm leaving, Bobby, I'll wait for you outside."

After he left, I asked Sonny what sort of parole he was on. Life parole he told me, and for what? Homicide. If violated he could go back to prison for life. "Well," I said, "what do you guys want to do?"

JB spoke softly, thoughtfully. "This detective is asking for one hundred thousand dollars. Tell him we'll give him seventy five hundred dollars. But we want his word that we'll never hear from him or see his face again."

On the street in front of the resturant, I asked the detective to explain why he had told me that this case was worth working. "This case was blown. You knew that, and you told me to work it. What's with that?"

"What did you expect me to say?"

I passed on the Indelicatos' offer.

"Sold," he said. "Good job," he told me. "You deserve something here too."

"The informant," I said. "I want the Baron."

"Sure. You knew, huh? Had a suspicion, that sort of thing?"

I nodded my head.

The detective was a hero cop, highly decorated; there was a half second of hesitation. I had been feeling this awful nagging guilt and wondered if he felt the same.

"I'll call you," I said. "Do that," he told me, and then he pinched my cheek.

THE
AWAKENING

The safest course is to do nothing against one's conscience. With this secret, we can enjoy life and have no fear of death.

— VOLTAIRE

It was the late sixties and all of a sudden, and for no apparent reason, a sea of heroin began flooding through the city. Dope was literally everywhere, compelling the police to fight off a never-ending stream of junkies, dealers, and gorillas who seemed to be rising up through the pavement like ghosts. Demons driven by the terrorizing addiction, gone from normal street-running addicts to stone evil, determined to find money and dope any way they could.

From neighborhood to neighborhood, precinct to precinct, it was the same. Herds of addicts prowled the street, high and sick junkies on every corner. Eventually we came to believe that this was all beyond repair. You could increase arrest numbers and double prosecutions, and double them again. None of it seemed to matter.

"Nobody, you'd better believe, gives a shit" was what Frank said, with wistful resignation.

"It's the guineas," the Baron told us. "They're flooding the market, driving down prices, building their customer base. You wait a month or so, they'll pull back product, prices will go through the roof, and we'll have a panic. You ever see a panic? Man, it's a kick; it's something to see."

On the Lower East Side of Manhattan, where Houston Street meets Avenue D, Frank and I met the Baron for the first time. He cruised up in a late-model black El Dorado, a glittery and stunning woman at his side. He sashayed from that car like Superfly. We talked, had a few laughs about his clothes and pimp hat and the woman in his car.

He told us she'd been a Playmate of the Month and asked us if we'd like a taste? Then he told us that he had been connected for years with the "fellas from Church Street" (the feds). He said he'd been an informant for the Bronx district attorney's office, Manhattan too. He knew scores of detectives and federal agents, called them all by their first names. He knew Vinny Albano, did some work for "that crazy bastard." He owned a Laundromat and a cab service in Yonkers. The Baron was a good-humored, fun-loving guy, and he'd recently been doing business with Stanley Simmons, Sonny Red's friend.

The man was the whole show, a large-scale street supplier. He'd give us cases, sure, as long as we gave him protection, and maybe some drugs, and possibly a way to turn a dollar every once in a while. "It's the guineas," he said. "They control all the dope. Da white guys."

"Let's go get them," I said.

"I'm ready," he told me.

The Baron had a smile you could see from half a block away, and he scared me to death.

At our next meeting I asked the Baron to give us a name, a

location, and a phone number. "You know what we want. Give us someone important," I told him.

The Baron had a clever way of speaking. His voice was a tour de force, learned from years of treachery. It was the way he survived in the street. "I got just the guy," he said, "guy paints houses and sells dope."

"A house painter?"

"A house painter that sells dope, big packages."

"Italian guy?"

"What else?"

I knew that the Baron was a fraud. He was a drug dealer and an informant, but maybe he was less of a phony than we were. The Baron came on without a disguise; he was precisely who and what he looked like. On the other hand, who and what was I? I was in a hurry. I wasn't thinking clearly, I couldn't sort it out.

There was something very dangerous in self-examination and I was starting to do a lot of it. There were moments when I looked hard at what I was doing, what I was becoming. There were reproachful voices in my head, sometimes soft, sometimes a screech. All this guilt was starting to really eat at me, yes indeed it was.

Startled, Gina would wake me in the middle of the night, asking what was wrong. She told me that I was moaning and grinding my teeth. I was dreaming, having nightmares about my brother, my father, seeing things in my mind's eye, things I cannot bear to describe; all kinds of stuff—about judges and jail, and sick junkies, and suicide.

I had this driving ambition to return to TPF, to the cop and man I once was, to the time in my life when I could take pride in myself, when all things seemed easy and clearly defined. I knew that I was shaking hands with the devil—I was squandering my most precious asset—and the indefensible horror was that I was not brainless. I knew better, but weak as it may sound, I didn't seem to be able to help myself.

My life in those days was a jumble of interconnecting double-dealing scams, deals, and seductions that were making me mentally and physically ill. But I simply could not find the resolve or the backbone or the means to do anything about it. I don't know how to tell you how complicated that made my life.

The way I looked infuriated me. I hated what I appeared to be. Couldn't stand my shoes—those lightweight loafers were killing me. I had worn desert boots all my life and swore I would again. I was comfortable in short-sleeved shirts and crew-neck sweaters, not Italian knits. I missed my chinos and jeans. And the goddamn pinky ring. I had never worn any kind of jewelry, and finally I got rid of that trinket. I'd stand in front of the mirror, looking at myself, asking myself, *What are you doing? Who are you?*

My cousin Johnny continued to call me. I'd stop in at The Lock and Key to see him and have a drink. I'd look around, wondering what the hell I was doing there. I told myself, *If I hear one more sad story about a wiseguy getting shook down by some detective, or another Bobby Darin or Englebert Humperdink song, I'll go nuts.* And now my newest best friend was the Baron. Wonderful.

"IT'S NOT RIGHT," I told Frank, "it can't be right. The Baron is a major mover." In Brooklyn we had informants who were dealers, but they all had heroin habits themselves. This joker, the Baron, was a businessman, the real thing.

"So true and so what," Frank said, "We're hunting big-time drug dealers now. You expect to get what the Baron can give us from a junkie, or maybe a social worker? The Baron and people like the Baron are who we have to deal with now."

"We both know it's not right," I told him.

"Don't start," he said.

MEANWHILE, WE PUT in a wiretap on the house painter. It turned out that Joseph Mastro was indeed a supplier, but in reality he was merely a background figure and gofer for his boss, a man named Frank Santamaria.

Santamaria was ostensibly a painting contractor; in reality he was a major drug dealer. He lived with his wife in East Islip, on Long Island. These two characters spoke every day, and some of their conversation was in Sicilian. I brought that Sicilian conversation to my father's sister Angie. She would listen to the tapes and say, "Ooooh, these are bad men."

Aunt Angie would laugh and shake her head and translate, telling me to be careful, these people were gangsters. One afternoon, after listening to conversation from the night before, she looked at me, and then she played the tape over again. "It's the wife," she said. "The wife, Lee, she's the boss."

I checked and found that Lee Santamaria, Frank's wife, had once been married to a man named Joseph Condalucci. They had two daughters, Marion and Carol, and one son, John, aka Johnny Candy. Both the daughters were married to wiseguys: Carol to Joseph Gernie Jr., Marion to Salvatore "Sally Moon" Tomasetti. Both men were significant drug dealers with international connections.

Lee's son, John Candy Condalucci, and her son-in-law Sally Moon were both doing prison time on a drug case. In time we found that Sally Moon's lieutenant, a man named Al Felici, was now running the business.

As all the players began to fit together, my mind was ablaze with possibilities. This was it, the beginning of the big one. If we persevered and stayed with it, there was no telling where this case could lead.

We put in a second wiretap on Santamaria, a third one on Felici, and set up surveillances. Now we had three taps working, and they went on and on—month after bloody month. Every night I'd go home in a haze of weariness and anticipation.

We decided to let movements of small packages slide, gathering intelligence and waiting for something big to give. Late one night, while I was sitting on the Santamaria wire, a call came in. It was Carol, Lee's daughter, and she was hysterically crying, screaming, "They killed him, those fucking bastards murdered my Joey."

Softly, and with complete emotional control, Lee said, "Carol, calm down, these walls have ears." Carol's screams grew louder, but then suddenly ceased altogether when her mother said, "Bite your tongue, Carol. I wish from my heart I could take your pain, but I can't. You have to do it. Bite your tongue."

Lee Santamaria was one very tough lady. Her son-in-law had been shot to death in a Bronx restaurant, but like a Sicilain holy woman at an altar rail, she lost not an iota of self-control.

The heart of this case beat on Manhattan's Pleasant Avenue, the Italian enclave in East Harlem. It was in that wiseguy-infested neighborhood that Lee had been born and raised. There were more major drug dealers in East Harlem than anywhere else in the city. Our Lady of Mount Carmel, the local church, was euphemistically referred to as "Our Lady of the Three Kilos."

In time we identified all the important players. They included Frank "Shish" DiSimone and Armand Cassoria. Both men lived in New Jersey, but they had sprung from that Pleasant Avenue neighborhood and still hung out there.

Shish drove a new Mercedes and had his home in the town of Edison. Armand lived in a gated mansion in Fort Lee. Half Sicilian, half Corsican, Armand Cassoria and Frank DiSimone were the real deal. Now all we had to do was find the dope.

We put in all kinds of hours and worked seven days a week. I loved every minute of it. Dedicating myself like that was a salve for my soul. I had been sleeping badly, feeling depressed and guilty. Now all that was lessening. My sense of self-worth was returning.

Wasn't all this committed work proof that I was a good guy? Some of the smug confidence returned to my step. I was a top-flight New York City narcotics detective, breathing right down the necks of some of the country's major narcotics violators. I was one of the best of the best, and I had earned the right to feel that way. Given the opportunity, I could put one helluva case together. Maybe even a bigger and more important case than the French Connection. And money was not the driving force; money was not what I was about. For me, this case was an opportunity, a form of personal and professional rebirth. The feelings of culpability and worthlessness and the sickness of heart made heavy by guilt had melted away.

Our team had the thickest case folder in the office. Surveillances and intelligence reports, photos, criminal records, associations, a flow chart that went from the street dealer right up to the importer.

All the SIU bosses recognized what we were onto and shared my enthusiasm. Nevertheless, in spite of everything, my partners were growing antsy.

Gene became unbelievably restless; he was all the time angry, telling me that too many people knew about our case. We were putting in too much time and effort and there were no arrests in the offing. Frank too grew edgy, and Jack Bergersen asked to leave the team. In the fall, Gene D'Arpe was transferred out of the Narcotics Bureau altogether. Now it was just Frank and me and that was fine.

It was Christmas Eve. Frank was out of town on vacation; I couldn't get anyone to fill in, so I set up on one of our targets by myself. There had been several guarded conversations between Al Felici and Shish. It was the holiday season, and I was convinced that something significant was going down.

Around eight o'clock at night, I tailed Felici from his house to a diner on White Plains Road in the Bronx. In the parking lot of that diner, a new Mercedes sat waiting. Behind the wheel of that car was Shish.

Felici walked from his car and got into the Mercedes. Out of my car, standing in a light snowfall, I could make out Felici handing DiSimone a package wrapped in Christmas paper. It was a box six inches high and about two feet long. As Shish opened that package, I moved closer and looked at them through the windshield.

The collar of my coat was up around my ears; my hand was on the pistol in my pocket. If that package contained drugs, I had already convinced myself that I was going to arrest both of these guys.

From what I could see, there had to be close to a million dollars in that box in neatly stacked bills. The two men twisted in their seats to look at me, while I stared at them. I turned and walked away, thinking—*Where the hell are the fucking drugs?*

EARLY ONE MORNING, an SIU sergeant, Jack Hourigan, telephoned me at home. "Incredible news," he said. "We have a new commanding officer. A young captain and a rising star in the department. His name is Tange, Captain Dan Tange, and he's called for a meeting. He wants us all in the office this afternoon at one."

Captain Tange was young, fit, and attractive. A former motorcycle cop, he told us that he had once worked Internal Affairs. He knew the game, he said.

"Maybe some of you think you're getting away with it," he told us. "Maybe some of you still think you will. A guilty conscience needs no accuser, and I see a lot of uncomfortable faces in this room. I'm here to tell you it's over. I catch any of you off-base I'll lock you up myself." The captain was expressive, animated; he had a warm and pleasant smile, and he got everyone's attention.

Tange was in his early forties, but he had a fresh look that made him seem even younger. "Think of this as an opportunity," he told us, "a new beginning." All that was in the past would remain in the past. He promised better equipment and more money to pay informants, seized drug dealers' cars to use in surveillances, and more supervisor participation in our cases.

He expected to see one member of each team in the office every day. He wanted weekly typewritten reports on what we were doing and what we hoped to accomplish. He spoke slowly, with certainty; his eyes gleamed with passion.

"Have no doubt," he said, "I will find out who the good and bad are among you." As he spoke, there were detectives in that room who wanted to hide, to shrink into nothingness. I was one of them.

He told us that he was in the process of going over all our open cases. "I'll be talking to each of you separately," he said. "I'm telling you, be straight with me, and you will do well here. Fool with me at your own peril, and that is a promise."

Someone said the captain had studied for the priesthood, that he attended church three times a week. Someone else said, "Fuck him."

After the meeting, off we went, Frank and I to the Villa Roma for lunch. "This guy is terrific," I said. "What a change. Maybe there's hope. Really, I think we finally lucked out."

"Are you nuts?"

"C'mon. You can't fool me. I know you feel exactly the way I do. I know you've had enough of this bullshit too."

"What the hell are you talking about?" Frank said.

"Maybe we can do the job now; I mean really do the job."

Frank Mandato's ability to see through people, and me in particular was ruthless in its power.

"Don't try and make me feel guilty," he said. "Don't lay that shit on me. We had a long talk about money before we started working together. I told you then, you could make up your own mind, do what you thought was right, and I'd never hold it against you. Remember?"

I said I did—and I did, but the truth was, back at that time I had come to feel that all of this was fated. I believed that sooner or later I was bound to go along. I thought I had no choice. If I wanted to be accepted into a very private club, a group that meant everything to me, I had to conform.

Back then I assumed that Frank meant what he had said about not holding it against me if I told him no, no way, I'm not getting involved. Except it seemed to me that he was lying to himself. I had gone through partner after partner, and it was always the same story. Somehow it was Frank telling me I could make up my own mind that made me believe, past all doubt, that it would be the same story again. Even today, those words *Do what you think is right* sound less like a chance at a decision than a direction. It's the last lie we tell ourselves before jumping onto the proverbial slippery slope.

But it's no use, is it? No matter what I liked to think of myself, that I really didn't want to, that I wasn't, I did and I was—and no matter how much I'd like to, it's simply not possible to change history.

I told Frank that I was feeling really loose around the edges. I couldn't seem to find any footing, and I was beating myself to a pulp. "Cut it out," he said, "just cut it out. For Christ sake, look around you and stop kidding yourself."

Captain Tange was going to change things, I told him. He told me that Tange would not change a thing. "The man worked in Motorcycle; those guys didn't carry extra bullets on their belts, they carried change purses."

That's when Frank told me that he too was losing interest in our case. He said that Gene had been right all along, working Italians was a nightmare. It was way too difficult and time-consuming. He'd been thinking, and what he decided was that we should drop the wiseguys and start using an old Cuban informant of ours.

Frank and I knew each other, understood each other, worked better as a team than most of the other detectives in our unit. We never argued, rarely disagreed. We joked that the women in our lives, the women we slept with, didn't know us as well as we knew each other.

I told him to please forget South Americans; we were going to nail the people we were working on. We could make this case. I said that all we needed was a little patience, and maybe one more wiretap. If we hung tough, we'd put together a case greater and more important than the French Connection case.

That particular dream of mine would not settle.

Frank puffed his cheeks and blew; whenever I'd worn him too thin, or worn him out, he had the habit of puffing his cheeks and blowing. Recently, Frank had been putting me in mind of Puff the Magic Dragon.

He smiled at me—it was Frank's own secret kind of smile, as if he knew things about me that no one else did. He pinched my cheek. "You're a nut case," he said, "you know that, don't you?"

"Wiseguys," I said. "Mafia dealers are who we're working, and that's where we'll stay."

THERE WAS A vast and essential difference between Mafia drug operations and South American, and the difference was supply and money. To begin with, mafiosi rarely came into personal contact with the drugs. Catching them with their hands on a package was all but impossible. Mafia cartels had been in the drug trade for years, it seemed like generations. With their connections in the Far East and Europe they had access to a limitless supply of heroin. Their business was based on the capability to always deliver. Theirs was a consignment business. Mafia dealers extended credit and waited for payment. Foreign distributors trusted them and were willing to wait for their money too.

South Americans did a cash-and-carry business. Their prices were lower, and they moved through the drug world with carloads of dope and money. In the countries of their origin, the police were a business expense and no threat at all.

Everyone wanted to work South Americans. In either case, and at the end of the day, American addicts became the victims of the most lucrative criminal activity known to man.

The stakes in the drug business were so high that entire governments were corrupted. So it was no surprise that an American police captain, an essentially decent man, with all sorts of talent and promise, that he too could misplace his moral compass.

IT WAS EARLY in the morning when I took a call from Sergeant Hourigan. He told me to hurry into the office. The new captain was meeting with each team leader, and he wanted to see me.

"By the way," he said, "the worm has turned in the apple."

"What does that mean?"

"You'll see."

Throughout the department, everyone thought the chances were good that Captain Daniel Tange could be the next police commissioner. Erudite, attractive, and a born leader, with a reputation for honesty, and dedication to the work, he was a natural. He was waiting for me in his office.

I was revved up. A new beginning, a whole new ballgame. The captain looked at me for a long time. Then he leaned back in his chair and smiled, telling me that he had read my case; as a matter of fact he'd read it several times. "One helluva case," he said. "This is an amazing amount of work. When are you going to make a collar?"

I had no way of knowing, and I told him so. We left the building and went for a walk down near the river. Tange was warm and friendly. He asked if I needed any help. I told him that I was thinking of putting in another wiretap. I could use some additional help. "No problem," he said, "whatever you need, just ask."

That's when he told me that he had bought a piece of property out east on Long Island. He was in the process of building a house.

"I'm in a bit over my head," he said. "That means you now have a new partner. Do you understand what I'm saying?"

I didn't say anything.

"I want you to go through Sergeant Hourigan. He'll be my bagman."

His words stunned me. For a second I felt paralyzed. Instead of wiping the SIU slate clean and starting fresh, it was going to be more of the same. Only this time a bit more organized, more systematized.

Standing there with the captain, looking out at the East River, I thought of Jerry Schremph. How would he have reacted to all this? What would he have thought of this captain and me? The hypocrisy of it all, the irony. Instead of making a decision right then and there—choosing to change my life—I shrugged my shoulders and said, "Sure, whatever you say."

I got right back onto the case. Frank was exasperated—he told me to call him when I was ready to make a hit. The hit never came. All the wiretaps went dead. The activity ceased—more than a year's worth of work had been for nothing.

"I don't know what to say," I told the captain. "My wires are dead. There is no movement in the case. I don't know what happened."

"I do," he told me. "I figured it out; you sold the case."

"I did not," I said. "I'd never do that." I was embarrassed and insulted. I tried to explain about the hours I put in, the holidays I'd missed, the partners I was losing one after the other, that I had good intentions and that I wanted nothing more than to make that case. I never would have sold it.

All that was true.

"Well," he said, "apparently somebody did. Maybe you should reach out to these guys. Find out if there is any more money there." Then he smiled a great warm grin. "Think about South Americans," he said. "Cubans and Colombians, they're the ticket."

I eventually found out that my case had indeed been sold—three separate times. It was two detectives from my office and one from the Bronx district attorney's office, each in his own time and in his own way—and for his own reasons. Their reasons totaled about one hundred thousand dollars. More or less.

"Your own big mouth," Joe Nunziata told me. "It's your fault; you talk too much, ask too many questions—and trust too many people. You know you can't trust cops." It was an in-joke. But it made me hate those guys, all of them, the way you hate terrorists—or child abusers, a deep, burning loathing, the kind that doesn't go away.

The feds would eventually make a case against Shish, an international case. They nailed Frank DiSimone with 70 kilos of pure heroin, a seizure bigger and more important than the French Connection. I should have felt a certain vindication, a confirmation that I had been right all along. All I felt was betrayed and beaten.

———

LET ME BE clear: police work was not a job to me, it was my life, and I was beginning to hate what my life had become, but it was the only life I knew.

I was tiptoeing through my days on a thin wire, a circus stunt, and constantly just this side of catastrophe. I cannot say I was over the edge. But undoubtedly something was very wrong when I couldn't find sleep until dawn, grinding my teeth to nubs. I had the feeling I was living in one of those dreams where you are convinced something terrifying is going to happen, that it's only a question of when and where.

I didn't see any way out. So I made a decision to play everything close to the vest. I would be careful and keep my head up until I could find a magical way to turn all this around.

Eddie Mamet and I had worked together in Brooklyn; he was a weird and wonderful guy and a good undercover cop. One day at the office, Mamet told me that he'd met a Sergeant Durk at a Shomrim Society meeting. He told me that Durk had some terrific information about the big-time drug dealers on Pleasant Avenue.

"Trust me," Mamet said. "Durk is a good guy, and I think he can help you."

The name sounded familar, Sergeant David Durk. "Where does he work?" I asked.

"The Department of Investigations."

By reputation, the DOI was a do-nothing office, and everyone who worked there—the lawyers, the investigators, and the supervisors—had heavyweight political connections.

Whoops! I knew exactly who Durk was. "This is the guy that worked with Serpico, isn't he?"

"Right," Mamet said, "but you can trust him. I wouldn't bring him here if I didn't think that you could trust him."

"You brought him here?"

"He's waiting in the hallway."

The enduring code in the department was to have nothing whatsoever to do with anyone who worked in an internal affairs unit. Even though the DOI did not investigate cops per se, they were an internal investigating unit. Simply to have a conversation with someone like a David Durk would bring you puzzled stares and questions regarding your sanity.

But I was still smarting from the sale of my case. I would have given anything to get another shot at the Pleasant Avenue dealers. I would have lain down with Satan himself for information on those people.

I liked him immediately.

Durk was articulate, well-dressed, open, and attractive. He was straightforward, telling me that he hated working in the DOI and wanted to get a temporary assignment to SIU.

"Fat fucking chance."

"What?" He hadn't heard me.

"Right," I said.

Maybe he did work in an office that spent its time investigating the theft of city-owned tools and paints. On the other hand, he had an informant who knew plenty about Pleasant Avenue. He could sort out all the players that operated there. He showed me some notes he had taken, a flow chart.

Durk had it all. He had as much and more than I had put together in a year's worth of investigations, although he hadn't put it together correctly. Durk's informant was all over the lot, but he had all the names, locations, and phone numbers. The man was a gold mine of high-level narcotics information.

"If I could get access to this informant, we could do some important things," I told him, and that was to become something of a refrain for the remainder of that day and late into the night.

Captain Tange came out of his office and called to me. Behind a closed door in the captain's office I came on with an impressive spiel about Durk's informant.

Tange was the smartest boss I'd ever had, or at least I thought he was. "This Durk is a dangerous guy," he said. "The only reason he's here is to embarrass us. I want you to get rid of him."

I told Tange I didn't think that was true; all the same, I'd love to get a hold of Durk's informant. "Screw the informant," he said. "You get that pain in the ass out of this office, is that clear?"

"Sure."

Durk had made it clear: no Durk, no informant.

That night I was alone with Durk in his West Side apartment. He had wall-to-wall books and great posters. The son of a physician, he told me that he had graduated from Amherst College and spent a year at Columbia Law School. He was a spellbinding talker. Immediately I wanted to believe that it didn't matter what our histories were, that we had common ground. It was a love of the job—not the job of the SIU, the job of the TPF.

We sat in his living room, David on a chair in front of a wall of books, me on a sofa facing him. Suddenly he was into a tirade. He went on about the majesty of police work and how important it was to find like-minded people to do this work.

I was impressed.

He explained how he had taken Frank Serpico by the hand and helped him expose the corruption in the public morals units.

Again, I was impressed.

We talked about politicians and commissioners. We argued over comparative responsibilities, about district attorneys, about judges. He made jokes I didn't like about cops being penguins.

Durk was a flatterer. He said that Eddie Mamet had told him what a great detective I was. How honest.

Right.

As the night wore on, he began to sound like one of those people who thought you knew nothing and would spend their time telling you what you needed to know. He had a few glasses of wine and began to rant, and soon he was sounding paranoid, wild and irresponsible, like a nut.

246 | ALL THE CENTURIONS

Durk was full of brash ambitions and full of himself. He explained that he had a confrontational personality, and that brought him his share of enemies. But he had access to the media, and that made him impossible to ignore.

After a while, listening to David, I couldn't help but feel a deep sense of sympathy for him. There were conflicts raging within David Durk that were worse, possible, than the frenzy whirling inside of me. All this ranting and raving while trying to maintain some humanity.

It was clear to me that there was much that Durk understood about the men and women who worked this job, but just as much that he didn't. He couldn't. Considering the world he lived in, it was simply not possible. Durk was highly educated. He came from money, and his wife too came from a well-to-do family. David Durk and the average cop were poles apart.

It was well past midnight, and I understood that there was no way I was getting access to his informant. Still, by then, that was okay. I'd met David Durk, the moving force behind Frank Serpico, and I'd had a tiny peek into certain possibilities.

THERE WAS ONE more teaming, one more chance for me to permit myself feelings about possibilities. It didn't take long before I knew it would be more of the same.

Detectives Dave Cody and Les Wolff joined Frank and me. At first I thought that maybe this team could make important cases and stay out of trouble. It was possible, I thought, that we could leave behind the kinds of degrading activities that so many of us had come to accept as business as usual. Maybe we could do things that would make us all proud. I was living on possibilities.

Les and Dave had been partners in the Harlem narcotics group. Before that, Les had worked uniformed patrol in East Harlem, and it didn't take him long to let us know that he had heard the SIU could make him rich.

Who could blame Les? The Narcotics Bureau, and the SIU in particular, was a topsy-turvy world where much of the conversation had to do with making cases and money; and not necessarily in that order.

Dave was older than the rest of us. A frail and easygoing man, he had worked a number of years in PMD. Dave Cody was that classic, the Irish bachelor son who remained at home with his mother and enjoyed his pint. He had come to the SIU only hoping to survive his remaining years in the department.

We worked well together; we changed our focus from Italians and moved on to South Americans. The team made cases, good seizures, and had some wild times on the Upper West Side of Manhattan. We constantly crossed paths with other SIU teams and federal narcotics agents; everyone was setting illegal wiretaps. I heard stories of cops wiretapping entire sections of the city, and of amazing seizures of drugs and money.

The sense of foreboding returned to my life, more powerful than it had been before. Everybody was running wild—cops, agents, prosecutors, defense lawyers, and drug dealers. Things were getting worse. A sense that we were mercenaries in a give-no-quarter war seemed to permeate all of narcotics enforcement. There was a loss of all standards, all sense of right and wrong.

One time we hit a cocaine connection on 118th Street in Spanish Harlem. He was a good-sized Cuban dealer, a businessman who owned several bodegas in Harlem. We found a substantial amount of drugs, arrested him, and he let me know that he was willing to cooperate.

When I met him the following day to discuss his cooperation, he was furious with me. He said he would never work together with us. He told me that we were small-time thieves, explaining that during the search of his store and apartment, someone had stolen his dead father's watch. It was a cheap watch, but it was engraved to his father. And then there was his son's camera, and a pair of alligator shoes.

Alligator shoes?

I called a team meeting and told everyone that I wanted everything back, no questions asked.

"C'mon," I said, "what the hell are we, fucking burglars? Give me the stuff back."

I asked the clerical man, Ciro Pastore, to keep an eye on my inbox. One of my partners, not Frank, thank God, returned the camera and watch. I returned them to the Cuban dealer. "Thanks, but no thanks," he said. "I'll go to jail before I'd work with you guys." I didn't blame him.

At home, with my family, I was growing more short-tempered and impatient. I had little time for my wife and children, none for my brother. My mind was always on fire, always drifting, positive that sooner or later the life I was living would explode. I believed with all my heart that this lunacy was a volcano, and it was coming to a head and was bound to erupt, burying all of us.

I wasn't much of a drinker, but I took a crack at it. It helped.

Meanwhile, Serpico and Durk were making an enormous splash. An investigative committee called the Knapp Commission was established to investigate police corruption. How about that? I used to wonder. Wasn't anyone paying attention? Did everyone believe that we could go on without shame or fear doing the things we were doing without someone taking notice? We must have, because everyone kept doing it. And some were doing things that were beyond my wildest imagination.

YOU KNOW, IT'S funny the things you remember. Like the night I walked off the elevator at the Brooklyn district attorney's office. As soon as the doors slid open, I was met with the sound of applause. Whooping and hollering, laughter, people jumping on every side, as if the Dodgers were still around and they'd won the pennant.

Pete Perazzo, the DA's narcotics sergeant, slid by me saying, "Ser-

pico's been shot. Somebody shot that rat cocksucker in the head."
Then he went on to slap palms with other detectives in the crowd,
leaving me to wonder just what form of mass insanity had taken hold
here.

For several months, Frank and I had been working at the DA's office. It was a temporary assignment. I told Frank that I loved it, and
I did. I thought that there were real possibilities, maybe a chance at
a whole new career. The strained tensions of life in the SIU had
been, for the time being, replaced by a clean investigator's job.

Perazzo had asked me to help him upgrade his narcotics unit and
maybe make some cases. I redid their files and made new ones, pro-
filing all the major Brooklyn narcotics violators. I opened an intelligence file on the Grand Colombian Lines. Their ships coming up
from Cartegena docked weekly at the Brooklyn piers, and I had information that for years seamen on those ships had been used as
drug couriers.

We opened a case, got a wiretap, and made some arrests. The
ADAs were delighted with the activity, giving me high hopes that I
could escape the SIU and find a permanent assignment with the DA's
squad.

One day Frank Serpico and David Durk made an appearance,
and I spent some time with them. They asked me to drive with them
into Manhattan, to go along while they met with one of the Manhattan district attorneys.

At the foot of the Brooklyn Bridge, a cop was directing traffic.
Serpico said, "David, whadaya think, how long would it take you to
make a case against that guy?" Durk said five minutes. Serpico said
two—a joke in which I could find no humor. It was just a little
chitchat—both of them being flippant. I knew it was nothing more
than lighthearted BS. These were two bright guys, both of them
struggling for control of their relationship, both of them thinking it
was trendy to shock.

Serpico in particular could be an extremely likeable character, but he should have gone Krishna instead of cop. Durk was far more serious and far more strident.

The night Serpico was shot, I spoke with two or three of the young detectives who had been assigned by the DA to work with me. "Listen," I told them, "it's not amusing that Serpico's been shot. He was shot doing narcotics work, he was one of us." (Serpico had recently been transferred into the Narcotics Bureau.) They all agreed, acknowledging that their reaction was thoughtless, maybe even worse than that; but everybody was doing it.

The following afternoon I went to the hospital to visit Serpico. While there, I ran into his uniformed police guard, who told me that he hated this job. I said, "What, being a cop?" He said, "No, guarding this asshole."

Durk was waiting in Serpico's room along with a woman flight attendant Serpico had been dating. To his credit, Durk gave off a heavy trust-me, you-can-talk-to-me vibe. The man was a magnet for all sorts of people with stories to tell. On that day he was happy to see me, but he seemed wary and uptight.

He said that they were going to give Serpico his gold detective's shield and that it was about time. Durk looked pale and drawn, the realization taking hold that it would be Frank Serpico who would emerge as the hero of this piece, and he, Durk, would be the forgotten one.

As for Serpico, other than a crashing headache, he said he felt fine. He actually looked pretty good for a guy who'd been shot in the face and was a hairbreath away from being dead. His head was swollen and looked as though someone had bounced a bat off it. His eyes were bloodshot and watering heavily.

"I doubt you feel fine," I told him. He said, "The drugs, man, these drugs are fantastic." I smiled, thinking, *This hippy cop deserves a better fate than this.*

Getting his gold detective's shield had been the single most motivating force in Frank Serpico's life. For years he had been trying to put the pieces together. Now a .25-caliber bullet that fragmented at his cheekbone and spun behind his right ear had done the work for him. I asked him if there was anything that I could do. He said no, everyone's been great. I asked if he thought the cops were implicated in his shooting. "No," he said, "no—a guy named Mambo, a drug dealer with a shitty little gun."

Ten shots were fired in that Brooklyn hallway. The detectives with Serpico behaved heroically, firing their guns and trying to drag him from in front of Mambo's door. Everywhere you went, you heard, "The cops were responsible for Serpico being shot." And everywhere Serpico went, he never said they weren't.

Durk and Serpico were the driving forces behind the creation of the Knapp Commission. It was a committee with the authority to investigate the police department in the early seventies. It had been part of their lives for over a year.

Both men had been telling whoever would listen about the rampant corruption in the NYPD. They told police supervisors, journalists, assistant district attorneys, and still they were having trouble getting their story out. It seemed to make them both a bit loony.

Their joint enthusiasm made you feel that nothing else in their lives mattered. Nothing other than the fact that someday they could be superstars. Already they had met with Robert Redford and Paul Newman, the actors considering a movie based on their shared ordeal.

So if in the months that followed their meetings with Newman and Redford it didn't work out, and the interest in Serpico as a wounded and solitary figure increased, it was unfair to Durk. He was, after all, the initial impetus for all the corruption investigations that would follow.

As I was leaving the hospital that day, Durk told me he had mentioned my name to a Knapp Commission lawyer. "I told him you were the only honest detective in the Narcotics Bureau," he said.

For a long time I just stared at David Durk. "Thanks," I said. "You're a real pal."

Back at the Brooklyn district attorney's office, an agitated Sergeant Perazzo asked me to come into his office. He told me that I had done some good work there. He was impressed, he said—and then he told me that was not the only reason he'd brought me to Brooklyn. He opened his desk drawer, saying, "I expect to see something; I've expected to see something ever since I brought you here. But look, my desk drawer is empty."

Another boss that wanted money. It was, as they say, the perfect ending to a very bizarre day.

I REMEMBER THE burning down deep inside me, how full I was of indignation and anger, but mostly what I remember is that I was scared stiff.

I was sitting on a wooden chair at the Knapp Commission office, a treacherous setting for a cop; looking around, I felt a bitter rage, all these lawyers, investigators, and technical people—all this to investigate the police department. Something was wrong with all that. What about the courts—the corrupt judges, assistant district attorneys, bail bondsmen, the defense bar? The entire wacky system was a mess. Why choose only the police to investigate?

I was ready to flee. There was nothing keeping me in that office—but there was something. It was a restless curiosity. The longer I waited in Nick Scoppetta's outer office, the more I worried, and soon I was feeling like a man who knew he was about to be told by his doctor that they had found a lump the size of a baseball in his lung.

I knew I was not a target. Nevertheless, for a detective with my history, this was not a place to be. A sense of my own guilt kept drilling into me. It was like when I was a kid and waiting for confession, waiting for absolution for all those venial and mortal sins. The Knapp Commission was the site of an inquisition—it was no church, no confessional. If I could have figured some dignified way out of that office, I would have run like Hermes, the god of thieves, who was Mercury, the messenger of the Olympians.

When we shook hands, I recognized Scoppetta as an ADA from the Manhattan courts. He had the kind of look that once seen, you remember. His nose gave the impression that he'd once been a prizefighter, and he had kept himself in good shape.

When we met he was soft-spoken, relaxed, and friendly. He smiled when I told him that this commission was bullshit. I said I'd bet he was smart enough to know that there was nothing that wasn't for sale in New York's courtrooms. Why was he wasting his time investigating cops, the least culpable in a very corrupt system?

He was disappointed. He said that Durk and Serpico had recommended that he speak to the only honest detective in the Narcotics Bureau. They had told him I could be helpful; yet here I was defending cops—and attacking him.

In the years to come, I was to find several personal heroes who would in essence save my life. Nick Scoppetta was the first and maybe the most important. He looked at me, listened to me, and I like to believe that something special clicked between us.

To this day I'm not sure just what it was he caught sight of in me. Nevertheless, in his eyes I glimpsed sympathetic understanding, and at that critical time in my life, it was exactly what I needed.

That night I ended up in Scoppetta's West Side apartment. We ate steak and drank wine at his kitchen table, Nick and I and George Carros, an IRS agent on loan to Knapp. We talked law enforcement, corruption, politics, and family until late into the night.

I did a lot of the talking.

I was bitter and I was scared—my conversation rambled. I felt that something was about to break loose inside me, and I was barely able to control myself.

You were a worthless, corrupt shithead if you had done the things I had done. But I refused to be judged that way—I simply would not accept that hideous view of myself. Clearly I'd made some terrible mistakes, but I cared too much and worked too hard. I'd put myself in harm's way too many times and forsaken too much of a normal family life to be assessed that harshly.

In some bizarre way, I saw myself as an embodiment of the NYPD itself. I was not about to admit to these two noncops all the things I'd seen and done. They wouldn't understand—and if they did understand, they didn't have the power to forgive. I didn't think anyone did.

That first night my emotions were jumping from fury to panic to dread. There was an infection inside of me, I could feel actual sickness—and after a while I had to get out of that apartment. We agreed to get together again the following night. For what, I wasn't sure, but I knew I would be there.

As I was leaving, Nick said, "You seem to know an awful lot about corruption."

"I've been a cop for ten years, a narcotics detective for seven. I'd have to be deaf, dumb, and blind not to."

"Have you yourself been involved?"

"Absolutely not."

"Good."

We met again the following night. This time I was more accusatory, and so was he.

"Are you telling me that you worked in the Manhattan district attorney's office all those years, and you never saw any corruption?" I said.

"Hogan's office was absolutely clean, I'm sure of it."

"Bullshit! They've always had a gambling pad in that place and wiretaps, and cases have been sold from there."

I was guessing, but it was an educated guess. I had heard of detectives and more than one ADA who were rumored to be corrupt in the Manhattan DA's office. And their gambling pad was legendary and no secret.

"And you," he said, "you expect me to believe that you know all this stuff about citywide corruption, and you've never been involved yourself?"

"That's right."

"Bullshit!"

"You know," I said, "maybe cases and wiretaps were being sold all around you, and you never noticed; that is possible, isn't it?"

"Possible but unlikely."

"I think very possible."

Nick began mentioning names—many detectives' names that I knew; some I'd worked with, all of them touched by one form of corruption or another.

"Great detectives," I said, "all those guys are top-flight cops." I believed it; at least I believed it regarding most of the names he mentioned.

Then he got into an emotional rant about corrupt cops, how the system was rife with them—and how terribly sad that was. I answered that cops were followers, not leaders. If it was required of them to swim in an ocean of shit, how could you expect them to come up smelling like a rose?

"Weak," Nick said, "that's a really weak excuse."

It was the best I had. "Look," I said, "it's the truth. You give cops inspired, honest leadership, a court system that's not bought and paid for, honest politicians, you'll have honest cops, but the opposite is also true."

I told him that I'd seen it both ways, and that's the way it was. Nick said, "If you've seen it, you could do something about it."

"I would never have anything to do with the Knapp Commission," I told him. "You guys may be well motivated, and all that jazz. But unless you go out after all the others involved in the criminal justice system, it's all a sham, and you know it."

Nick raised his hands, a small surrender.

He opened a bottle of wine, and for the moment we changed the subject. Nick told me that he was a part-time photographer, and then showed me some of his pictures. He did stunning work in black and white. He'd been raised in an orphanage and had a brother whom he loved, a man who had had his own share of tribulations.

I talked about my own brother, Ritchie, and I talked about my father, how disappointed he was in both his sons. I told him how I had once felt about being a cop, and how I felt now.

There is something about talking on the subject of youthful dreams and ambitions over a glass of wine and Vivaldi. It isn't the light buzz of the wine or the soothing music or the human bonding that somehow always arises in extraordinary times. It's not even the understanding that you share similar personal histories. If anything, there is a specific kind of human connection, a certain kind of respect that is established. And that's the way it was with Nick and me.

I had always loved classical guitar, and he was taking lessons. He was a compassionate and thoughtful man; he put me in mind of Mario Cuomo. Both of them took me back to the very best of the priests of my youth. But just like the governor, Nick's seeming naïveté was startling. I liked him very much.

"You know," Nick said, "I think we could do that, an across-the-board investigation into the criminal justice system. We would go federal; do other, more important things than the Knapp Commission. You would be a cop again, the cop you always wanted to be."

"I am that cop."

"I'm not so sure."

I was beginning to feel sick again. "What do you know?" I said.

"I know you wouldn't be here, and we wouldn't be having this conversation, if you didn't want to do something."

For two days, the agent George Carros had been sitting and listening and speaking only enough to agree to something or other or join in on a joke. A New Yorker, he'd grown up on the West Side of

Manhattan in Hell's Kitchen. With a full head of curly brown hair, half Irish and half Greek, George was a big man, heavyset, with arms like fence posts and a cheery temperament. His honesty impressed me. He told me that he had done some boxing, but he was no street cop. His job was to investigate corrupt IRS agents. His gun, he said, was a ballpoint pen.

I liked him and saw no treachery in him. The going, federal part, I figured, was probably his idea.

"I've been listening to you for two days," George said. "It's clear to me you want to say something, to tell us something. I'm wondering when?"

"Not tonight," I told him, "maybe not ever, but we'll meet again tomorrow night—and maybe then. Maybe."

The following night I said, "Look, you tell me what you'd like me to do—and then I'll tell you what I will and will not do."

I'd been haunted for years—an absolute basket case for months. I was barely sleeping at all now—lost, looking for an answer, a guidepost, a way to turn my life around. I thought that possibly I'd found it. I continued to live on possibilities.

Nick said, "Tell us everything you know."

I told them not to go there. "I'm no informant," I said. In some peculiar way, nothing was more important than how these two men viewed me. Ultimately it would be the way I viewed myself. "No one caught me doing anything wrong. I'm not here because I'm under a hammer," I told them.

"He's no informant," George said. I smiled at him, and George winked at me.

"I'll never point a finger," I told them. "I won't mention names, do anything like that. But maybe I could work undercover, and we could make cases. I will never, ever implicate my partners, or work against people that I've known," I told them. "The moment that subject is even approached, I'm done, it's over."

There were reassurances and then some quick off-the-cuff questions that I refused to answer, followed by uncertain looks and more questions that made me squirm. I delivered some thought-out lies.

Finally I told them that I had personally been involved in a total of three acts of misconduct. Those acts concerned me, by myself.

It was a question of credibility.

How could I say that I had never been involved in any acts of corruption? After seven years in the Narcotics Bureau, I didn't expect that anyone would believe that. But to admit everything would mean implicating my partners, and that was never going to happen. Still, any admissions once made cannot be unsaid. I probably should have taken the Fifth. Confession, any admission of wrongdoing, always brings with it a certain amount of self-destruction. And for me, there were still uncertain reasons.

In any case, I had already gone too far, said way too much. Oddly, though, it was almost a pleasant unburdening. There was this sense of letting go, a kind of freedom in it.

"Three cases of misconduct?"

"Yes."

A stern, surprised look from Nick, and suddenly a burning need in me to be somewhere else.

"What else?" Nick asked.

"When push comes to shove, I'll do this only with the consent of the police commissioner."

Stakes were getting higher. If I didn't have the PC on board, and in my corner, things could get dicey, if nothing else. Of that I was certain.

"No one else," Nick said. "We can let no one else know."

"The chief of detectives," I said.

"Out of the question. I trust Commissioner Pat Murphy completely; anyone else, and you might be a dead man."

I didn't say anything.

Then the enthusiasm took over—we were actually going to try and do something. Just what, was the question.

Nick asked, "What sort of cases could we make?"

"You name it, we can do it," I told him.

He said that was too vague. He wanted something specific. He'd have to go to the highest levels of the Justice Department.

"We need their support," he said. "In order to get it, I have to be armed with information that will grab their attention."

"What if you told them just about every wiretap in this city is for sale, and I know how to buy them? Then say, that's just for starters."

Stunned silence, then: "You're serious?"

I nodded.

Nick hugged me. George hugged both of us.

I remember the feeling of turmoil in my stomach, a kind of excitement—and fiery self-pity—and no small amount of terror.

Nick and George were both elated, overjoyed—but my mind was elsewhere. I was thinking of how other cops were bound to view me, the kind of reaction I was letting myself in for.

No matter what my rationale, if we were successful, my actions would be thought of as a betrayal, a betrayal worse than any betrayal. I had been accepted, transported with smiles and hugs into a very special club—I was trusted. It was far, far worse than anything Serpico had done. Serpico was, in reality, an outsider—not one of us, he set out to deceive no one.

All of a sudden I was reduced to the position of a kid in weepy grief. "I'm no informant," I shouted, a sound so full of fear and self-pity I shocked even myself. "Don't try and make me an informant. I'm a New York City police detective, and we are going to conduct an investigation. That's what this is—nothing more—nothing less."

I'm not sure my passion won them over; then again it was me not them I was trying to convince.

Nick grabbed my shoulders. "Of course," he said.

"No one will call you an informant," George said.

I thought that I'd need more time; I wanted to think this through. My life was changing too fast, I was feeling paralyzed, losing control. Another day—maybe two. I said, "I need a little time."

There was some small talk, some grumbled warnings about not confiding in anyone. I did my best to reassure both of them that I was 99 percent sure I'd go along.

"It's the one percent that concerns me," Nick said as we walked to my car. He asked for a promise that I would not speak to anyone at all about any of this.

I had long since convinced myself that I really didn't have to sleep, I didn't have to go home, and I rarely had to tell the truth. I told Nick that I'd tell no one.

Nick Scoppetta kept, it seemed to me by will alone, a look of deep concern on his face. During the past couple of days and nights, it had been a continuous, encouraging, occasionally uncomfortable sensation for me to look at him.

THEY CAME FOR me two nights later.

George Carros and another federal agent arrived at my house. They picked me up in a government car and we drove to the Waldorf-Astoria to meet, they said, a most important man in the Justice Department.

Once before, I had been at the Waldorf-Astoria. In the garage. On that night it was a rallying point for TPF cops guarding the president. As we rolled into that same garage, I felt this eerie, dreamlike sensation, as though all of a sudden I had slipped into a spy movie.

The room was full of faces staring at me, faces that were tight-lipped and unsmiling: Nick, Mike Armstrong (the chief counsel for the Knapp Commission), several agents—and Deputy Attorney General Will Wilson; he explained that he was standing in for Attorney General John Mitchell. The AG, he said, would have loved to be there and meet me, but he was downstairs making a speech.

Wilson was a stylish, elegant man, tall and thin, with an appealing Texas drawl. "We're proud of you, son. I'm here to tell you that your country appreciates what it is you are going to do."

I didn't know what to say; I didn't say anything.

"The people in this room are good, honorable people. They will support you," he said. "You should never think that you are alone. Let me ask you, do you think that Mayor John Lindsay is aware of the extent of corruption that exists in his city?"

"I couldn't say for sure—but it certainly wouldn't surprise me."

"Me either, son, me either."

Imagine how it was. I wanted to reconsider a decision made when I was not thinking too clearly—then someone only steps removed from the president tells me that he's pleased by my decision, that it was a hard, dangerous, and couragous decision, that he would support me, filling me with the kind of pride that comes when you are convinced you are doing honorable work for your country.

It was a spy movie.

That's when I knew that in my life, I hadn't felt anything until I felt the patriotic feeling in that room.

Someone said you could steal Lindsay's shoes and he'd never know it. Someone laughed—and someone else was not pleased that I had overheard all that.

The following day, Nick brought me to meet Henry Ruth. He was the man in charge of New York City's Criminal Justice Coordinating Committee. Ruth was a close personal and professional friend of the police commissioner. When it came to Police Commissioner Patrick Murphy, no one was neutral. There was downright hero worship or absolute contempt. Henry Ruth was a fan.

"The PC wants you to know that you have his support. I want you to know that I personally feel you are a brave man, and I'm proud to meet you."

That did it.

For no reason that I understood—I wept. "I'm no informant," I said. "God, please, don't let the police commissioner think of me as an informant."

Nick put his arm around me; Henry Ruth, for a second, was unnerved. He told me, as best he could, about his feelings, how sad this all was—and how necessary. He was a decent, unassuming, soft-spoken man. He convinced me that he cared about me. I wanted him to be sure and tell the police commissioner that I was not going to betray the department. That we were not going to focus on the police. It would be an investigation into the criminal justice system in New York.

"You needn't worry," he said. "We all understand."

At that moment, Henry Ruth's and Nick's presence, their warm-hearted words, were more real to me as a personification of clemency than of themselves, and I found myself thinking once more that maybe, just maybe, I could be created again, free of my past.

I spent the following day walking the beach of Long Island Sound. It finally settled in my mind that I would, in fact, set out on this marathon of an investigation. I could not have anticipated that I'd be forced to run faster and further, with more reckless abandon, than I ever had. Even so, I would learn, yet again, that no matter how hard or how fast or how far I ran, there was no way I could outrun yesterday.

FOR FIFTEEN MINUTES he told me how much it meant for him to work with me, how many adventures, how many near misses we'd shared, how many laughs and horrors, and how proud he was to have had me as a partner. But no matter how earnest Frank Mandato tried to look, all the time something uneasy showed, letting me see how worried he was.

"That fucking whack-job Durk and that goofball Serpico—how'd you get yourself involved with people like that?" he said.

I told him that I wasn't involved with Durk or Serpico, and then I went on to explain my fears, my dread, how unnatural it was for me to do some of the things we had done. I tried to reassure Frank that I wasn't blaming him; I couldn't blame anyone but myself. I had chosen that life, but I was tired of it—so worn out by it that my brain was twisted, and if I didn't straighten out my head, I'd go insane. I wanted to talk to him about my brother, my father, about my nightmares, about TPF, but I couldn't get to it.

"What are you thinking of doing?" he said. "Christ, I know you. I can't figure out what the hell you think you could do to ease your conscience."

I was embarrassed; I didn't know what to say.

"Just remember that we all have families, and nobody wants to get jammed up. Getting jammed up is horrible."

"I know that," I told him.

"I believe you do, but I also know that you're always looking for a pat on the head, willing to put yourself in situations and places you don't belong for a pat on the head."

"That's not it."

"I'm worried that it might be. Do you think these people know or care about what they're asking you to do?"

"Look," I said, "I had to tell you, I had to let you know what I was thinking."

He stuck out his index finger and his thumb. "Aren't you afraid that someone will walk up behind you and blow your brains all over the fucking street?"

"If you say something, maybe somebody will," I told him.

"Never. It will never be me," he said. "The last person you have to worry about is me."

He made good on his word. Frank Mandato never passed on our conversation. He never betrayed me. My partner.

Torn between the desire to do the undercover job just right and a need to show Nick Scoppetta and all the others in a firsthand way the world narcotics detectives endured in, I went all out. I allowed my body, my car, my telephone to be wired for sound. In all the important ways, I threw caution to the wind.

MUCH OF MY memory of the early stages of the investigation is blurred. I was troubled and anxious beyond belief, and such anxiety blows holes in your memory of things.

My car was sent to Bell & Howell and returned fully wired. A telescopic microphone was built into the ceiling, and a tape recorder concealed in the wall of the trunk. They installed an on-off switch in the seat belt.

The technicians at Bell & Howell were so goddamn clever, they made a belt that I could wear under my trousers next to my skin. It was a soft and supple belt, the underside lined with Velcro. When that belt was pulled tight, it became a second skin. A hand search would never uncover it. A hair-thin wire, with a microphone the size and shape of the tip of a pinky, ran from the belt up my chest to a spot two or three inches below my Adam's apple. That too was taped to my skin, and without a strip search it was undetectable.

After a test or two the belt and wire appeared to work perfectly, *appeared to* being the operative words.

IT WAS LATE in the evening, and I was doing all I could not to draw attention to myself. I was sitting in the backseat of Mikey Coco's brand-spanking-new Mercedes. Mikey was driving, a detective by the name of Bernie Geik was riding shotgun. I sat in the backseat, bent forward at the waist, groping at my stomach, probing for the on-off switch. I couldn't get to it. In order to protect against an unintentional shutdown of the transmitter, the switch had been taped in the on position. I remember how much it hurt, how I was sweating, how much I wanted to scream.

The transmitter sat in an open-ended pocket; it had somehow

turned in the belt, its blunt end pressing up against my stomach. It was hot—and getting hotter all the time, burning me, burning a hole in me.

We'd been riding around for two hours talking about life, the FBI, and how Geik had access to FBI intelligence files and most of the wiretaps the PD was installing. How, for a price, he could be of help to Mikey.

Mikey Coco was an important wiseguy. He was a gruff, affable, and bighearted man. He was also a suspect in seven Mafia killings. Business was business, and in Mikey Coco's world, one thing had nothing to do with the other.

Of all the wiseguys I had ever met, he was the most interesting, the most introspective—and probably the most dangerous.

Geik said, "Something stinks in here."

"This is a brand-new car," Mickey said. "It doesn't even have a hundred miles on it. Someone must have stepped in dog shit or something. That smell is horrible."

My head was spinning—my flesh was burning—I was trying to hold it together, but I knew I couldn't last much longer. It occurred to me that maybe I deserved this, that this burning skin of mine was part of the deal. A bit of the old Catholic penance. I gave myself over to the pain. It was terrible, but it was the only way to go. I had no options.

Mikey pulled the car to the curb, asking us to step out and check our shoes. The stars were out, there was a full moon, Sinatra's "September Song" was coming from Mikey's tape deck—and the smell of burning flesh permeated the air.

"Jesus Christ," Mikey said, "you're burning up." He put his hand against my cheek. "Bobby," he said, "you have a helluva fever."

I was in such a state of agitation that I could barely stand still. "Get me back to my car. I feel terrible," I told him.

In the men's room of the Baychester Diner, I removed that belt in a slow, painful, and torturous way; a portion of my skin clung to the transmitter. I stared at that piece of equipment that held a piece of me, thinking that simply surviving this night was blessing enough, something of an omen. The federal agents that were supposed to back me up had long since faded into the night. They were nowhere to be found. That too was an omen.

I came to terms with the fact that I had better get some real cops with me. Get some men who had their shit together—street detectives and street agents, not former IRS inspectors. Carros and the others were earnest, sure they were, but they weren't observant; they lacked imagination. The street was an alien world to them. They were, after all, accountants.

NICK SCOPPETTA'S NORMALLY enthusiastic, optimistic, and supportive cadence had all but disappeared. It was as though, all of sudden, he was embarrassed. His face was pale, the look in his eyes unsure. When he saw my wound, there was shock and dismay. "How could you stand the pain?" he asked me. "I don't know," I told him. I really didn't know.

"They lost you," he said. "You ended up out on your own, and the agents only got part of a recording. That could jeopardize the case."

In the past, Nick had worked investigations using detectives from the Manhattan district attorney's squad, good investigators and top-flight street cops. These federal men were different. They were white-collar investigators, men who had a habit of hesitating; all the time afraid they'd somehow jeopardize the case if they got too close. Such habits, I told Nick, could jeopardize me.

We needed field agents, real cops, I told him. I mentioned the name of a DEA agent I'd bumped into in Brooklyn by the name of Lee Volmer. Lee was a Texan; he'd once been a Houston cop, a street guy, and he could be trusted. "And," I said, "I'd love to have Aaron Mazen."

Nick felt that because Mazen was a detective captain, a company man, he might be perfectly honest, but there was no way he could be trusted to keep this investigation confidential. I argued that point, but Nick wouldn't hear of it. He overruled me.

So for the time being, we kept things as they were. Nick went about setting up an office and began coordinating his plans with an assistant U.S. attorney, a man by the name of Michael Shaw.

Because I could not be seen with Nick, or near Nick's office, we held our strategy meetings at Mike Shaw's Brooklyn Heights apartment on Willow Street.

Edward Michael Shaw, the AUSA in charge of the official corruption unit of the Southern District of New York, was thirty-five years old, Harvard educated, with thick, prematurely graying hair, thin and six feet five inches tall, a good-looking man who listened more than he spoke. When he talked, his words were thought out and self-assured. A very impressive guy.

While Nick and Mike discussed potential areas for the investigation, I studied Mike Shaw, wondering who he was, trying to figure what sort of world he lived in. Mike was so unconnected to me, so different from anyone that I had ever known, I couldn't help but wonder if a man like that could have any understanding of me at all.

At times Mike seemed to have the solemn personality of an Episcopalian minister. Mostly he had the air of someone who was resolute and absolutely forthright.

Listening to him and Nick, I discovered a newfound respect for the legal profession. These were truly dedicated men, men who were surprisingly similar in their intolerance of any form of corruption, no matter what the reason. They saw themselves as the operative definitions of honesty and fair play.

So different were they from the local DAs and defense attorneys I'd dealt with that they were unrecognizable as members of the same profession. Sitting on the sofa in Mike's apartment, I'd ask myself, *What would these two men think if they knew my whole history?* Could it be that I'd waited too long to try and turn my life around? I had a notion that probably I had. Then I'd tell myself, *These men are decent, kind, and thoughtful people; surely they would understand.* It was early in the investigation, and it was already starting to get very complicated.

I WAS REASSIGNED to the SIU and did my best to stay away from my old partners and friends. In the evenings, I would sit together with Nick and Mike as they determined what we should do next. Soon the early enthusiasm I had felt for the investigation was replaced with a kind of what-have-you-done? sensation. The understanding took hold of how relentless and uncompromising an internal inquiry could be.

I had not told the truth about the extent of my prior misconduct. That could be a problem; I knew that someday that could be a very serious problem.

The concept of lying to protect others, and myself as well, was complicated. I had to think harder, and the harder I thought, the more I persuaded myself to follow my own conscience. I'd do what I thought was right—and what I thought was right was to keep quiet.

As the days wore on, I found no peace or pleasure in the investigation. Although I can't be certain, I believe that I was on the edge of real depression. Again I was finding it hard to sleep, waking in the middle of the night in a sweating panic.

During the day, in the SIU office, I'd find myself staring at the men working at their desks, feeling a burning sensation in my chest, my stomach in knots, this awful guilt eating at me.

I could not shake feeling that Frank was right. I was a foolish and hopeless person, always putting myself in places and situations where I didn't belong. Always searching for that pat on the head. At night, in bed, I'd lie awake wondering why I continued to do the things I did.

I had been assigned two new partners, Jim Sheridan and Bill Hubert, and a sergeant by the name of Norm Cohen. Immediately I was certain that all three would be future actors in my recurring nightmares.

Both Sheridan and Hubert had worked in the Harlem narcotics group. They had recently been promoted to the SIU. Both were dedicated and hard-nosed detectives who had brought down a good number of street dealers. Now they were in the big leagues—and a bit out of their depth.

"No more rooftops," I told them. "No more backyards and basements, no more sick junkies. Here we go after the major players."

"I'm told you work guineas," Sheridan said with a great big smile and the broadest, deepest brogue I'd ever heard.

"You got it," I told him.

"I'm gonna like the SIU," he said. "Son," he told me, "I'm ready to kick some ass."

Jesus, Jesus, Jesus, I thought, *an Irish soldier boy. God help me, I'm going to love this guy.*

Bill Hubert was a New York City police detective, but the city was not his home. He lived a schizophrenic life, his days spent among the streams, farms, hills, and valleys of upper Westchester County. An outdoorsman, he fished for trout and hunted wild turkey and white-tailed deer. Nights he spent fighting the drug war in upper Manhattan—stalking drug dealers. This required some serious commuting, but no matter. When it was time to work, Bill got into his pickup and headed south into the city. A little Hank Williams on his tape deck, denim jeans and jacket, a flannel shirt; plain and simple—which was how he liked things.

A few days after we'd teamed up, I asked the Baron for some help. He came up with a target in the Bronx.

"Italian guy?" I asked him.

"They're the people with the dope," he told me.

We began surveillance of a midlevel heroin dealer named Joseph Andretta. Using SIU tools of the trade, we tapped his phone. Never mind that it was an illegal wiretap, it was the way it was done, which made neither Nick nor Mike happy and kicked off much debate and consternation in the offices of the Southern District.

I explained that taking drugs and a connection off the street was the chief measure of success in the SIU. Violating some dope dealer's civil rights meant nothing, making the collar everything.

If this investigation was to have any chance at success, it was essential that I behave precisely the way everyone else did.

to make a move—to order a package of drugs.

My partners wanted to be my newest best friends. Before I knew it, a familiar, inescapable energy took over. They invited me to join them for dinner, they wanted me to meet their families, they telephoned me all the time at home, asking how I was doing, wondering why I seemed so distant. Both of them tried to ripen a friendship that for my sanity, I needed to let die on the vine. I hadn't taken any of this into consideration. Partners were partners—old and new, that relationship was special. It was torture.

I constantly lied to them, saying that I had other plans, things I had to do. And that was true. I had meetings—tactics sessions with Nick and Mike.

Mike had given me a target, a corrupt bail bondsman (talk about a tautology), a man the Southern District was interested in. I had to find the time to probe in that direction. There were only so many hours in the day—my candle was flaming at both ends.

Our SIU team began moving on the Andretta case.

The Baron, as usual, was right on target. Andretta was a midlevel dealer; more precisely, he was a gofer for a Mafia associate by the name of Joseph Marchese. I told the Baron to make a move on Andretta; he telephoned him ordering an eighth of a kilo of heroin. Andretta then telephoned Marchese and set up a meet.

"You mean it's going to be that easy?" Hubert said.

"Well, we have to nail them with the package, and that's never easy."

It went down like clockwork.

Andretta showed up with his bodyguard. Marchese was waiting with the heroin. Sergeant Cohen and Bill jumped Marchese. Sheridan and I grabbed Andretta and his guard. After cuffing Andretta, I looked up, I spotted Marchese, a rough, thick-necked and brutish guy, swinging Cohen around as though the sergeant were a rag doll.

When I ran across the street to lend a hand, Cohen called out to me. "It's all right," he shouted. "This guy's okay, he just doesn't want to go into the station house."

"Well that's just too bad, isn't it."

When all of us rolled into the squad room of the Bronx station house, Sergeant Cohen walked off, making a move of his own, a little song and dance, whispering with Marchese.

Sheridan and Hubert were beside themselves with glee. They were riotous and irreverent; they loved this. Both men had worked years in Harlem, kicking in hundreds of street-level dealers' doors. Now, after only a couple of weeks in the SIU, they had collard the man who symbolized to them all that Harlem misery.

Cohen took my arm, led me off, and told me that Marchese had offered him money to be set free. "Listen," he said, "I'd like to go for it, but I'm not so sure about this Hubert character. And I'm not so sure about you."

"Really?" I said. "Well then let's forget it."

Sheridan came over and joined us, asking what was going on, and I told him he knew what was going on. "This guy, man," Sheridan said, "this guy has plenty of money."

Then Marchese came by. He told us that he had to get out of the station house. He owed people in this precinct money, and he wanted out of there. He offered us four thousand dollars.

"Sold," Cohen said.

Bill Hubert, when he spoke, spoke with the authority of a man who stood for certain values. I listened to him, hearing the pain in his voice. "What are we going to do?" he said. "Let the connection go and collar the gofers? Is that what you want to do?"

"He's a businessman," Cohen said. "Hell, the man owns a taxicab company in Yonkers."

"That's bullshit," Hubert told him.

"We're cutting him loose," Cohen told him.

Hubert's head was down, his chin resting on his breastbone, his eyes staring at the floor.

"You don't belong in the SIU," Cohen said then. "You should be back in Harlem, chasing niggers over rooftops."

Hubert turned to me—his eyes were glassy, pleading with me.

"Bill, I can't help you here," I told him. "This has to be your decision. But whatever you say, I'll back you up."

Silence from him.

"You want to collar this guy," I said, "let's do it. If you want to go along with the sergeant, that's okay with me too."

"I hate this," he said. "This is the best collar I've ever made—and we're going to cut the bum loose. I don't believe it. Bob," he whispered, "I'll do whatever you do, just don't make me talk to that fucking sergeant, or I tell ya, I'll knock him on his ass."

After a long and painful pause, he said, "What do you think I should do?"

"Don't ask me that," I told him.

"Christ, if I don't go along, he'll have me back in the field group and out of SIU. Then it's back to uniform. What choice do I have?"

I'd expected something like this. Still, I never anticipated what a horror it would be to go through it. I had an important story, the tale of how a young, honest cop can get turned around. Except now I had to make the case. A case that in all fairness should not be made.

How does a sincere young cop like Bill Hubert, a guy who just wants to get along, find the strength to stand up under the relentless pressure from a superior officer, a man whose every word sounds like a threat?

And what was my role in all this?

I decided not to interfere; for the time being, I'd let things take their natural course.

So I went with Marchese to pick up the money. We rode in my car, and the tapes whirled, and our conversation was recorded. I couldn't wait to play it for Nick.

Nick studied me, in his sweater and slacks, his chin resting on his fist. A strange thing to watch, hardly any response at all. Finally a knowing nod of the head. I tried to explain, to put into plain words a superior officer's power, the fear of losing a job that you loved, the awful feeling of being lost and frightened.

"But in the end, he took the money," Nick said. "The point is, he had no choice," I told him. He said, "How do you know that?" And I told him, "I'm telling you," and he said, "That's just not good enough."

The next day, I put Bill Hubert in my car and we went for a ride. I threw the switch in the seat belt and the tape rolled.

"How do you feel about what happened yesterday. Tell me, how do you feel?"

"I didn't sleep at all last night," he said. "I've never done anything like this before, and you'd better believe I'll never do it again. I want no part of this shit."

I asked him what he'd like to do. He told me that if it were not for Jim and me, he'd burn Cohen. He'd report him. That's when he said, "I want to get out of this office."

He seemed sad and worn out, there were gloomy bags under his eyes, the look of somebody who hadn't slept. "I love this work," he said. "But not at these prices." Then he told me he had a fantasy of getting transferred to the Intelligence Division. But that was doomed to failure; you needed serious pull to get an assignment there.

I told him to be patient, just be patient. He looked at me as though he wasn't sure what to make of me.

That night I played the tape for Nick. He accused me of arranging an exculpatory conversation. That was not my job.

"C'mon, Nick," I said, "c'mon." "I understand," he told me, "I'll try to be of some help. But don't count on it." Two weeks later, Bill Hubert telephoned me at home. He told me that he'd been transferred to Intelligence. "I don't know how you did it," he said, "but Jesus Christ, Jesus Christ, man, am I happy."

Nick said he had nothing to do with it. I didn't believe him. But no matter, Bill Hubert was safe, and another detective joined our team.

Stanley Glazer, an ex-PMD cop, slick and smooth and 100 percent a money guy. He was a man with a winning and friendly personality. He had shoulder-length hair and the habit of smoking cigarette after cigarette, using a spiffy teak cigarette holder, allowing his ash to grow and grow. One time his ash fell into a cup of Jim Sheridan's coffee. It caused the big Irishman to steam up, his nostrils flaring. He told Stanley that he was fucking with his shit, explained that he would not have his shit fucked with.

A thing developed between these two disparate men, and I was obliged to become the shock absorber. Stanley believed that Jim was not very smart but was very dangerous. Stanley's smooth and sleek style was a huge irritant to Jim. I expected that at any moment the big Irishman would lose it and toss old Stanley out the SIU office window.

Working together, we made some interesting cases. There was the Cuban ex-CIA operative selling a kilo of morphine base. That ended in a chase in the Lincoln Tunnel and Jim firing a shot. Then there was the dawn raid of a heroin packaging plant on Atlantic Avenue in Brooklyn, half a dozen detectives standing on the street, a newly assigned lieutenant, Jim, Stanley, and me.

I tried the street-level door. It was locked, locked and reinforced. That door was not opening.

I suggested that we go to the local firehouse and borrow one of their door jacks. Jim Sheridan told everyone to step aside. Jim was one big strong guy. I expected that he'd try to shoulder the door. I told him it was impossible. I'd felt the door and knew from experience that King Kong could not budge that type of steel door.

"Everybody step back," Jim said with the quiet confidence of a man who had maintained a mystical life. He drew his pistol, took careful aim, and fired a shot at the door's lock. Everyone dove for cover.

"In the movies," I yelled. "Jim, that only works in the movies."

The new lieutenant was not amused, but everyone else thought it was a helluva way to start the day. When Jim cocked his gun the second time, we all grabbed him, saying, "Easy does it, big guy, easy does it." It seemed like a good idea.

During this time, I regarded every day I got through with my sanity intact as a plus. Incredibly, I managed to do a lot of work. SIU cases and the corruption investigation moved into high gear.

There was a big-money fixer lawyer by the name of Ben Ciola in the Bronx, and he had two clients, a pair of brothers who were Mafia wannabes; they owned and operated a private carting company.

Early in the morning, not much past daybreak, the brothers picked up garbage in and around the Hunts Point Market. As the day wore on they sold junk in the form of heroin.

I'd arrested them. Their lawyer, Ciola, offered me sixty thousand dollars to change my testimony. It was easy enough; or so it seemed.

I was careless. I hadn't realized that there was a need for caution with the brothers. One day, like a pair of professional dancers, they took hold of me and turned me around, searching me. Four hands fluttering, moving up my legs and around my back, they smiled while they did it, but they were deadly serious.

I was wearing the wire, and when they ran their hands over the microphone they felt it and asked what it was. I brought out my religious medal; they stared at the medal for a moment studying it. They nodded—and went no further.

The years I'd worked undercover buying dope, I always had the belief that I could manage most situations. I thought it was all in the head—the ability to control your fear. I considered myself skilled at that sort of thing. Lucky was what I was, and luck can always run out.

The Knapp Commission hearings were in full swing. Their shocking disclosures of widespread police corruption filled the headlines. They were a daily presence on local and national TV. It raised the level of paranoia in the city.

I was so self-absorbed that I didn't realize just how tense and suspicious everyone was.

One night, after dinner at Mike Shaw's apartment, Mike showed me a folder with two photos in it. One photo was of a bail bondsman and the other of a private detective who worked for the bondsman. These brothers in arms were at the center of a highly organized case-fixing scam in the Manhattan criminal and supreme courts. The government had made a subornation of perjury case against them. It was a weak case, with little chance of success—the operation was still going strong.

From the outset, my aim was to expose the extent of corruption that existed around the police, making their world a foul place, drawing them in, causing many of them to behave in ways that were foreign to their nature.

Up to this point in the investigation, there had been no single thing I could point to, no particular case that would clearly demonstrate the extent of it all. Suddenly, here it was.

I had heard the rumors about this particular crew. You made an important case in Manhattan, and someone would contact you, asking if you wanted to sell it.

The talk was that they were adept at getting to DAs, to lawyers and judges. It was said that they could fix any case at the drop of a hat. I could go after them, but there was a problem, a serious problem: their point man was a police detective.

As I saw it, there was no need for our investigation to focus on the police. The Knapp Commission, Serpico, and Durk were doing that. Still, as our own investigation progressed, the widening distance between what I had told myself and the reality kept growing— slightly at first, then alarmingly, reaching crisis proportions.

I asked around about the detective, about the bail bondsman, about the private investigator. Everyone I spoke to, in and out of the SIU, warned that this crew was treacherous. They saw the Manhattan Criminal Court building as a bank, and they were there to make steady withdrawals. They knew all the tricks.

The detective's name was Lamatina, and the private investigator was DeStefano. They were both named Nick. The bondsmen were using the detective as a bird dog. He was their hook into the police department.

Meetings were arranged with the two Nicks.

At first they were uneasy, worried after hearing all the buzz about turncoat cops and informants coming out of the Knapp Commission hearings.

Undercover work is the art of controlling scenarios; so I took care not to push, allowing them to ask all the questions. I made sure I didn't have all the answer, only a willingness to be of help.

I told them that I had a connection in the federal courthouse, someone who would sell confidential information. All of a sudden the two of them were as thrilled as a pair of minks in heat.

Mike Shaw thought my idea was imaginative, but not very funny.

Lamatina took on the tedious job of searching me, which made perfect sense from the two Nicks' point of view. These were dangerous times, and it was wise to trust no one. Sometimes Lamatina would do the job; other times he'd let the search slide. Sometimes I wore a wire, sometimes I didn't, a decision I made for no good reason other than some Zen-like reflection.

One night, Lamatina pulled me into the men's room of an Italian resturant. He apologized, explaining that it was something he had promised the others he would do. Actually, Lamatina was a sweet and gentle guy—another cop who had somehow lost his way. He grabbed my ass and felt my chest. I told him to cut it out, and he did. I was wearing a wire, and that was an incredibly close call.

To make a show of their expertise and extensive clout, both men boasted that they had lawyers, judges, and DAs in their pocket. They were arrogant and proud, telling me that their record of success spoke for itself. At one early meeting, they outlined a case they had been working on for quite some time.

A major drug dealer had been arrested with a sizable amount of cocaine. He was willing to pay big money not to do jail time. If I registered him as an informant and gave him credit for cases he had nothing to with, he wouldn't go to jail. We could all make a lot of money.

They had done this sort of thing many times before, and it had always been successful. The drug dealer's lawyer and the DA were prepared to go along, they said. "We have a judge too," they told me.

I doubted that—and wasn't all that convinced about the DA. I figured if they had a DA and a judge on their payroll, why would they need me? They said that they needed someone active, somebody who made important drug cases, to register their guy as an informant. I would then give him credit for four or five arrests—tell his lawyer and the DA about his assistance. The DA would inform the judge, our boy gets a suspended sentence, and he walks away a free man.

Registered informants who had proved their value and had been arrested generally walked away from their cases. It was all part of the give and take, a cop-shop game.

The entire situation had been banging around for over a year. The drug dealer was becoming impatient; the Nicks were hot to move on it.

"Why not," I said. "Let's do it."

Wired, I met with the drug dealer and his lawyer. They backed the Nicks' story, even going so far as implicating a DA. When I spoke to the DA, he told me, "I would never get involved in anything that took this long to get done."

Nick and Mike were ecstatic. We were scoring big-time: drug dealers, lawyers, DAs, maybe even a judge. If I could manage this, I could handle the next thing, and the next thing was major. The most important target yet. Another meeting was arranged with the two Nicks.

There was something in the air on that muggy Friday afternoon in July, something out of the ordinary, and if I had been paying attention, it would have put me instantly on my guard. But I wasn't.

As soon as I got to the corner of Grand and Elizabeth Streets in Little Italy, I saw panic on Nick Lamatina's face. The other Nick was there too; he was wide-eyed and pissed off, a look that said, You fuck, you prick, I'm going to kill you.

I was wired and didn't have my gun with me. Sometimes I carried my gun and sometimes I didn't. Don't ask, I don't know.

Straight away, Lamatina began searching me; the other Nick made it clear that he was holding a gun in his pocket. The neighborhood street was jam-packed, but in those days such Little Italy encounters were not all that unusual.

Nervous and sweating onlookers merely averted their heads. New York City. "Where's your gun?" Lamatina barked.

I'd left my gun in the trunk of my car—another virtuoso move.

Neither of the Nicks believed the gun-in-the-trunk-of-the-car story. They had heard that I'd been arrested and my gun had been taken from me. That I was cooperating with the Knapp Commission. All this they had been told by a friend in the Bronx district attorney's office. Their source, they said, had inside information. He warned that a detective with the first initial B would be testifying at open hearings the following day.

"B is you," DeStefano said. "You're Bob, you're B, and we're gonna fucking kill you."

"What? You're crazy."

I thought, *Oh, fuck, they are crazy.* Both of them were grabbing onto me, pushing me, shouting, wild reckless eyes staring at me.

Things got worse. They began dragging me along the street, heading for, I assumed, one of the blocks where there were deserted lofts. These two guys were determined to put my lights out.

"Get your hands off me, Nick," I said. "What the fuck is wrong with you two?"

I was wearing the wire. I figured they were so out of control that if they managed to get me to a place where they could search, they'd find it. That would be bad, oh yeah—that would be very bad.

"Hey, cut it out, you fucking guys, let go of me." I yelled, screamed, whined. I didn't think I was whining. I'd never whine. But later, when I replayed the tape, it was a whine all right.

Then I spotted him—he was standing across the street with a container of coffee in his hand, watching us as I watched him. At first he appeared uninterested, calm, and about ready to walk off. Then he tilted his head to get a better look, his eyes squinting. He seemed curious and puzzled.

"See that guy?" I said. "That guy across the street. Go and talk to him—he'll vouch for me."

I knew the extent of fear and respect Sonny Red commanded all over Little Italy, throughout the wiseguy world for that matter.

They both turned to look, Lamatina saying, "Who's that? I don't know him."

The other Nick said, "That's Sonny Red. You know him?"

"He'll vouch for me," I said.

Lamatina held me by the arm, while DeStefano ran across the street. After a very short conversation with Sonny Red, he hurried back to us, head down, his hands in his pockets, making up his mind.

Sonny Red smiled at me, and then he waved his hand.

"What did he say?" Lamatina asked.

"I said, 'We think Bobby is a rat, and we're gonna clip him.' He said, 'If he's a rat, you should clip him.' Then he said, 'You'd better be right, because he's a friend of mine.' "

"So?" Lamatina said.

"So, you know who that guy is? He said Bobby is a friend of his, a friend of his. No way I'm fucking with that guy, no way. I'll take my chances on Bobby here."

Alphonse "Sonny Red" Indelicato, one of the top Mafia leaders in New York City, in some people's eyes perceived as a villain, in the film *Donnie Brasco* portrayed as a very evil man. In one significant moment of my life, he was a knight in shining armor.

The federal agents who were backing me up and theoretically protecting me were again nowhere to be found. A police officer and a bail bondsman—two officers of the court—wanted to kill me. There was unquestionably a paradox there, some serious irony.

After a while, the two Nicks were smiling; everyone felt great relief. I had no time to consider the paradox or the irony, or even thank Sonny Red. I was late again for a meeting at the SIU office.

I telephoned from a street pay phone and spoke to Jim Sheridan. I told him in a general way what had happened. He told me to wait where I was, he'd be right there—he was bringing other detectives with him.

"We'll find those creep bastards," he said. "We'll find them and kick their guinea asses."

"It's okay, Jim," I said. "I'm okay. I'll talk to you later."

I was not okay, I was anything but okay. Hearing Jim's voice, that great brogue, his genuine concern—I was embarrassed, in a funk of gloom, struggling to understand what in the hell I was doing. I felt heartsick and guilty, like the worst sort of human being. I was a fraud and a phony, a betrayer.

When I hung up the telephone, I tried lighting a cigarette, tried smiling. I was thinking that turning one's life around was much more easily said than done.

Was it possible? Sure it was possible, but when it was achieved at the expense of others, you ended up an absolute cretin. I needed to talk to Nick and Mike.

That night, after some truly painful and tense conversation at Mike's apartment, I learned a lot more about the men who were behind the titles. Set aside their personal history and social class, these were essentially two very decent guys. And the extent to which they understood my situation—my personal agony—proved it.

I could see it in their eyes. Their voices took on new tones of commitment, trepidation, and understanding. I was profoundly impressed, and after a while I knew that no matter what, I had to see this investigation through to the end.

I WENT ON making SIU and corruption cases. My backups and support system changed. Bernie McCrossen, a young, bright, Bronx Irish street cop, came on board. He made an impression with his quick-witted ability to get close to me in the street. Vinny Murano, a burly knock-around patrol cop from Queens and my Long Island neighbor, joined us. And there was Lee Volmer, the DEA agent and ex-Houston cop; with a curt nod and advice to be careful of the former IRS inspectors, he too was attached to the team.

It was a relief. I felt as though I had partners now, real cops watching my back. There was at last a sense of camaraderie—and commitment.

I reconnected with the two Nicks, and they introduced me to a corrupt criminal defense lawyer. He was one of the most active narcotics lawyers in the city. Smart, an aggressive defender of top drug dealers. For years he had been outfoxing the government, often with perjured alibi testimony arranged by Nick DeStefano and others.

His name was Edmund Rosner. He was a superstar, the foremost thorn in the government's side, making a travesty of the law, of judicial procedure, and tweaking the noses of the U.S. attorneys.

In court, Rosner was loud and arrogant. He strutted his stuff.

Testimony was altered, witnesses disappeared, and drug dealers paid him big money.

He delivered acquittals.

When we met, I found Rosner guarded and soft-spoken, vain, with a deep and passionate sense of self-righteousness. He had a profound hatred of the government.

Mike Shaw told me that if nothing else happened in our investigation, nothing other than making a genuine, prosecutable federal case against Eddie Rosner, we would have won the day.

We made the case.

Rosner paid money to get access to secret grand jury testimony. Making the case was not all that difficult. But then I knew nothing about real power and money. Knew nothing about the extent of Rosner's hatred of the government. Nothing about the potent forces willing to take his side.

I never bothered to think about it. I saw the Rosner case as just another case against another corrupt lawyer. I had no clue what a trial against the likes of Eddie Rosner would mean for me personally. I'm sure that Nick Scoppetta and Mike Shaw didn't think too much about it either.

The fabric of each case was essentially the same: conversation, as much recorded as possible, the transfer of money, or a promise of money to be paid. With Rosner, we had all the elements. I assumed we had a very strong case. And then it was time to move on. Other things were happening, other cases to be made. And I was going to do everything possible within the margins of my ability to get them done.

Except what I was doing was wrong, ethically and personally, just wrong. The investigation itself was vital and long overdue. It was as clear to me as it was to everyone else involved that the back of corruption in New York City could not be broken with one investigation. Still, ours certainly would get everyone's attention.

That was good.

The fact that I had hidden the extent of my own misconduct was wrong. I didn't see it at the time—I assumed that since I had volunteered, since no one had ever caught me doing anything wrong, then I couldn't be expected to admit such things. Who in their right mind would? I believed that I could protect my partners and at the same time keep secret my own history. But I was wrong about that too.

In uniform, and then again in the Narcotics Bureau, I had testified in hundreds of cases, and such questions were never asked.

My experiences were limited to the state court; I'd find federal court a whole new ball game. I had convinced myself that I was a special case. I was willing to put my life on the line to prove that the whole system was rotten. That too was wrong.

There were many good and honorable people in the system—people like Nick and Mike and many others. The truth was, I had never come across them.

I suppose I always knew that taking on the undercover investigation was just looking for trouble. Nevertheless, in the bizarre playground that was my mind, there had always been something absolute and unchanging, and that was the belief that somehow I'd always survive. But that was wrong too.

Before long trouble would come, and it would find me, and it would be more—much more—than I could handle.

HE HAD BEEN sitting in a chair at Mike Shaw's apartment listening to a conversation between Mike, Nick, and me. He sat there staring at me, studying me, and making me extremely nervous. I wondered just who this character was and what his role was in all this.

He was young—too young to be very important. Mike told me he was a rising star in the U.S. Attorney's Office, maybe the brightest assistant in the office, someone that I was bound to connect with. Unlike some of the others, he could relate to me—understand me. He was, after all, an Italian American from Brooklyn.

His name was Rudy Giuliani, and after we talked a bit, I found him friendly and open. He had a great warm smile. Rudy explained how important the Rosner case was, that what we were doing would make it possible for the criminal justice system to do what it was designed to do. Offer justice.

Even now, when I think back on it, I remember his face so full of youthful exuberance. He was, in fact, four years younger than I was and he had plenty of hair.

On that day, he seemed disheveled—he looked tired and not terribly comfortable at Mike's apartment. He told me that when the covert work of this investigation had run its course, the cases would need to be prepared for trial. He'd be there, along with other assistant U.S. attorneys. He said we'd have one helluva time.

All the while I'm thinking, *Will Mike be there—will Nick?* He shook my hand; he had a firm and confident grip.

"We'll have plenty of work to do," he said. He seemed so sure of himself; I couldn't help but like him.

Days, weeks, and months went by. I was wearing thin. Each new case had an element that would turn my stomach to knots. I was getting numb, and my luck was starting to run out.

ONE AFTERNOON GEORGE Carros and his supervisor from the Drug Enforcement Administration, a guy named Tom Taylor, brought me to an apartment on the Upper West Side of Manhattan. They told me it was Taylor's brother's apartment.

Tom Taylor, like Carros, had been an IRS inspector. He liked to boast that once he had been a New York City cop. "It took me nine years, but I got a college education. All thanks to the NYPD. Then I went to the IRS."

The apartment was dark and dull; Taylor smelled of drink. I didn't like him very much. In the IRS, and now in the DEA, he had been an internal investigator, working corrupt agents.

"We'd like you to tell the U.S. attorneys that you no longer want to work for them. It's not natural; it's not their job to run an investigation. They prosecute the cases, they don't investigate them. Tell them you want to report to us," Taylor told me.

He was baffled and confused by my behavior. I seemed to like answering to Mike Shaw and Nick Scoppetta; they weren't cops, they weren't agents.

"We need you to get with the program," he said. "You tell the attorneys that you'll only report to us. We'll make them turn over the investigation. Hell, we're putting up all the money. We're using our agents to back you up, and when it's over, the U.S. attorney will get all the credit."

His eyes were wide; there was anger there, and resentment too. I looked at Carros. He shrugged.

"Will you do it?" Taylor asked.

When I told him how I felt about the prosecutors, Nick and Mike and Rudy, I was met with stony silence or mirthful derision.

"We'll be better friends than they'll be," he said.

I said. "I'll think about it."

I didn't have to think about it. Carros was a decent guy; he did his job as best he could and went home. Taylor was treacherous—a ruthless self-promoter. He knew nothing about the cases we'd made, nothing about what we were trying to accomplish. He was a man totally devoid of charm and compassion, a man with few scruples and fewer friends. No one you'd want to root for.

The way I looked at him, the way I shook my head, the way I smiled—all on its own, my smile could do strange things. I understood very well that something terrible had happened that afternoon. I had created for myself a powerful enemy.

All during the following weekend, Taylor phoned me two or three times a day, asking if I'd given more thought to his suggestion. I repeated that I was happy with the way things had been progressing. Finally he sighed and said, "Well it's your decision. I hope you'll be happy with it."

I REMEMBER A Saturday morning, along the roadside brilliant beds of blue, yellow, and red tulips, pockets of azalea and rhododendron in full bloom that seemed to go on and on and on, in the air the serene perfume of a southern spring.

I was in Washington, D.C., to meet a man named Andrew Tartiglino—the man in charge of the DEA's inspection and intelligence services.

I had been the lead undercover for almost two years. The investigation had gone on with increasing intensity, and I had grown weary. There was a coldness inside of me. I wasn't myself—didn't remember when I had been myself, I had managed to get so many things wrong. I felt hollow and vacant. My life was never-ending intrigue and subterfuge. I was living a LeCarré novel, and as the pages turned, the light at the end of the tunnel was, in fact, that oncoming train.

Andrew Tartiglino was a man who smiled often, a wide, gracious sort of smile, but his eyes showed neither mirth nor self-consciousness nor uneasiness. It was the kind of esoteric smile that I had seen on the faces of many men who were in charge of intelligence and internal affairs units. The puppeteers, they all had that kind of chilly, gloomy smile that seemed to say, "I know what you're up to. You can't fool me, I've seen it all."

When Tartiglino was angry, making his point, there was nothing you could say or do but curl up and try to make yourself small. If you had a point of your own, there was nothing you could say or do to change his mind, nothing at all.

Rumor had it, Tartiglino made his reputation by traveling to France to arrest his best friend, an agent who the DEA believed had gone bad. To those who knew him, Tartiglino was the best there was, the Michael Jordan of internal investigations, a Machiavelli of political intrigue.

On that morning, he greeted me at his office door and seemed exuberant, going on about the investigation and how it was turning into something special—far more special than any of us had thought possible. He had a spacious office with sofas, flags, and plaques on the wall, telephones and video connections to every city on earth.

When I think of him quickly, I see a not very tall, stocky man, powerfully built, with a soft voice. I had the strangest kind of feeling in his company, looking at him and thinking about how much power he wielded. He was a man who was uncompromising in his determination to root out all corruption.

People said he was without pity, cold as ice, a man without a heart. The fact is he had an impossible job. Tartiglino was responsible for safeguarding the integrity of America's Drug Enforcement Administration.

No small task.

His offbeat ideas and absolute single-mindness alarmed me, but I couldn't help but admire him.

That day, he set about telling me how impressed he was at what I had accomplished, how pleased and proud he was of me. Then he said, "I think you're fucking around."

At most of my undercover meetings I'd wear a wire, and many of the recent recordings had been unintelligible. "You sound like Donald Duck," he told me. "You know what I think? I think, subconsciously, you're trying to protect people by running your hand across the microphone."

He was smiling.

I shook my head.

"Have you ever been on the box?" he said.

For a long time I had realized how insanely dangerous this investigation could be, seen the possibility of my ending up one of the targets. By that point, my own personal motives for getting involved were inconsequential. The investigation had taken on a life of its own. There were powerful forces at play.

"A lie detector test? I'll take one if you like."

Tartiglino smiled again.

"Look," he said, "I understand. Two hundred meetings more or less, close calls and scary moments—who wouldn't understand. You were bound to get burned out."

That's when he told me he was going to bring someone in to help me. "The best undercover agent in the world." Not the best in New York or L.A., or even Europe, for that matter—the best in the world.

Well, they were going to have to show me. "Let's see what you got," I told him. He smiled and wagged his head. "I'm looking forward to you two meeting," he said.

"Me too," I told him.

HIS NAME WAS Santo Barrio. We called him Sandy. And he was the most dazzling undercover agent I ever ran into.

He spoke four languages—French, Italian, Spanish, and English—and had the slightest trace of an accent. He had the streamlined look of a movie star—European shirts, slacks, shoes, dark eyes, always suntanned, with a classic Roman face. Sandy was gregarious and confident, and for several months we worked well together. I was extremely impressed.

Sandy Barrio and I discussed many things—always about work, "a mission," he called it, never about me, never about him, either directly or obliquely. On those rare occasions when conversation about his or my personal life arose, he would carefully turn the conversation toward other subjects. Or he would simply grow silent and wait for the mood to change.

Sometimes I noticed a real chill between us, and I couldn't figure out what it could be. I would catch him staring at me, and wonder what he was thinking.

Then one night, in a restaurant about two blocks from the

Federal Building in lower Manhattan, Sandy said he didn't understand cops like me. His father was a cop in Italy. As for himself, he had been an agent of one form or other all his adult life. "Look," he said, "I like you—but you scare me. You're too close to the street. I'll work with you, but I don't want to be your friend. Okay?" He seemed uncomfortable.

I shrugged my shoulders—my feelings were hurt and I didn't know what to say.

"Tartiglino thinks you're real good," he said, "and maybe, when this is all over, you'll come with us. But as far as I'm concerned, there's the good guys and the bad guys, no gray area in between. Somehow, it seems to me, you've been dancing in the gray area way too long."

I appreciated his candor. He was being honest, but too much honesty can be painful and grating.

"You worked in Paris," I told him. "In London, Vegas, Toronto, and Rome. I worked the streets of East Harlem, the South Bronx, Brooklyn—walk in my shoes for a while, smartass."

There was a long pause before I told him that I liked him too. But if he was judging me, he could go fuck himself.

I remember how he smiled, but his manner didn't carry it off. We paid the bill and left the restaurant.

THE PLAN WAS simple. The government would arrange for Sandy to be arrested in Queens for possession of a gun. He would then dive into the vortex of fixers and intrigue, that sunlit world full of shady people in Queens County, and try to pay his way through the system.

Everyone was apprehensive, unsure how Sandy would make out. I had no misgivings. I'd seen Sandy and Queens County in action. I was convinced he'd be successful.

Word was leaked that Sandy was an organized crime figure—a wiseguy with plenty of money, and criminal operations in both Detroit and Las Vegas. By the time his gun case got to the grand jury, Sandy was paying a fixer lawyer, who in turn paid the assistant district attorney. It was the ADA in charge of the grand jury.

It was one helluva case. It lifted the investigation, gave it the potential of moving into important areas. This particular assistant DA, everyone thought, would cooperate. If he did, his information would be a fast track to the power brokers—the kings of corruption in New York City.

Then a time was set for Sandy to meet Sergeant Perazzo from the Brooklyn district attorney's office. It was the same sergeant who had been so jubilant when Serpico had been shot. The same sergeant who ceaselessly opened his desk drawer, asking me for money.

Perazzo loved wiseguys; he especially loved Sandy—and Sandy's money. He opened his drawer and made Sandy feel welcome. Sandy ate guys like him for breakfast.

Around that time the government brought in another undercover agent, a man we came to know as Carlo Dondolo, although that was probably not his name.

Dondolo was not an agent; he was a paid informant. An Italian national, he told me that he ran a nightclub in Beirut, Lebanon. Dondolo boasted that he moved drugs, big-time drugs. His conversation was always tinged with ridicule and hostility; he had a dark heart—an evil sprit.

Sandy knew Dondolo. He told me he had done some work with him in Europe. He said that Dondolo was a snake.

The idea was to send Carlo Dondolo through the Manhattan courts. Like Sandy, he would be arrested and then try to buy his way to freedom.

SANDY TELEPHONED PERAZZO and let him know that an international drug dealer had checked into the Americana Hotel. The dealer's name was Carlo Dondolo. Dondolo, he told him, was carrying a sample of a multi-kilo shipment of heroin. Dondolo was planning to move the drugs into the United States.

Perazzo needed someone with citywide jurisdiction to capture Dondolo. He picked up his phone and began to dial my number. Someone stopped him and told him to call Joe Nunziata instead.

Evil fate, no other words for it, horrible luck.

Joe grabbed Dondolo at the Americana. He took his passport, which had been stamped in cities like Rome, Marseilles, and Beirut. When he opened Dondolo's phone book he found names and phone numbers of high-level American heroin dealers. He also found an ounce of pure heroin sewed into the lining of Dondolo's suit.

Joe arrested him, but there was a snag. Nunziata no longer worked in the SIU; he was on temporary assignment to a federal and city joint narcotics strike force. Their cases were prosecuted in federal court. Wrong arresting officer, wrong courthouse. It could have ended there—but it didn't.

Dondolo told Joe that he was willing to cooperate and give up major international dealers. Visions of the biggest cases ever must have spun through Joe's head. Joe delivered Dondolo to Washington.

Alone with Andrew Tartiglino, Dondolo told him that although the original scheme had fallen apart, he could make a case against Joe and his partner. He could sense it, he said. "Do it," Tartiglino told him.

Carlo Dondolo was short, stocky, and foul-mouthed. He was a cocky man shrouded in the most vindictive sort of persuasiveness. Not long after his arrest, we gathered at a safe house on Sutton Place in Manhattan. It was an upscale building, a luxurious apartment paid for by the DEA.

The details of who was there are lost in my memory. I do remember Dondolo, Sandy, and several federal agents and NYPD people. We used the apartment for strategy sessions, and one or two of the federal agents slept there. The phone was constantly in use.

That day there was a heated conversation about what Dondolo's objective was. By my lights, it was not the two detectives.

"I can do it," he said. "These guys are cheap low-life thieves."

"That's not true," I told him, "and that's not your job."

"Your friend," he said, "I understand." He smiled.

"Look," I said, "Nunziata is not going to take money from you. But what he will do is tail you—and he'll tail you right here. You'd better watch your back, smartass; you could burn all of us."

Dondolo had been staying at the Americana Hotel, but he loved spending time at the Sutton Place address. "Me? You think these amateurs could follow me? The best cops in the world have tried to tail me. These New York cops are bullshit."

That's what he said—"bullshit." And he said it with the kind of smile and tone of voice that made my skin crawl.

A young blond agent was there—a real low-key and quiet guy. To me he looked like a California surfer. He'd been brought in from Southeast Asia to help with the investigation. The agent left us and went to the basement of the building to use the washing machine. While washing his clothes, he checked around and discovered a wiretap. How long the bullshit amateurs had had the safe house phones tapped no one could tell. Judging by the amount of used tape, it was very recent.

"Good looking out, Carlo," the agent said. "Because of you, we might all have to di-di the fuck outta here."

I had never heard that expression before, *di-di*; someone said it was Vietnamese.

Humiliated now, and angry, Dondolo said that he was going to offer the two cops money to return his passport. "Watch," he said, "they'll take it."

"Fuck you, man. You know, fuck you. We'll be lucky if you didn't blow this whole thing," I told him.

Someone said, "Let him try it." I don't remember who. I do

remember walking to a window that looked out over Sutton Place. I could see boats in the harbor, and the skyline of Brooklyn off in the distance. We weren't far from the U.N. building—a few blocks from the street and precinct where, on that day of wild combat, I had met Joe.

All I thought about was that great big smile, on that great big horse.

Suddenly, my whole history began rising up in me. A burning pain, like a bomb in my stomach, had gone off when Dondolo said he would offer Joe money.

"He'll never go for it," I told Dondolo. "This scam of yours won't work."

"Let him try it," Sandy said.

"Nunziata believes he's a major international dealer," I told them. "He thinks Carlo will cooperate and make him huge cases. He's not going to take money from him and then allow him to flee the country. It won't happen."

"Sure it will," Dondolo said.

I told Carlo he should go screw himself. Then I left the apartment, went to my car, and headed for home.

Dondolo's plan was to meet Joe that night and offer him money for the return of his passport. Then he would flee the country. And of course and for sure, I had no idea how Joe would handle it.

On my ride to Long Island, I ran scenario after scenario through my mind. I wanted to drive to Joe's house in Queens and warn him. But I couldn't bring myself to do that. Someone could be watching his house. For all I knew, someone could be watching me.

I tried to convince myself that Joe would rebuff Dondolo's offer. In spite of everything, Dondolo presented the possibilities of gigantic drug seizures and huge cases. Joe would let the money slide, he had to, it made sense.

The last time I had seen Joe he looked wasted. I suppose we both did. It had been a very long day for both of us. My SIU team had been on a dealer by the name of Peter Corso. We'd been on him for some time and were getting closer to an arrest.

We had the details right. We'd identified Corso's connection, a man named Jacques Bless. We had them both pinned down and were waiting for a move. But when the move came, we were late. It happens.

Suffering the frustration of being just minutes behind Corso, we raced from midtown to downtown, but in the end we were too far behind. Corso delivered a package of heroin to his customer. His customer was an informant who worked for Joe. And Joe, that Dean Martin grin in place, was waiting.

Late that night, at a West Street diner, Joe and I met for coffee and conversation. First we went through all the rituals of friends who hadn't seen each other in a while. He loved his new assignment at the joint strike force, he didn't miss SIU. He'd been working this particular case for a while and was pleased with the collar. "We were five minutes behind you," I told him.

He smiled.

"I know Corso's connection," I told him. "How about you?"

He smiled.

"You don't have a clue," I said.

"And if I don't? My gut tells me you're not going to tell me."

I told him his gut was always right. "How come we never worked together, Joe? How come we never teamed up?"

He shrugged.

"Forget it," I said. "I understand."

"Yeah, but listen. Are you going to tell me Corso's connection?"

"Maybe."

Until late into the night we sat together at the diner, had something to eat, and talked of life and loves, the job. He stared at me often, and there were long, embarrassing silent moments. When I told him who Corso's connection was, he hugged me.

Later I would hear a story about a peculiar gathering of SIU detectives in a Queens bar. There were thirteen or fourteen people standing around drinking and talking. Someone said he'd heard a rumor that I was working for some internal affairs unit. That's what he'd heard. Then someone said that I should be killed, clipped, whacked. Something should be done.

Joe spoke, and when Joe Nunziata had something to say, everyone listened. "If Bob Leuci's a rat," he said, "then I'm a rat. If you want to get to him, you'll have to get past me."

Joe.

I sat at my kitchen table hour after hour, the phone and Joe's number in front of me. When I could take it no longer—when I thought I would absolutely lose my mind—I made a decision. It was the only decision I could make. I had no options.

I could hear Gina moving around upstairs, playing with the children, and I called to her.

"I'm going to make a telephone call," I told her. "I'll hand you the phone. When someone answers, simply say, 'Don't go.' Say that and hang up."

I dialed Joe's number; the phone rang, and rang some more. No answer, no answering machine. I waited awhile and tried again; still no answer.

Joe met Dondolo at Friar Tuck's restaurant in midtown. They had met there before. A couple of nights earlier, Joe had introduced Carlo to a waitress friend of his. Taking the woman aside, he had given her some money and told her to go home with Carlo. "But," he said, "tell him to take you anywhere but the Americana Hotel."

That night Carlo grabbed hold of the waitress, got into a taxi, and went straight to the safe house.

Bingo.

In goes Joe's wiretap—a wiretap he didn't take the time to check.

They sat in the back of the restaurant, Carlo, Joe, and Joe's strike force partner. Carlo was speaking Italian, going on with the Sons of Italy routine. "We have a bond, a special bond—the same blood, we understand each other." That sort of manipulative bullshit rap.

"I need to get to Italy," he told them. "It's business—I have to be there. You help me get my passport and you have my word, we'll make cases. I'll make you famous."

Carlo put four thousand dollars on the table, saying that they were brothers and that the bread they broke and ate together cemented that relationship.

Joe told him that he didn't want the money; it wasn't about money. Dondolo said he knew that four thousand dollars was no money at all. Joe told Dondolo that he wasn't insulted, that was not the point. It wasn't about the money. He said that what they had was more important than money. Sure, he'd get him his passport; they had a special friendship.

Dondolo made promises, then said he had plenty of money. This few thousand dollars meant nothing to him—nothing more than an expression of gratitude. It was Joe's friendship that he valued. Joe made reassurances. The money sat next to the bread on the table.

The men smiled at each other, great big friendly grins. This was so good, way too good, and Joe wanted it so much. Like a deceived lover, he wanted so much to believe. He took the money.

Destiny is so random, so formless, so huge is the cost of the reckless decisions we make. Joe made his decision, and the penalty of that decision was his life. When you've let loose your moral anchor, you're in the hands of fate, and fate is never, ever kind.

They didn't wait; they picked Joe up that night and brought him and his partner to the U.S. Attorney's Office.

Nick and Mike, other assistant U.S. attorneys, and several federal agents were there. Joe explained, tried to justify taking Dondolo's money. He said he was out to make a bribery case against Dondolo.

"That's not going to work," they told him. "That kind of explanation, well, it's tantamount to a confession." They had tapes and witnesses, and they had Carlo Dondolo.

Joe could cooperate. Excluding a miracle, that was the only way he could save himself. They stayed after him, questioning him, and then they let him go at five o'clock in the morning.

Over the course of the next few days, there were a number of meetings. Nick thought he was making progress. He believed there was a real possibility that Joe would cooperate and save himself.

Once proud Joe, the lion of the SIU, was now caged and put on for show. His spirit gone, he was a broken man. I knew Joe suffered with a bad case of colitis, and all that stress must have left him in horrible pain.

Tartiglino flew in from Washington, and there was one final meeting in a hotel room near LaGuardia Airport. Nick told me the meeting started off badly. Joe continued to maintain his innocence—rambling and panic-stricken. Tartiglino told Joe, "Okay, you say you're innocent, that you've never done anything illegal. We'll give you a test. You pass and maybe you can change our minds.

"I want you to call Sonny Grosso," he told him. "You tell Grosso that the feds are onto us. Mention a case; tell him we have a problem with that case. Tell him that you and he and Eddie Egan need to get together to talk about the case—about the problem. Let's see what he says."

Joe refused. Seeing Tartiglino, the number two man in DEA, there conducting an interrogation, I'm sure he concluded that there was much more to all this than Carlo Dondolo. Joe had already spoken to a lawyer—more than one—and the consensus was, he had a viable entrapment defense. So when Tartiglino brought up Sonny Grosso and Eddie Egan, the French Connection detectives, as far as Joe was concerned, the problem was not Dondolo. The French Connection case was Tartiglino's target. Now, that was the major leagues. His problems with Carlo Dondolo paled in comparison.

Joe had never worked a case with Egan and Grosso. I'm sure he believed that Tartiglino must have known that. He would reason that it was not some obscure case Tartiglino was interested in—it was something else, and that something else had to be the French Connection.

All this was conjecture, jamming Joe's head. His life was now a scene of carnage. Unknown fears were ripping him apart.

Tartiglino told Joe that he had few options—really he didn't have any. He could cooperate, go to jail, or kill himself.

Andrew Tartiglino was not an evil man. There may have been a better way to phrase Joe's options, but on that particular afternoon he didn't come up with one. In any event, he'd been around so long, seen the drug wars create so many casualties, he knew that Joe Nunziata was not the first, and by no means would he be the last.

They gave Joe one more day to consider his options.

Nick had this feeling—a real belief that Joe would relent and cooperate. He was realistic about it, but he had this feeling.

That night, Joe wrote a long, grief-filled letter. He explained that his partner had nothing to do with the Dondolo situation. He also continued to proclaim his own innocence. He told his wife, Anne, about the letter, and then he put it in the trunk of his car.

Joe drove, his strike force partner sat in the passenger seat. They were on their way to meet with Nick Scoppetta. Joe had seen it all before. He had read about cops' arrests in the newspapers, seen pictures of cops with their jackets covering their heads on television. He had heard all the stories about disgrace and humiliation. All of it he'd seen before.

Joe was taking his time, driving through the old neighborhood, circling round and round the Williamsburg streets, counting off the stickball sewers. Nobody hit a Spaldeen like Joe, three sewers easy. He passed the stoops where he had sat as a kid, the candy store where he played the jukebox and listened to Little Anthony doing "Earth Angel."

His partner was getting nervous. They were late and he didn't want to be late. Joe pulled to the curb and told him to go in the candy store and telephone Scoppetta. "Tell him we're on our way."

Joe's partner opened the car door; Joe tried a smile and said that everything was going to be okay. He'd work it out. He'd fix it.

When his partner left the car, Joe took his gun and shot himself through the heart.

I don't remember anything about that day. They told me I vomited on the courthouse steps, and when they brought me to see Nick Scoppetta, he cried, and I cried—but I don't remember any of it.

I see Joe all the time. Like my father, my brother, and my mother, he may be gone, but he's a constant presence in my life. But the day he died—I don't remember at all.

MOUNTING
CASUALTIES

He came into the grand jury witness room, spotted me—
and smiled. He walked up to me, and he hugged me.
One of those routines old friends do. A real, warm hug.
Aside from the fact that we liked each other, we really
had not been that good friends. This was a new Sandy.

I remember the way he grinned at me, started to speak but then
stopped. He wagged his head and smiled some more. Sandy was in
an expansive mood. And tanned—he looked good. Sandy always
looked good. He was certainly exotic amid the button-down con-
formity of the U.S. Attorney's Office. I envied him his tan, his confident, carefree manner.

"I was wrong about you," he said. "Really off-base. I want to tell
you I'm sorry."

Our investigation had ended months earlier. It ended essentially
the way I always expected it would end. The Queens ADA—the man
against whom Sandy had made a case—was about to cooperate. The
likelihood of cases being made against judges, politicos—all the
icons and nobility of New York City sleaze—suddenly became a
genuine possibility.

Then something happened. Somebody leaked the story of the investigation to the media, and the once grand investigation came to an instant halt.

In short—we got sold out. Probably by someone who thought that the investigation had gone far enough. Wiseguys, bail bondsmen, cops, and fixer street lawyers were fine. Start to focus on the real power brokers and it was Whoa! Wait a minute. Enough.

Nick Scoppetta and Mike Shaw had both moved on. Nick became the commissioner of the Department of Investigations, and Mike was named head of a new federal organized crime strike force in the Eastern District.

Mike had only been there a short time when he asked me to recommend an undercover agent to work the garment center. A Jewish guy, he said. I told him that he couldn't do better than my former SIU partner Les Wolf. I knew that Les would do a first-rate job. And it was a good safe place for Les to hide while the department went through the turmoil of internal investigations.

That day at the grand jury, Sandy had arrived in the company of two DEA agents from Mexico. Right away, we four understood each other—at least on one level. We had all done undercover work. Except they were still doing it. I was being protected by nine New York City police bodyguards and living on Governors Island.

Governors Island is a speck of land in Upper New York Bay, purchased from the Indians for two ax heads, a string of beads, and some nails. All my time was spent with bodyguards on the island or with various assistant U.S. attorneys preparing cases. Sandy was still in combat, fighting the drug war. My days in the street were over.

Once you leave the action, things turn around. You're not a part of it anymore. You're working a desk, and you forfeit something. No matter how hard you try, you can't be part of it. That's how I felt standing with Sandy and his fellow agents; but I felt something else too. The change in Sandy was enormous. We walked into the hall arm in arm, like a pair of loving brothers.

"I never understood you," he said. "What made you tick. I do now. I was wrong—and I want to tell you how bad I feel."

He had his arm around my shoulder and he was holding tight to me. "You're going to be okay," he said. "I saw the *Life* magazine piece—and it said you're going to be okay."

Loudon Wainwright, a magnificent columnist and truly wonderful man, had written a story about the investigation and about me that had appeared in *Life* magazine.

"Okay?" I said. "I suppose I'm going to be okay. I live on an island and I'm never alone. I have bodyguards twenty-four hours a day. I get to see my family sometimes on weekends, and most cops in New York City hate me."

"I doubt they hate you," he told me, and I said, "It isn't over."

"Mexico," Sandy said, "now that place is spooky, spooky beyond belief. You think East Harlem, the South Bronx, and Brooklyn are wild, you should see Mexico."

I told him I'd heard, and I'd heard something else too. People in his agency were not happy with him—Taylor and Carros—the same people who were not happy with me, and for the same reasons. They were resentful of Sandy's relationship with the U.S. attorneys. "Be careful," I told him, "Taylor has Tartiglino's ear."

"Tartiglino knows him for what he is," he said. "A creep."

"Gold-plated," I told him.

Grabbing and shaking my hand, he said that when this was all over, maybe we could work together again. "Not likely—but a nice idea," I told him.

I remember standing with my arms folded, staring at Sandy, feeling a grip of sentiment, a real feeling of affection, for someone in harm's way. I could feel it then, the presence of unavoidable danger. I can feel it still today.

About six months later, I received a telephone call from Richard Benvenisti. Rick was one of the many young and brilliant lawyers who came out of the Southern District. He was competition for

Rudy Giuliani. Smart as hell, independent, with a gentle way about him. At the time he was dating Mary Travis, of Peter, Paul and Mary. One sparkling Manhattan afternoon they invited me for lunch at the Waldorf-Astoria.

They were an attention-grabbing couple, Mary close to six feet tall, Rick somewhere around five-five, five-six. Mary Travis was a bit wigged-out, radicalized, turned on by the political state of the country. Rick was about as laid-back as you could get without pharmaceuticals, the kind of guy who could slide into his own head and disappear for a while.

Recently I watched Rick on television defending a president who sadly could not be defended. Rick, the voice of the Democratic National Committee. One of the things everyone said about him was that he was as smart as Rudy, and that was saying a lot.

On the telephone that day there was the sound of anguish in Rick's voice. The call went something like this:

"Bob, if I asked you, could you be a character witness for Sandy?"

Rick and Sandy had been close friends. Then Sandy fell in love with a woman Rick had been dating, divorced his wife, and married her. Apparently their friendship had withstood all that.

"The answer is of course. But why would Sandy Barrio need me of all people as a character witness?"

A long pause and then; "Sandy's been arrested in Texas."

When the mental picture of Sandy in handcuffs took hold, I let out a moan of pain and disbelief. "C'mon," I said, "you're kidding, not Sandy."

Rick explained that Sandy had been working with an informant on the Texas border, a Canadian drug dealer he had been developing as a source. Trouble was, the guy was already an informant for DEA inspections. The Canadian maneuvered Sandy. He promised Sandy he could give up multi-kilo loads of heroin and coke, laying out that he wanted part of the package in return. Apparently Sandy went for it. It was a setup, one of DEA's masterpieces.

I was staggered.

"It's bullshit," I said, "total bullshit, some DEA power struggle. It's what they do."

"They have video and tape recordings," Rick told me. "It's a strong case. They're holding him without bail in a Texas jail."

Sandy, you're so experienced, so smart, you've been around this madness so long, how could you fall for this? As Rick kept talking, I kept thinking maybe this was a joke, hoping it was a joke. I half expected Sandy to pick up an extension, laughing and calling out my name, telling me, "We got you on that one, eh? Got you good."

And then I was thinking, *Sandy, you went to the Sorbonne, for Christ sake. How could you blow it like this? How could you fall for such an obvious setup?* Of course these were all rhetorical questions. It had been years since I held any illusions. Still, it was hard for me to believe. Suddenly I felt a terrible sense of sadness and pity for Sandy, and I blamed this phony drug war for what we had all become.

Sandy's wife, Maryann, was a lawyer. Sandy told her that the DEA wouldn't dare take him to trial. They couldn't, because what they were accusing him of was something they all did.

Time proved Sandy right. In jail he took a bite of a peanut butter sandwich, fell down in convulsions, went into a coma, and died. Initial tests said strychnine poisoning. Four weeks later an autopsy would say death by asphyxiation, telling the world that Sandy died when he choked on a peanut butter sandwich. I suppose I could have accepted that story at face value; but I didn't.

EARLY IN THE morning, we'd take the ferry from Governors Island, and my bodyguards would deliver me to the courthouse. I'd stay until late into the night, organizing cases with a variety of prosecutors, feeling a wrench in my stomach when I heard them predict difficult and dirty trials.

My family had been moved to a two-bedroom hunting cabin we had in the Catskills. U.S. marshals guarded them around the clock.

On weekends I would be driven north to be with them. Gina, it seemed, was holding up well.

Alone in the wilderness, she cooked meals for the marshals, made sure Anthony and Santina did their schoolwork, and tried to adjust to a life for which they were totally unprepared.

All the U.S. attorneys worked late. They were a committed and dedicated bunch. Even so, Rudy Giuliani stood out from all the others. It seemed to me the man never went home. A good listener, calm, a man of exceptional intellect, he'd spend hour after hour with me, talking about the cases, my life, his life, baseball, food, politics, women, and survival—my survival.

Both our wives were named Gina, and there was something missing in both our marriages. I found Rudy a thoughtful, caring, and concerned friend. But there was a bit more—a feeling. Sometimes he'd ask a question in an ill-at-ease way, anticipating an answer. It was my testimony concerning my admissions of prior misconduct. Was I telling the whole story?

Would you? I wanted to ask him. Would he—or anyone else— parade all the horrible things they'd done in their life for the world to see? Tell me, for what possible purpose, and for what possible good? The unspoken question was often in his eyes. Rudy was intuitive, he was probing, but I wouldn't go near it, and finally he didn't press. Not then he didn't.

Through all this time, everyone was telling me that there was the potential for a number of high-profile trials, all of them with top-flight defense lawyers. Things, they said, would not go easy for me.

Alone, at night, I'd wonder how I would survive all this. With thoughts such as these, I would try to fall asleep.

I had already gone through one trial with the lawyer Eddie Rosner. There had been a conviction, but the trial was a humdinger, a million times worse than anything I could have imagined. Even though I had plenty of trial experience in state court, none of it could have prepared me for the days and days of cross-examination I endured in that federal courthouse.

Rosner's defense lawyer was Al Krieger, one of New York's leading criminal defense attorneys. One day he would defend John Gotti. The focus of Krieger's defense, as it turned out, had less to do with proving Rosner's innocence than with attacking and discrediting me.

Bob Morvillo and Elliot Sagor, the prosecutors in the case, prepared me well. But there was no way they could have prepared me for the onslaught on my character and credibility that Krieger was prepared to unleash. He battered me and battered me, and battered me some more.

"Detective, have you ever given drugs to your informants?"

"No."

"Have you ever used illegal wiretapping?"

"No."

Have you—? Have you—? Have you—? Have you—?

No. No. No. No.

"Have you ever taken women, prostitutes, drug addicts to motels to have sex?" "No"—and at least that was true.

"Okay. Let's go over what you have done. Those three things."

Jesus.

I never understood what any of that had to do with the case at hand. I never lied on the stand—never perjured myself in order to convict someone. That too was true—but that question went unasked.

Rosner's defense team paraded into court just about all my informants. How they were able to find them was a miracle, but they did, and those old informants of mine, all of them getting paid very well, marched into court testifying that I had given them drugs. Nevertheless, at the end of the day, we had recordings. And the simple fact remained—Rosner was guilty.

When at last the trial ended, I cannot tell you how relieved I was, but my relief was short-lived.

One morning Elliot Sagor, looking as though he were about to enter purgatory, told me that Rosner had put in for an appeal. He had hired, as his appellate attorney, a professor by the name of Alan Dershowitz.

"So what?" I said. "Who's he?"

"You'll find out," he said, and boy—did I ever.

Months went by—then more months. I was full time preparing for the Rosner appeal hearing and other cases. Unable to get home for weeks at a time, my nerves were totally shot. I was crazed, on the very edge of losing control, that dizzying, sick sensation taking up residence in my head and chest again.

Dershowitz had hired a former SIU detective, Frank King, Joe's ex-partner, as a private investigator. And they had the Baron.

Frank King was paying him for testimony. The Baron contacted me at the U.S. Attorney's Office and told me he was broke. He needed the money—he hoped I would understand.

I understood, I told him. I did. Then I told him to tell the truth. "Don't inflate it. The truth," I said, "is probably worth plenty to these guys." He said he wouldn't embellish anything—but he did.

One night, I told Elliot that I was exhausted, missing my family, and that I was going home. "No you're not," he told me. "You'll stay right here until we finish, and we're a long way from being finished." I lost it—and turned his desk over. From underneath his desk, Elliot telephoned Bob Morvillo and told him that they should give me some time off, I was becoming unglued.

There was a snowstorm that night. The turnpike north was closed, so the government arranged for me to be flown home by helicoptor. My bodyguards drove me to the midtown helipad. When I stepped up onto the helicopter, I was taken aback. A former SIU detective was the copilot.

When he turned back, guiding me to my seat and giving me a headset, I said, "Mickey, what the hell are you doing here?"

Mickey Tobin had been an active detective in the SIU; he'd left for the Customs Department not long after I was transferred into the unit. He was a well-liked and key player in the SIU. As we lifted off, I asked him if I was sitting on an ejection seat. He laughed and told me that I should sit back and relax. "Enjoy the ride," he said.

The snow had stopped falling, there were no clouds, the lit-up city was at peace, and the East River was bathed in brilliant star and moonlight. It was a small hellicoptor, with room for no more than three or four people; a clear bubble sitting on an engine. In a single smooth leap, we rose into the night sky, over the Fifty-ninth Street Bridge, up and over Manhattan, and then for fun we flew under the George Washington Bridge. It was one helluva ride.

Mickey was enjoying himself, pointing out interesting things to see. The pilot, a Vietnam veteran, was thrilled. He loved flying and hadn't been able to do much for some time.

Through my headset, the pilot told me that we were going to follow the New York State Turnpike north, then go west at Cairo and look for lights on a field in Freehold.

There were high hills, small mountains—I told him to be careful. He said the only thing he was worried about was the fact that he'd never landed on a snow-covered field before. That, he said, could be tricky.

"Hey," I told him, "at least when we go in, nobody will be shooting at you."

The pilot laughed, but his laugh came out deadpan and remote. He explained that when we got to the field, he would get as close to the ground as possible. "But you'll have to jump—I'm not going to land."

"Sure," I said, thinking, *Whoa!*

Federal marshalls had circled the field with their cars; we could make out their headlights from miles away. As we came down, the landscape was sparkling white. Snow blew up; I couldn't tell ground from air—everything was white.

The helicopter hovered a moment. Mickey reached back and opened the door. He smiled. I shook his hand, telling him that I appreciated what he and the pilot had done for me. Mickey said, "We appreciate what it is you're doing, good luck." I jumped.

I was about three feet off the ground, amazing.

IT CAME ON as a whisper inside my head. "Do it," it said, "you can do it." Joe and I had talked about it all the time, planned all the details. You turn your wrist toward your heart; *boom*—it's done—*fini*. I never believed I had the courage, not really. I certainly could not do it through the mouth—not in the head. That would be bad, no fun at all. An inherited trait, they say, a birthright you leave the family, a Hemingway legacy. Not true in my case. A clear, free decision—difficult certainly, but doable. Only why do it alone? Make all that pain and suffering meaningful—take some contemptible creature along, do a service for humanity.

Valium helps—like heroin, a wonder drug. Drop 20, 25 milligrams, wait a minute, let it kick in, find the contemptible creature, then *bang!* Now the hard part; take your time, don't rush it, through the chest, in the heart, not in the mouth. *Bang!* Problems over.

I was at the Southern District courthouse, alone in an office, when Tom Taylor walked in. It was early in the afternoon; he seemed already lit up—wearing an odd grin. "Geeze, would you believe it," he said. "Last night Dave Cody killed himself. Your ex-partner shot himself in the head."

Taylor looked at me looking at him, hesitated a second, then spun on his heel and left the room in a quick schoolgirl-like trot.

First I found the Valium. The trick was to stay calm. No way to tell how many pills I swallowed, but there were more than enough. Then I found my gun, put it in my belt, and walked out of the office.

My bodyguards were not around; someone had taken them off—probably to a meeting of some sort—a conference on how to deal with Bob Leuci now.

The hallway was empty. No one was around. Taylor had hightailed it. An elevator door slid open—a tiny elevator; I'd never before seen one like it. Cowering in the corner was a small man in a gray suit. He almost smiled, and pointed with his chin to a sign that said Judges Elevator. I nodded and he said, "Come aboard."

He stepped off at the next floor. I got off in the garage. For a while things flashed in and out, there were blank spots. I found myself standing at the center of the Brooklyn Bridge. I wasn't about to jump—no, no! It was going to be *bang! bang!* Then came the slide—I crossed the threshold of the void. The next thing I remember, someone had her arm around me, saying, "Something's wrong, Bob, what is it?"

It was Margaret Shaw—Mike's wife. She'd been out running when she spotted me coming off the bridge. I don't recall what I said. I remember her telling me that she was going to call Mike. She'd take me home and telephone Mike. Then the Valium took over and would not let go.

IT HAD ALL begun to crumble about a year earlier. It was a banner headline in every newspaper and the lead story on local and national TV. Following the break of the story, even though I continued my routine of preparing for hearings and trials, I knew that no matter what I had been through, all that had happened was a walk in the park compared to what lay ahead.

It was weird how it started, really bizarre.

His name was James Farley—everyone called him JJ.

Rape has nothing to do with sex and less than nothing to do with a man's ability to find a sexual partner. Nevertheless, when the SIU's best-looking detective got arrested for rape, it was a shocker.

On a quiet, tree-lined street of row houses in suburban Nassau County, JJ had tried out his act as an Allstate Insurance salesman. A pretty young housewife had let him in; it was awkward talking about insurance at the back door.

An encore performance—JJ had run the same scam at least a dozen times before. This time Nassau County detectives were waiting.

A week or two later, Nassau police searched JJ's house. They were stunned to find police department property-clerk envelopes containing narcotics evidence scattered about.

It was not unusual, JJ told the cops. SIU was a citywide unit. Sometimes he worked in one borough and had court in another. He lived on Long Island, making the logistics of picking up and returning evidence a nightmare. So for convenience' sake, he held on to the evidence until something brought him into Manhattan, when he could return it.

"Isn't that a violation of the rules and procedures?"

JJ was about to be charged with a dozen rapes, so a rules violation was hardly a major concern. Besides, he told them, everyone did it.

He was right.

Nassau County police notified the NYPD, who in turn notified William Bonacum, the commanding officer of the Narcotics Bureau.

I had known Bonacum when he was an administrative lieutenant in the TPF—a straight shooter, smart, a stickler for the rules, and tough as nails. Now his sole mission was to straighten out the Narcotics Bureau.

Bonacum didn't like the sound of it, evidence lying around. First he called for an inspection of the property clerk's inventory book. He told them to check all the narcotics evidence that had been signed out and not returned in a timely fashion. Examine the large seizures first, he told them.

Clerks rummaged around and found that three years earlier, in March of 1969, a Detective Nuzziato had signed out the 50 kilos of the French Connection heroin. There was no return signature. And there was no Detective Nuzziato; there was a Nunziata.

Frantic, they searched the evidence lockers. They hunted through all the nooks and crannies of that eight-foot-thick-walled, antiquated building on Broom Street. Finally they found a steamer trunk containing plastic bags of white powder. It was the French Connection evidence—but not all of if. The remainder they discovered in a blue suitcase. Everybody was relieved. It was all the evidence from the French Connection case.

There were a total of 50 kilo packages. Then the chemists at the police lab shattered all relief. The packages were crawling with flour beetles. Flour beetles don't eat heroin—flour beetles die when they eat heroin. These flour beetles were quite chubby, and contentedly scampering about.

In all, 97 pounds of pure heroin had been stolen from the police department property clerk's office. The heroin had been replaced with flour and starch. That was only the tip of the iceberg; more seizures waited to be checked.

The inventory lasted three weeks. It wasn't long before they realized that something very serious had gone wrong. When the smoke finally settled, the police commissioner, looking totally mind-blown, read the results.

Someone or some persons had stolen nearly 400 pounds of heroin and cocaine from the New York City Police Department. In six separate withdrawals between 1969 and 1972, 261 pounds of heroin and 137 pounds of cocaine had been replaced with flour and cornstarch. This quantity represented one-fifth of all the narcotics seized by the department since 1961. The value of the stolen narcotics, at street prices, was estimated at seventy million dollars, far surpassing any bank or jewelry robbery in American history, including the famous Brinks robbery. And, since the Police Department had been burning confiscated heroin no longer needed as evidence without a chemical analysis, perhaps hundreds more pounds of narcotics had been removed, replaced with flour, and cremated.

The six withdrawals formed no identifiable pattern, except that the narcotics had been signed out by a Detective Nuzziato or Nunziata.

— GREGORY WALLANCE, *Pappa's Game*

When I heard the news, for a long while it was hard for me to focus. I was shaken, alternating between rage and disbelief. I knew that every single prosecutor in New York City would work double overtime on a crime with the scope of this one, and there was no telling where such an investigation could lead.

Like a gargantuan sewer backing up, the stench would spread everywhere—I could count on it. Whatever justification I had tried to make concerning my own behavior and the behavior of other detectives who had gone along simply to get along had not a prayer of falling on sympathetic ears.

Every prosecutor, all the law enforcement officials, every single journalist would look at me and every other detective who had ever worked in the SIU with complete disgust. And who could blame them? It was an absolute horror.

The police department put together a large task force to investigate the theft. Heading it was an intelligent and experienced investigator, a captain by the name of Joseph Comperiati. Comperiati had the look and the ticks of Peter Faulk's Colombo character. Joe C, as he was called, gave the world around him a gaze of oblique analysis, always polite, always searching. His second in command was Lieutenant Walter Stone. Easygoing and as soft-spoken as Joe C, Stone and Comperiati were two of the NYPD's best.

Joe Nunziata's signature was compared with the signatures in the property clerk's logbook. They were forgeries. Like all current and many former narcotics detectives, I was asked to quickly sign Joe's name six times. Then I was to write out a badge number, any badge number.

So it began. I knew that without an informant inside the rip-off, this was bound to be an infinitely difficult case to break. Some people thought that it might take as long as six months. It took five years.

Federal prosecutors from the Eastern and Southern Districts of New York, and the new special state prosecutor, Maurice Nadjari, at different times held jurisdiction over the investigation. There were wiretaps and grand juries that folded into other grand juries. Indictments for other crimes were brought. The hope was that those indictments would be hammers over the heads of possible cooperating witnesses.

It was a brutal and mean business, an all-out purge. The SIU—and just about everyone who had ever worked there—was a target. For months I was put through the mill, in the mornings by the NYPD's Internal Affairs people, in the afternoons by investigators and prosecutors from the special state prosecutor's office. Late in the day, people from the Southern District would question me. In the evenings, Tom Puccio from the Eastern District would come on-stage. It was as if they blamed me for their inability to break the case.

I didn't know anything about it. I knew that convincing them of that would be an art. They all believed that I was hiding a past filled with sordid ugliness, and information about the how and who of the theft could be a part of all that.

Three acts of misconduct? Bullshit!

We're going through all the SIU files, they said. We're pulling in informants and defendants in all the SIU cases, yours too. The detectives are dropping like flies, they're all getting indicted for this and that; we're seeing to that little game. They'll cooperate—all of them will roll over—and some already have, and those that have are pointing a finger at you. Three acts they say—c'mon? He's Babyface.

That was how it was, five, sometime six days a week, twelve to fourteen hours a day. My bodyguards thought I was either made of steel or brain-dead. "How do you do it?" they'd ask. Day in, day out the same questions, and with every breath the anger and disbelief growing, threatening.

No matter what happens, I thought, *I'll always have* bang! *Then* bang *again.* For the first bang, the target list was mounting; that was a problem.

HE WAS A Sephardic Jew, dark-featured and handsome with shadowy, expressionless eyes, eyes that were impossible to read. His name was Maurice Nadjari, and for more than ten years he had been a star ADA in the Manhattan District Attorney's Office. After the Knapp Commission hearings, the governor had appointed him special state prosecutor. His mandate, root out all corruption in New York City.

Nadjari's office and his grand jury were in Tower Two at the World Trade Center. You went into that grand jury room and it was not unlike standing in front of a firing squad. You went in, you were indicted, case closed. Next.

Maurice Nadjari went after police corruption, sure he did, but cops were not where his passion lay. Nadjari wanted the politicians. He set his sights high. His list of indictments was impressive, a Republican county chairman, a Democratic chairman, a congressman, judges, the district attorney of Queens.

Maurice Nadjari fought his way into the throne rooms and was targeting the royalty of political duplicity in the city. They labeled him a zealot, and some on his staff certainly were. The appellate courts ultimately overturned many of his convictions. But the man was a true believer. I liked and admired him, but I knew his days were numbered.

I was sitting in his office surrounded by investigators and several of his prosecutors. We'd been talking about the French Connection theft, about who I thought had done it. I didn't know. The mood in the room was somber. I had a sense of being watched, studied.

The Baron had given a deposition to Dershowitz; in it he said that I had given him drugs wrapped in a property clerk envelope. He'd taken a lie detector test. First they found him to be a liar, tried again, and the second time discovered that he was untestable.

Hook the Baron up, ask a question, and the machine went *hummmmm*—a flat line. No surprise there.

I wondered how and why the Baron had come up with such a peculiar story. Then I remembered that a week or so after Joe's suicide I was in the SIU office, and Frank King, one of Joe's old partners, had come after me. He asked why I was so upset about Joe's death. Joe, he said, was a rat and was going to cooperate.

"He killed himself—shot himself. Where the hell is your heart?" I asked him.

King and Joe had been partners, close friends I'd thought. Joe had introduced us. Early on, it was King telling me I should put an end to the Babyface jazz that he'd been hearing on the West Side. It was King who was now Dershowitz's investigator and working for Eddie Rosner. It was King who was paying the Baron, King telling him to come up with the phony allegation about the property clerk's envelope. I felt a twinge of recognition—every wiseguy I'd ever met had mentioned his name. Frank King was more wiseguy than cop. Frank King could have stolen those drugs. He had the balls, but lacked imagination. Who could have given him the idea? Who else? I didn't want to think about it.

Nadjari came into the office. I remember the way he looked at me, his smile. "Well," he said, "what do you think of the Baron's deposition?"

"Listen," I said, "none of that's true."

I could feel the room go silent—real quiet, heads turned. "Give me a lie detector test, sodium pentothal, hypnotism, truth serum, do whatever you like."

Nadjari's smile faded, he nodded. "I believe you," he said. His eyes were calm and attentive. "So who do you think, got any ideas?"

"No." I did and I didn't. The truth was, it was all speculation—my mind marking off some of the ifs and maybes. I thought it best to keep my thoughts to myself.

RUDY'S PROSECUTOR'S VOICE traveled the range of disbelief—and then anger. He was no fan of Maurice Nadjari. He was sitting behind his desk when I told him that I had offered the special prosecutor a chance to give me a lie detector test regarding the French Connection case.

"First of all," he said, "you don't take lie detector tests. You're a basket case—a nervous wreck. God only knows how such a test would turn out."

"I know nothing about that theft—how could it turn out badly?"

"No tests. Listen, you're going to have to go over to the Eastern District and see Puccio. They're going to indict your partner, Les Wolff. They're charging an entire team of SIU detectives, and Wolff is one of the team."

I felt as though a trap door had opened and I had fallen through. For a while we sat silent, staring at each other. I tried a mind-clearing trick, a little TM. Deep breaths, stay calm, and hang in there.

At one point Rudy said, "Dershowitz and his team can parade in here with junkie after junkie, dope dealer after dope dealer, telling us stories about you. It won't go anywhere. But let one detective come in and corroborate any of those stories, implicate you in anything you haven't told us, anything illegal, and I can't protect you. You'll be indicted. Don't let all you've done, all you've been through, be for nothing. Don't let that happen."

I said it wouldn't.

———

TOM PUCCIO WAS the chief of the Criminal Division of the Eastern District of New York—Brooklyn, Queens, and Long Island. The Southern District was Manhattan, the Bronx, and several lower counties of upstate New York. The Southern District had the accepted superstars; they made the vast majority of high-profile cases. There were people who didn't even know that there was an Eastern District and that it had a U.S. attorney.

I imagined a competition, a basketball or softball game, and uniforms: Southern District in the home white and blue, Eastern District in gray. Only a game, a little friendly competition—Harvard vs. St. Johns, but maybe more than that, Ivy League vs. Working Class.

We know Leuci is your guy. Well, we have him here now, and it's our move. Entirely my imagination, of course, but maybe that's what Puccio was thinking—a tweak of Rudy's nose.

It was a bad afternoon, one of the many bad afternoons I had spent in Puccio's outer office. It was a small space, barely room for two desks; the phones never stopped ringing, people never stopped coming and going.

We'd already been sitting for two hours. My bodyguards, John Farley and Don Makofsky—two motorcycle cops—skimming through magazines, barely concentrating, glancing at me and shaking their heads. We'd been together a long time, three years. At first they were careful with me, unsure of who I was, what I was about. Then for a long time they'd talk to me, asking about the hows and whys and what-the-hell-fors.

At times I had as many as nine bodyguards. Now we were down to six—sleeping together, eating together, me watching and listening to them as they kept an eye on me. All of them good solid regular cops, going through this with me one day at a time, saying reassuring things, each of them stubbornly protective. There had been stories—information about an attempted hit, one out of Las Vegas. "Let them come," they said, "we're ready, all of us. Let them fucking come."

I hated Puccio for putting me through this—making me wait, and wait, and wait. It gave you the willies, just sitting there.

Don Makofsky was trying to explain front-end wobble to me.

"Say you're on a bike chasing someone, and he's going eighty, ninety miles an hour, making you push a hundred. The front end of the motorcycle begins to wobble, scares the crap out of you. How can you take this?" he said. "How the hell do you deal with these pricks, day in, day out?"

"Calm down," I said. "Take it easy; it'll all be over soon, I can feel it." I was wrong.

There was a look of schoolboy innocence about Puccio and he was out of whack—one shoulder gave the impression it was higher than the other, or maybe it was simply the way he sat and stood. Painfully thin, he had seven hairs, I counted them, and they were combed across a polished, pale scalp. In his tortoiseshell glasses, his physical appearance was so far removed from the stereotype of a hardnosed prosecutor that it was laughable. All the same, you laughed at Tom Puccio at your peril.

He was a talented man and an amazingly hard worker. It was a given that AUSAs put in long hours, but Puccio took it to another level, and then two or three levels higher.

Maybe he worked hard simply to make the case, maybe to impress his colleagues, maybe for the fun of it or because that was the way he always did things. He'd spend hours on the smallest details, more hours on the big ones. As far as the French Connection theft was concerned, he was relentless. Puccio was consumed with the need to know who thought of it, who put it together, who pulled it off. And who would be the linchpin, once pulled, that would bring it down.

He had someone in mind. Based on information from informants, from wiretaps and bugs, from net-worth statements and income tax returns, the evidence was very damaging. Everything pointed at Frank King, and Puccio was convinced that King had been a major player in the thefts.

There were others, one, maybe two other cops and one of the country's major drug dealers—a man by the name of Vincent Pappa. A lifelong drug dealer, Pappa did not fit the mold. Although the radiance of power hung all around him, he lived a quiet, family-oriented life.

Pappa was not an inducted member of the Mafia, but he knew every mafioso in the city. And they knew and respected him. Even though he was a drug dealer, Vinny Pappa had the reputation of being an honorable man. He was the perfect connection to buy and move the stolen French Connection drugs.

Then—an amazing twist of fate.

Bill Hubert—the detective I had worked with in SIU, the same young man I had asked Nick to help have transferred to the Intelligence Division, the one who lived in the country, hunted and fished during the day and chased drug dealers at night—he ensnared a big one.

He stopped a car that Vinny Pappa was driving. When Hubert searched the trunk of that car, he found close to a million dollars in cash. First Pappa said he didn't know anything about the money, had no idea who could have put it in his car—thought it was probably counterfeit. When that didn't fly, he offered Billy Hubert some or all of the money. Billy arrested him. It was reflex, no hesitation, not a single moment of uncertainty. Given the opportunity, I always knew exactly what he would do.

That money showed up in Pappa's car not long after a load of drugs had mysteriously walked out of the property clerk's office. It couldn't be a coincidence. The money, along with information picked up off wiretaps, pointed directly at Pappa and King.

Tom Puccio believed he was putting the pieces together. He tended the investigation like a magic lamp, but there are no magic lamps, and believing is a long way from proving. Puccio knew that he had to make a solid federal case against Frank King, get a conviction, and use the sledgehammer of that conviction and sentence to force cooperation.

It was all a matter of connecting the dots. Detective Wolff will lead to Detective McClean; Detective McClean will lead to Frank King, and Frank King to the mystery man who forged Joe's signature and signed out the French Connection drugs.

Finally I got into Puccio's office, sat in a chair opposite him, saw him smile, knowing his smile was meaningless, heard him tell me he'd indicted all these detectives and that he needed my help to understand what kind of men they were.

"Are they all liars? Are the things they are saying about you true?"

"Is what true?"

"What they're telling me about you?"

"Like what?"

"Things."

His office door opened, and a Hispanic man stood there. I didn't recognize him. He looked at me, then he spit on the floor and left.

"Who the hell was that?" I said.

"You don't know?"

I didn't.

"You arrested him four years ago. You, Wolff, Frank Mandato, and Cody; you arrested him for drugs. Then you arrested him again, along with his wife, when she came to the station house offering a five-thousand-dollar bribe."

I remembered.

"He said that one of your team stole four hundred dollars from him."

"We arrested him for five-thousand-dollar bribery."

"Yes, yes—but he says you stole four hundred dollars from him."

"And you believe him?"

"Why would he lie?"

"Maybe he thinks I made a pass at his wife. Maybe he's a fucking drug dealer and he hates cops. I don't know. He's totally full of shit. But you want to believe him. Am I right?"

Puccio smiled.

"So I'm right."

An hour after we left Puccio's office, my two bodyguards and I sat together in the anteroom of DEA headquarters off Columbus Circle. It was a bureaucratic and most important-appearing place. Agents came and went. We sat and waited. At length George Carros came out and told John and Don to wait. Then he led me into Tom Taylor's office.

"Do you know something?" I asked George on the way in.

"I have no part in this," George told me, and I believed him. He seemed distressed, out of sorts, and that did not bode well for me.

Pen-pusher dreamland—Taylor had been promoted to assistant regional director. I'm thinking there wasn't a field agent in DEA who didn't know more about how to fight the drug war than this ex–IRS agent goofball. Regional director my ass.

Taylor despised me because I didn't tell the U.S. attorneys that I wanted him and the DEA to run the investigation. Had I done that, when the investigation ended it would have guaranteed him major press coverage.

His superiors had put him on the spot, and he hadn't come through. For that he blamed me. The man was a bully, and he was dying to bring me down. He would teach me a lesson and shove it in the face of the Southern District.

"You're a liar," Taylor started out. "I'm sending you a message from Puccio. You don't tell us everything—what you've done and who you've done it with—by five o'clock this afternoon, Puccio is going to indict you."

"For what?"

"For that four-hundred-dollar rip-off of the drug dealer, that's what."

"I didn't do it."

"You're a liar."

"You're an asshole."

I'm figuring he's bullshitting; I'm hoping he's bullshitting, thinking that Puccio would have said something. For a moment I felt myself losing ground, dropping through some sort of crack in the universe. My knees were trembling.

Anything was possible—they could indict me. Taylor could convince Puccio to do it. I knew that they could indict the Gingerbread Man if they had a mind to.

"You're a crook," he said, "and all you care about are your prosecutor friends in the Southern District."

"I used to be a crook. That was a long time ago. You're a fraud—and you'll always be an asshole."

All the while I was in Taylor's office, George never looked at me. He stood at the window, staring out, thinking, I suppose, about how this had all started in Nick Scoppetta's apartment those long years ago.

"You have till five o'clock," Taylor said.

"Right, five o'clock," I said—and left.

In the waiting room, I found John and Don. They were nervous wrecks. Me too. John said, "We didn't know what to do. If they took you, what would we do?" Don said, "Ey, I'm a cop, ordered not to let you out of my sight; there would have been trouble."

That brought a smile—a nervous smile but a smile nonetheless. He meant it.

"Let me tell you," I said. "That asshole tries to take me, I pop him on the spot—then maybe I shoot myself, or maybe shoot him and give you my gun."

"Give me your gun," Don said. "Give me your gun. Don't shoot yourself over that shit-bird. Better yet, shoot him, then put up a little struggle and let us disarm you. We get a medal, maybe a promotion." Cop comedy.

There were more smiles and some laughter on the way back to the Southern District, back to Rudy's office. But the laughter was phony and hollow, the smiles forced. There was just too much that was scary—unknown and unknowable.

Things were going from dire to dismal, then to unbearable. The morning and afternoon with Puccio and Taylor proved that there were too many skeletons, minefields everywhere.

Puccio once told me that had I been working for him, he'd have had me take the Fifth. Forget the three acts of misconduct, don't admit anything, and take the Fifth. Could've worked. Maybe. Probably not.

By the end of the day, I felt drained and vulnerable, thinking, *If they arrest me, what will I do?* What could I do? I was mumbling to myself. The light was going out, I could feel it—such thoughts always brought Joe's face to mind. Jerry Schremph too.

Dying too young may be a tragedy, but living through this daily lunacy was crushing and demeaning—it was a sordid way to live. My chest pains were back, my jaw was killing me, clenching and grinding. Arty Monty, one of my best friends in life and one of my bodyguards, told me, "Man, when you're sleeping—do you know what you sound like?"

We parked on the street in front of the Southern District courthouse and went inside. I found Rudy sitting behind his desk.

Right from the start, way back when I'd met him at Mike Shaw's apartment, Rudy had always treated me in a warm and friendly way. There was always a smile. Partly, I figured, it was our mutual heritage. Raised in a large Italian family, it seemed that he understood me, how excruciating this investigation had been for me. But on that day he disappointed, frightened, and surprised me.

He had known about Puccio and Taylor's devious little mind game. No, Puccio was not going to indict me at five o'clock. But there were all sorts of wild cards out there. "You can't hang tough forever," he said. "Something, or someone, is bound to give way."

"I'll never implicate my partners, I won't do it."

"Don't you understand that simply saying that indicates to me that there are other things you haven't told us? We're your partners now, the Southern District. This is where your loyalty should be. Time is running out on you."

"You knew about all this, this Taylor and Puccio game?" He nodded, and I said, "I'm going home."

"You can't keep this up."

"That right?"

"Yes."

I HAD SOLD the Catskill cabin and the Long Island house and bought a home just outside of Washington, D.C., in Vienna, Virginia.

Gina and the children loved it; compared with the cabin in the hills it was a palace. It was a small brick ranch house, with two bathrooms, a working kitchen, kind and thoughtful neighbors. In the Catskills, there was but one bathroom—Gina, the children, and nine federal marshals, twenty-four hours a day.

The plans were that I'd stay put on Govenors Island during the week and fly to Virginia on the weekends. When I finished with the hearings and trials and then put a neat bow on the investigation, I'd move full-time to Virginia.

Shortly after we moved, I had several meetings in Washington with Tartiglino. He was gracious and generous, genuinely concerned about my family. I would be on loan from the NYPD to the DEA. Tartiglino thought I could buy drugs on the Mexican border. It would have been great; Sandy and me, just wonderful.

The DEA may have had characters like Taylor, but they also had men like Tartiglino, men who had actually fought the drug wars, hard men, true—uncompromising, absolutely, but men who understood.

Tartiglino helped me to get settled in Virginia. He may have had his doubts, but I know he hoped that I'd survive the storm.

The night after the day with Puccio and Taylor, I left Rudy's office, and instead of going to Governors Island I went to my parents' house in Queens.

When I got into the house, I immediately telephoned Puccio, asking what the hell he was doing with me. I was not terribly stable, and I was wondering why, after all I had been through in the investigation, I was now being forced to worry about a federal prosecutor of his stature coming after me. Didn't my work with the Southern District matter? What was he thinking?

He replied that if I had lied to Rudy and the others in the Southern District, then that was on my head. He respected the work I'd done, all that we had accomplished, but that was in the past. This was a whole new ball game. He didn't seem angry, he seemed confident. I got off the phone and had a glass of my father's wine.

Knowing for sure where Tom Puccio stood in all this, much of the confusion left me and I began to feel simply fear.

If I got arrested, what would happen to my family? The investigation had resulted in major print and TV stories. If indeed it came to pass, my arrest would dwarf all that. My parents, Gina and the children, all the innocents would be swept up in my disgrace.

Don't think about that, I told myself; *don't think about that now.* But I thought about nothing else.

I had sat down with my bodyguards a few times—hell, more than a few times—and discussed the developing situation. I decided that I would put the question to them one more time. Then I'd speak to Les Wolff.

I had helped the NYPD people in charge decide who would be assigned to guard me. I wanted regular cops. Motorcycle cops to drive me, and mounted cops for the reason that in or out of uniform they always made a great appearance. And I wanted patrol cops from active precincts.

After the original nine, the six who were left were Don and John, the two motorcycle cops; Bill Fritz, a six-foot-three-inch and handsome mounted cop; John O'Donahue, a patrol cop from an active Bronx precinct, a young man who had aspirations of being first a prizefighter, second, an actor; Roger Bonafidi, born and raised in a tough Brooklyn neighborhood, an innately quiet man with loads of street smarts; and Art Monty. I had known Artie since sandbox. We'd grown up together in Tudor Village, gone off to the army together, and come to the police department around the same time. We all came from a common place and shared a love of the job. After three years of living together, we were all close friends.

They sat in my parents' living room, all six of them nodding, all of them quiet a long time. I brought them up to date.

"Look," I told them, "if I tell the truth, all the things I've ever done, I'll be implicating my partners." Frank had resigned from the job and was living in Florida. Dave Cody and Les Wolff were still working, but Les was now under indictment. "What I have to tell the government is no worse than what I have already admitted to. Although what I admitted to concerned only me. Over a year now, I've been banged around and interrogated by every prosecutor in the city and I've been able to hold it together. Almost everyone else in the SIU has cooperated, but not everyone. Some are still refusing to rally round Puccio, and it doesn't seem to me that any of those guys will fold. Still, if anyone comes forward and somehow links me to something, I'm in trouble. The Southern District will indict me."

"You've already committed perjury," Artie said. He waited, then he said, "You acknowledge more acts than you've already admitted on the stand—that's perjury."

I didn't think so. I wasn't positive, but it was my understanding that unless the lie had to do with the facts of the case and had a bearing on the outcome, it wasn't perjury. What I had lied about was not material to the cases—giving drugs to informants, illegal wiretaps. I wasn't sure. I didn't know.

They separated by age—it was fascinating.

John and Don, the motorcycle cops, and John O'D, the youngest of the six, argued the merits of standing firm and admitting nothing: You can't tell them a thing. How can you trust these characters? They'll all turn on you.

Roger, Bill Fritz, and Artie, older, with a lot more time in the job, were convinced that I should let it all out. If I didn't, someone, sooner or later, would burn me, and then where would I be? I had to think of my family first—anyone would.

They argued among themselves, and I listened. The discussion became loud and animated. It was a bitch of a decision, impossible. If nothing else, these men had been by my side through all of this, saw the horror as it developed day in, day out.

Finally they all looked at each other, then looked at me. They smiled, letting me know that they empathized with me, all of them wondering why I had gotten myself involved in the first place. "Well," I told them, "well now, that is a tough one."

Then it was time for three of them to leave. The other three would spend the night. My father came downstairs, asking what the commotion was all about. He knew only what he had read in the newspapers and seen on TV. I didn't want to involve him; I didn't think he could handle it.

I apologized for all the noise. He asked again what was going on, if he could be of any help. I told him it would be all right. I said that I'd handle it. That's when he said he could never forgive the people who testified at the House Un-American Activities Committee hearings. There was no room in his heart for people like that.

"That's helpful," I told him. But this was different, I said. You couldn't compare the two. He nodded.

Around nine or ten o'clock, Les Wolff showed up, and we went for a walk around the block, Artie and Bill Fritz following a few steps behind.

Les was furious—beyond furious. He couldn't believe that

Puccio had indicted him. I had recommended him for the strike force undercover job, and he'd done a fantastic job. He had worked for Mike Shaw and made all sorts of organized crime cases. He had worked his ass off, put himself in harm's way every day.

"How could Puccio toss that all aside?" he said. "More than a half-a-million-dollar government investigation—all that work shit-canned over allegations from some drug dealer? Fucking ridiculous."

I nodded—I didn't know what to say. We kept walking.

Shouting and rambling a little, Les said that Mike and another AUSA, a guy named Bill Aronwald, were livid with Puccio. They couldn't believe he'd indict on such flimsy evidence, ruin a year-long prize investigation on practically no evidence at all.

"That spick never put money in my hands," Les said. "Never, and Puccio knows it."

I was right away livid on his behalf. I told him that he should take a lie detector test. "Fuck you," he said. "You take one." I was all of a sudden depressed. So I told him about my adventure that day with Puccio, and the drug dealer, the guy we'd busted for drugs and bribery. "The bum is now saying we stole four hundred dollars from him. Puccio believes him."

"Fucking unbelieveable!"

"Puccio doesn't care about your case," I said. "He doesn't care about mine. Puccio's only concern is the French Connection. Puccio's only concern is Puccio."

"I'm fighting him," Les said. "I'll never give in to that fuck. Can I count on you?" Then he almost laughed. "You know what?" he said. "They can't hurt us. We tell 'em to fuck off—they can't do a fucking thing."

It was as if he were trying to convince not only me but himself too. I nodded, but I knew better, and I believed that Les knew better too. He hugged me, telling me he had never felt as close to me as he did at that minute. I hugged him, wishing him good luck, telling him, "Les, don't worry. I'll figure something out."

Artie Monty whispered in my ear, "Don't trust him—he's going down the tubes."

The following morning I flew to Virginia. All during the flight, I thought about Les. Puccio had indicted him without a moment's pause. The things Les took for granted were not worth a moment's consideration to Puccio. The fact that Les was working a dangerous and productive case, that he, Puccio, would essentially destroy that case, didn't mean a thing. It was as if he wanted the world to know that he was Tom Puccio, dragon slayer, and everyone had better stand back.

Although I hated Puccio for what he was doing to both Les and me, another thought skimmed through my mind. One way or the other, the French Connection theft was bound to bury all of us. The people who did it knew that it would. They recognized what they would bring down on all our heads. Apparently, that never registered—they didn't care. I was no fan of Tom Puccio. I believed this whole French Connection business was way more than simply doing his job. It had more to do with ego and some bizarre notion of competition. Puccio was Puccio, but I despised the degenerates who pulled off the property clerk theft.

When I got home there was a message from Rudy—he was coming into National Airport at six. He wanted me to meet him there. I caught Gina looking at me. "Is it bad?" she said.

"It can't be good," I told her.

Rudy arrived with Joe Jaffe in tow. I was happy to see Joe, I liked him. A low-key and quiet sort, Jaffe was an AUSA who had a good feel for cops. Tall and thin, with a wild head of very curly hair, he had a hippy quality to him. He was a close friend of Rudy's.

We had dinner, Gina left us alone, and it began.

"Puccio thinks you're a con man," Jaffe said. "He doesn't trust you."

Rudy sat still, watching, listening.

"I was an undercover cop in one form or another most of my

career. Being a con man comes with the territory, but I'm no con man. I can understand him thinking that—but it's not true. At least I hope it's not."

"I know who you are—what you are," Rudy said then. "You're a different man today than you were four or five years ago."

I didn't think so. "I'm not any different today than I was five years ago," I said. "I've always thought of myself as a good cop. I cared about people and did my job, and I did it well—better than most."

"Good cops don't steal," Jaffe said.

"You're right—of course you're right. Look," I said, "sometimes things happen—things that are beyond your control."

"C'mon," Joe said, "try that explanation on Dershowitz. See how that goes down."

He seemed angry and tense, and he was making me very uncomfortable. I looked at Rudy, as Rudy looked at him. Jaffe's impatience with me was clear; I hadn't expected that. I didn't know what I'd expected, but I certainly didn't expect to be attacked by Joe Jaffe.

I said I thought I had overcome my past with my particapation in the investigation. I had surrendered so much of what made my life meaningful: the respect and affection of the men I had worked with. More importantly, I had exposed a wide range of corruption—more than Serpico, more than anyone had ever done. I thought that would be enough.

There was nothing but silence from both of them.

I believed that I had run past my yesterdays, but belief will never be stronger than the truth. The truth was that dodging the past was simply not possible. So now what? Where do I go from here?

"The one thing I've learned is that adults are responsible for their acts," Joe said. "For what they do, no matter why they do it."

In my heart, I knew that these were words—just words that come from people who sit on the fringe of the action. The dreamers, and the politicians who want it both ways—they stand back with clean hands in the air while someone else does the dirty work.

Now I was frightened, and a little angry, but mostly frightened.

"C'mon," Rudy said, "let's you and me go for a walk." I was pleased, happy to be able to spend some time alone with him.

We walked the neighborhood. Rudy said that this was a nice area, a pleasant place to live. It was true, it was a nice neighborhood, but I was a New Yorker. I lived and died with the New York Giants. I hated Washington's team, and I'd been forced to listen to "Hail to the Redskins" more times than I could bear.

Rudy laughed—it was good to see him laugh. "You're in trouble," he said finally.

"I know that."

"Do you?"

"Of course. What's with Joe? We've always gotten along just fine. At least I thought we did."

"He doesn't believe you."

"And you, do you believe me?" He shook his head.

I set about explaining that when I began this investigation—when I agreed with Nick and Mike to go ahead—it was understood that I would never make cases against people that I knew. I would not implicate my partners. There was no need—there were so many other cases out there to make. " 'I'm no informant,' I told them. I would never do that."

"Look," Rudy said, "Mike and Nick had no idea where your investigation would lead. They had no right promising you anything but their support—and I doubt that they did."

"They did. Well, sort of."

"Sort of?"

"You know what I mean."

He put his arm around me. "Bob," he said, "I came down here to see you. I came down here to save you from yourself. There are dozens, and I mean dozens of detectives, sergeants, and lieutenats who are going to cooperate. If one—just one—implicates you in anything you haven't already told us, you'll be indicted and arrested. That would be a damn shame."

"Would they do it?" I asked him. "Do you really think the Southern District would actually indict me?"

"No one would like it. But I think we'd have to," he said. That's when the whole thing changed—and became clear.

I was so tired, worn out by the fervor of the past couple of days. My bones and muscles ached, and as we walked the silent streets of that Virginia neighborhood my anxiety was through the roof. I was going to be arrested, the hero undercover cop brought down to pariah. I felt numb. The emerging thought was that it was going to happen. I knew how it would twist my family's and my own future.

In some ways I was amazed that I had made it this far. The insane tenor of the times—getting past prosecutor after prosecutor day in, day out—it was remarkable. My energy was all but gone; it was my worst moment.

Bang! Bang! was no longer an inside joke played out in my head. To continue this life seemed insane. I wanted all of this, all of it, never to have taken place. But it had. It was done—as I was done.

Bang! is easy—or maybe not so easy. What happens to those you leave behind? No insurance, no pension—a selfish act, a personal escape hatch, and let everyone else hang. *Man oh man*, I thought, *what a fucking mess.*

Then all at once an extraordinary moment—a sudden recognition that maybe I did have one more shot. It was a possibility—one of those maybes—another what-if. One more.

"Rudy, can we talk hypothetically?"

He gave me a meaningful look; it was almost as if he were afraid of what I might say. "Hypothetically? We can't talk theory, Bob. You're my friend, I care about you, but I'm a U.S. attorney. You have to remember that."

"I need to talk hypothetically," I told him. "A what-if kind of thing. It's a what-if. Can't you be Rudy for a minute, and not a prosecutor?"

"Look, you make an admission to me, we're both screwed. I'd never let you testify. The way things stand right now, unless this is resolved, I doubt I'll let you testify again anyway."

"You're serious?"

"I don't know. It's not my decision to make."

"What if I managed to get all my partners to come in and cooperate? What if we came in together? Les Wolff has done all this work for the government. If he came in, don't you think something could be worked out? Say I get Frank Mandato to do the same, and Dave Cody too."

"You can do that?"

I was fuzzy, guessing. My goal was to see what could be salvaged. "I can try," I told him.

In his own way Rudy brought me back. His dismay was apparent, and his patience was wearing thin. When I mentioned my partners again, he stiffened.

"Bob, I'm not concerned about your partners. I'm worried about you."

"I want to be able to talk to my partners."

"Come in first—you have to tell us the truth. Do you understand?"

"I think I do."

"Well?"

In a tone of surrender, I told him that I'd come back to the city tomorrow and we'd talk.

"Everything."

"There's not all that much."

"I can't tell you how relieved I am."

"Really?"

"Yes." Pausing briefly, he said, "Tell me, did you ever murder anyone?"

"Rudy, give me a fucking break, will you? I never murdered any-one, I never sold dope, and I don't know a goddamn thing about the French Connection case."

He smiled and nodded his head. "Good," he said. "It's all right. We'll handle this; we'll get through this."

Later that night, I drove Rudy and Joe back to the airport. On the drive home, I considered ramming my car into an abutment on the George Washington Parkway. I was speeding enough to draw the at-tention of a parkway cop. He pulled me over and read me out, ask-ing what the hell I was trying to do—kill myself, maybe kill him too in the process? I had buried the speedometer.

I showed him my ID and then told him that I wasn't thinking, I was lost somewhere. I said I was sorry, I mean really sorry, for forc-ing him to chase me. It was difficult trying to explain, a New York City narcotics detective living in Virginia.

He was fair-skinned with a thin, unlined face. It was the face of an untroubled man, but in fact he too had his problems. He'd worked a narcotics task force with D.C. cops. He said it had cost him a wife and two children. He'd been reading the newspaper stories coming out of New York and asked if I was caught up in all that.

I nodded.

"I loved that drug job," he told me, "but did it ever screw me up." We exchanged numbers—and promised to go to a Redskin game to-gether. He had season tickets. I didn't tell him how much I hated the Redskins. I'd already told him enough.

When I got home, I telephoned Frank in Florida, then Les and Dave Cody. I tried to put in plain words what I was going to do. I told them that I had a plan, a good workable plan. "If we stand to-gether," I said, "we'd all survive this." I was convinced there was no other way out.

My assurances did not encourage any of them. Frank said, "Whatever you think. You know what's going on better than I do.

Whatever you think." Then he said, "What a fucking horror." Les was more to the point: "Fuck that—fuck you."

His voice poisoned by rage, Les was carefully nurturing a livid, self-rightous anger. I could not break through. I hoped that Dave Cody might.

I told Les to be patient. I asked him to trust me, told him my plan would work. "Fuck that," he said finally.

Dave agreed to meet me in New York. He understood, he said, sure he understood. Dave seemed sad and worn. His nephew, the one shining light in his life, had recently died of cancer. He was a teenager, a handsome, bright young man and a scholar athlete. The boy's death had crushed his heart. Now I was bringing him this news. Sure, he understood, he said, and not to worry—he'd talk to Les.

"We'll get through this; all of us together. We'll make it," he said finally.

When I finished all the calls, I sat at my kitchen table. I told myself that it was time for me to show real courage. The winds were too hot and too strong to survive. Except I could not find the guts for *bang!* Much less *bang! bang!* It simply was not there.

And so I flew to New York the following morning and spent the weekend with Rudy and Joe. I did my best to remember and retell the grubby details of all my misdeeds.

Rudy was so pleased he could scarcely control himself; there was nothing terribly shocking. The same sort of stuff others were admitting. Less than some, more than others. Not very much money—I was never about money.

On Monday, Frank came in and Dave Cody too. In my insufferable smugness, I was convinced that if we all stood together—let it all hang out, get it behind us—we would survive.

Rudy, I was certain, and the others in the Southern District would do all they could to help. I managed to convince myself that the light at the end of that tunnel was perhaps only a light. The truth once revealed will set you free. Sort of, maybe—it depends. Les Wolff was the wild card; he had to come in too.

Les was so outraged with the feds for targeting him, he was trancelike, not thinking clearly. He saw it as utter treachery. He'd already threatened to toss Tom Puccio out a window.

I understood and identified with him, but his fury narrowed his thinking. The idea that the feds had betrayed him—and now his partners would too—added fuel to his passion.

Without Les, my plan, such as it was, had no chance at success. If he didn't come in, it would set us all against one another. It would be devastating. Les's lawyer, Paul Goldberger, a first-rate New York criminal lawyer, made it clear that he would not defend a cooperating witness. That didn't help.

I sat down with Dave Cody, and we discussed how to approach Les. He was confident, positive, and a bit too cheery. He worried me. Dave had always been a heavy drinker. The sweetest of men. Since the death of his nephew, he had been drinking at a frightful pace.

"I can talk to Les; he'll get it from me—he'll understand."

"I'm not so sure," I said. "Let me go with you."

"No, no. Better just me. Better he gets it from me, Bob. He's very angry with you."

I understood, and I told him so. Still, if he could convince Les to come in, we could work this out. If Les calmed down and thought this all through, he would realize my plan could work. We could all survive this. I believed that then—and I believe that today.

Dave said, "That's what the prosecutors told me. I'll explain, he'll understand. Ey, Les is a smart guy."

Confident, Dave left me with a smile and a handshake and went off to meet Les. I should have gone with him. I never should have sent him off alone. Back then, I had no real understanding of alcoholism and depression—any comprehension at all of what Dave himself was going through. It was my outsized egotism. I was so convinced that if everyone followed my lead, we would all be fine.

Dave's meeting with Les went badly, could not have gone worse. I know this because two days later, I had a tear-filled, somewhat hysterical telephone conversation with Les. He continued to attack me and my friends in the government. Convinced that Dave had already made admissions to prosecutors that implicated him, Les saved his best body blows for Dave Cody. He tagged him a drunk, an alcoholic, someone no one in their right mind would listen to, not a soul would believe.

He was so outraged that there was not a scintilla of sympathy in his voice, not a shred of compassion for a man who had just put a pistol to his own head.

In the end, Les Wolff beat the Puccio case, and when I testified against him in Nadjari's state court, he was acquitted. It was a dark, brooding, and depressing case. The truth was, I was testifying against myself. It was the only trial I ever lost.

ULTIMATELY, LES WAS dismissed from the NYPD. The Dershowitz-Rosner appeal was turned down. There were several other trials, which all ended in convictions. My past misconduct was deemed cumulative and not pertinent. And then there was one last trial in the state court.

The defendants' attorney was Jack Evseroff.

Festooned with jewelry, Jack was a dazzler, always attired in one of a magnificent array of expensive and eccentric suits. I had met him when he was an assistant DA in Brooklyn and knew him to be brilliant performer in the courtroom.

I had been forced to contend with a number of the most talented and high-profile defense lawyers in the country, including Al

Krieger, Alan Dershowitz, and his co-counsel Ivan Fisher. Jack Evseroff may not have been as intellectual as some of those. In some ways, he was less prepared than the others. But in the heat and battle of a trial, he was a vicious street fighter with practiced showbiz routines that would wow juries.

And now he was armed with all my admissions. I knew I was in for long, hard days of cross-examination.

The day the trial began, Jack was given permission to speak to me in the witness room. He was friendly, gracious, and smiling. He reminded me of the old days, when he was an ADA, and how together we had put drug dealers in jail. How sad it was, he said, that we had to be here now. He spoke softly, telling me that he respected what I had done. He liked me, and wanted me to know that what he was about to do, he did professionally. He felt no personal malice toward me and wanted to make sure I understood all that.

I appreciated his position, and I told him so. Maybe, I said, just maybe, for old time's sake, he'd go easy with me. "Not a chance," he said, and he smiled.

Before he left the room he shook my hand, not like a friend, but like someone starting a car on a cold winter morning.

I was sworn in. Jack was speaking softly. First he asked how I was feeling. He said, "Detective, you look good and well rested."

I was anything but. Still, I thanked him. He turned his back to me and began walking toward the jury, his voice rising. "Tell us, Detective, how long have you been a member of the New York City police department?"

I'm thinking, *Here it comes.* "Fifteen years."

"And tell us, how many of those years were you assigned to the Narcotics Bureau?"

"About ten."

"You were famous—I mean I remember you were a very active detective. They used to refer to you as Babyface. Isn't that true?"

An objection that was overruled, and I answered that there was more than one Babyface. Jack still had not turned to look at me. He remained facing the jury, showing me only his back. "Yes," he said, "yes, yes, but you were the most famous Babyface."

Another objection that this time was sustained. Then suddenly Jack spun on his heel and looked at me in the most malicious and cold way, and his voice rose to a crescendo. "Tell this court, Detective, how much money did you steal as a narcotics detective? You don't have to be precise. Give us a round number."

Oy. "I don't know precisely."

He turned his back to me again, his hands on his hips, his voice ringing with scorn and mockery. "I'm not asking you to be precise. Give us your educated guess."

I looked at the defendants, and then looked at the jury. Jack had everyone spellbound. "I'm not sure," I said. "But I'll tell you what— I know it was not nearly as much as your fee for this case."

Everyone went batshit. The jury broke up—even the defendants began laughing. Jack Evseroff literally screamed for a mistrial. I was ordered off the stand and returned to the witness room.

The prosecutors lectured and harangued me. There was a great deal of noise in the room. Someone said troublemaker, someone else said smartass.

I leaned back in the chair, rested my head against the wall, and closed my eyes. Treacherous rest, sleep brought dreams. My mouth was dry, and I was very, very tired.

"He's taking Valium," someone said. "It's the drugs."

In my mind's eye, I could see the fixer lawyer from Queens who, when I was in the TPF, put the twenty dollars in my hand, the ADA in Brooklyn into whose hands I had put five hundred dollars. I thought about the fixer lawyer from the Bronx who wanted to give me thirty thousand if I changed my testimony. And the lawyer in Manhattan who, for a price, wanted his client registered as an informant. I thought about my days at the beach with Jerry and about my time in TPF. I thought about the drug addict Junior, who had named me Babyface, and about Joe Nunziata, about Frank and Les and Dave Cody. It was all a wonder.

"Hey," someone said, "hey, are you ready to get back out there?"

A football game, it was all very familiar.

The trial went on for three days. I was battered and bruised and reeling. Jack's attacks on me were ferocious, brutal, but like all the others, Jack Evseroff lost.

His defendants were guilty.

Jack Evseroff was right, it was all very sad.

DAYS ROLLED INTO weeks, weeks into months. My bodyguards left for new commands. Rudy went off to Washington as deputy attorney general. Puccio went on to investigate and prosecute Abscam. Abscam was an FBI undercover sting operation, FBI agents passing as Arab sheiks, throwing money at congressmen and senators. One day, sitting in his office, Puccio would tell me that if he had not been stopped, there would have been no one left in Congress. I believed him.

The police department didn't know what to do with me, where to assign me. I began lecturing at the police academy. Did a powerful little dog-and-pony show on the dangers of what I called the erosion process, how horrible and unforgiving it was to lose your sense of personal ethics and morality.

At the academy, I was a popular success—the only instructor the recruits invited out for a beer. Some of the brass abhorred the idea that rookies would use me as a role model, so my academy career ended.

A year went by, then another. I was assigned to work at the Internal Affairs training unit and then the Civilian Complaint Review Board. Although I did have one or two moments of confrontation, there was nothing terribly serious. Generally I was treated kindly, and during that time I met some of the most interesting and enter-taining cops.

I had committed myself to see it through. I'd go to work every day, keep my head up, and do my twenty years. For a street cop like me, the jobs themselves were hideous. Any real future for me in the police department seemed, at best, unlikely.

PRINCE OF THE CITY

After the Jack Evseroff trial, a *New York Daily News* headline went "I Hate Leuci List Grows." That was just a warm-up. Suddenly I understood clearly that there would be many stories. There were all sorts of people out to humiliate and disgrace me. A number had already begun to make me a piñata for revisionists. I was all the time trying to explain myself.

No, I wasn't under arrest.

Then they must have threatened you?

No, it was nothing like that.

Then why did you do it?

It's complicated—many reasons.

C'mon. That's not what I heard.

It wasn't long before I'd had enough of it. I mentally ticked off the list of characters who would probably do a book. Convinced that few, if any, would be fair and evenhanded, I asked around and was told that I'd better find a literary agent.

Her name was Esther Newberg. I said that I wanted my story told. I explained some of my life, and she told me a bit about her own. She had been there, oh yeah, right on that island on the terrible night. One of the "Boiler Room Girls."

When she told me this, she puckered her lips, and the faintest sign of a cynical smile crossed her face. Esther had experienced and understood the merciless power of the press, how an incident could be turned and twisted until it no longer resembled the truth. She was smart, and when aroused she had a habit of strumming her fingernails along the top of her desk. I was impressed by her lack of pretension and her humor, and right away liked her very much.

At first I let slip that I'd like the chance to write my own book. Tell the story of the investigation within the pages of a book I created.

"Well . . ."

"Why not?"

"Have you ever written a book before?"

"Of course not. But I've read any number of good books. Five or six at least."

"Do you trust me?"

"Yes."

"Then forget it. Find a journalist. Find someone with credibility, someone with standing, someone who has a track record. Be sure it's a writer who knows the police world."

I had an author in mind and told her so. I had recently read one of his books, *Target Blue*. I thought it had been very well done. It was an accurate insider's view of the workings of the upper echelons of the NYPD. His name was Robert Daley, and he had been a deputy police commissioner of public relations.

"We don't represent him."

"I'd like to speak to him anyway."

"Go ahead—can't hurt."

I telephoned Daley, and we met; it was an eventful day. We discussed the possibilities, all the ifs and maybes. If he did it, it would not be a puff piece. He'd do the research and all the reporting. He was not necessarily a fan, but I'd be treated fairly. That's all I asked, that I be treated honestly. He was a full-time writer, made his living from his work. I was a policeman—I had a job. There probably would not be much money, and the work would be hard—grueling hours of interviews. Was I willing to make the effort.

Yes, sure, let's do it.

It was a magnificent year, painful and magnificent. Painful reliving the investigation, magnificent spending time with Bob Daley, watching as he put a book together, learning just how difficult and demanding the work was.

Bob Daley lived in a lovely house in Connecticut with his wife, Peggy. Peggy Daley was a strikingly beautiful woman, born and raised in France. She arranged for Bob and me the most wonderful lunches.

Reliving the story was painful psychoanalysis, and after a difficult morning's work, those lunches with Debussy, Verdi, Puccini, and Ravel in the background became for me a quasi-religious experience.

There was nothing I loved better than to sit around and gaze at Bob and Peggy's beautiful gardens, sipping a glass of a wonderful wine as Bob tutored me. He taught me about French wines, classical music, and bullfighting. I listened to tales of his life in France and England. I enjoyed those moments, but I hated revisiting the decisions I had made before and during the investigation. I was still working in the police department—it was all so recent. Bob asked piercing questions, and I had severe problems dealing with my own answers.

All through that time, I learned to respect and admire Bob's work ethic. During that year we formed a special bond. Grounded in a Jesuit education, Bob Daley had strong moral integrity, and I was concerned that he would judge me harshly.

Collaborations are never easy, but ours was totally untroubled. We have known each other now going on three decades, and I don't remember one insensitive word ever passing between us. He was then, as he is now, a kind and generous man.

Back with the police department, I lectured occasionally at the academy and the Internal Affairs school. My lecture was long. I'd take the students step by step—introduce all the characters and examine the price of giving up one's moral anchor.

A sergeant with the New Jersey State Police sat in on one of my lectures. His name was Bob Delaney—today he's an NBA referee. Back then, he had just completed a complex and difficult two-year-long organized crime undercover job. He asked if I'd come give my talk at the New Jersey State Police Training Center in Sea Girt.

I was happy to do it. The need for catharsis drove me: I had a continuing need to work out in my mind the whys and ifs and hows of my story. A grave warning: Mislay your morality just one time, and chances are you won't get another try. But I was doing a book— and would probably make some money. The hypocrisy of all that was not lost on me. More guilt.

At the New Jersey State Police academy, I met Dan Russo. Dan was an FBI agent. He asked if I'd come to Quantico and share my story there. The catharsis went on. In time I would speak to thousands of police officers throughout the country. Some listened and learned, some didn't.

All during that time I had dinners and spent time with Rudy, with Nick, and Mike too. Everyone, it seemed, was doing well. The investigation and all that it entailed was receding. I'd survived; we had all survived. Now each and every one of them was ready to move on with their lives. As for me, I knew there was not much of a chance that I would ever be able to chase all the ghosts. The nightmares never went away.

One night, after a meal with Nick, sitting in a café alongside Central Park, he asked me if I thought it had all been worth it. Would I do it again?

"Would you?"

He smiled, shook his head, and turned away. "I think you've done something important," he said.

"Yeah, I guess so. But at what price?"

"You're better for it. That much is for sure, the PD and you, you're both better for it."

IT WAS A spring afternoon. I was in my office at the training center on Poplar Street in Brooklyn Heights, shooting the breeze. My phone rang—it was Esther Newberg.

"Sit down," she said.

"I'm sitting."

"Bob Bookman, ICM's book-to-movie agent, just phoned me. Are you ready?"

Silence from me.

"He's made a movie deal with Orion Films. It's a very, very good deal."

Her words drilled into me, lifted me, and spun me around. I wanted to react, to jump and shout, but I felt paralyzed. There were other cops in the room, men I had worked with for the past couple of years—calm men, educated, and easy to talk to, detectives who had looked past all that had happened and taken me in, good men who had lived with the book and all the publicity surrounding the publication and still remained friendly. There was even some of the old-style camaraderie—the binding element of cops.

But now a film—*Prince of the City* would be a movie. I didn't want to imagine what the department's and their reactions would be.

When I hung up the phone, I told them. "That was Esther Newberg. She tells me that they're going to make a movie of *Prince of the City*."

Suddenly I was getting a lot of "Geeze, that's great. That's fucking wonderful."

———

ONE WEEK LATER I was standing, looking out the window of the Beverly Hills Hotel. I could not quite convince myself of the reality of all this. Hollywood bristled with allure. All the clichés were true. It was nirvana, the city where your imagination ran riot, a fantasy come to life, the stuff of wonderful imaginings.

Through my hotel room window, it seemed a grand place indeed. It was all summery sunlight, and seventy degrees in the middle of the day. Wherever I looked there were palm trees alive with birds of a color and type that I had never seen before. The air was lush with exotic and tropical aromas. I was a million miles from Red Hook.

This was the city where Joseph Wambaugh had once carried a badge and gun. The city of Newman and Redford and Dustin Hoffman, Pacino and De Niro; of course none of those actors actually lived there.

Los Angeles was a city where most of the cops looked as though they'd just returned from a casting call. The men and women of all ages were young, thin, tanned, and seemed to smile all the time. It was as though in their well-groomed heads, wind chimes sang.

That night, Daley and I had been invited to dinner at the home of an important agent. It would be a fairly large gathering. There would be film stars, an important director and his wife, the head of a studio. There would be two other people, one of whom would one day head a television network, the other a mysterious woman. At least she was mysterious to me.

I'd like to tell you all their names. I'll refrain from doing so in the interest of their personal privacy, and in truth, it would serve no purpose.

Sitting next to me at the dinner table was Sean Connery. His name I'll use because he's one of my heroes, and on that night he performed like the elegant champion he is.

All during dinner, there was small talk and friendly chatter. Sean told me that some slug in Europe was impersonating his son. The guy was running up huge bills using his name. Sean was not happy.

In the midst of this conversation, the mystery woman sitting across from me—and putting away great amounts of wine—leaned toward me and whispered: "I'd like to pee on you."

Now to some, this may have been a new sexual fad, some L.A. hip-hop, but I'd never heard of such a thing. A fine-looking and sophisticated woman—it was probably a riveting and edifying cultural moment for her, the idea of pissing on a cop. I felt insulted and more than a bit annoyed.

"Excuse me?"

"You heard me." Said sweetly, a little smile.

"Take my word for it, it would be no fun for you. What you should do is go and piss on your boyfriend. The smiling guy at the far end of the table."

Piss on me? Piss on you.

Suddenly one of the guests gave the room the once-over, then came out with a fistful of joints. Pot—marijuana. I'd smoked before—didn't do well with it, but it was not that big a deal. Still, in that crowd, I felt embarrassed, not sure what to say.

Sean Connery stood up. "Listen," he said. "I think Bob is too much the gentleman to say anything, so I'm going to say it for him. Personally, I'm embarrassed by that, and I'm sure he is too. He is, after all, a police officer."

There was some good-natured laughter—people shook hands, the dope was put away—and everyone went home.

Back in New York during the weeks that followed, Orion hired director Sidney Lumet and screenwriter Jay Presson Allen. Each of them gave me schooling in how the business of Hollywood was in essence the pistonlike work of getting a movie made.

IT WAS THE day of my twenty-year anniversary—twenty years on the job. Chief Guido telephoned me and asked me to come to his office. Apprehension had haunted me for days. Now here it was, and the chief was right on the dot.

John Guido—the five-star superchief of the department's Inspectional Service Bureau. Some people said he was fanatical. I thought of him more as a whirling dervish. There were days he was kind to me, even supportive. Other days, he wanted to string me up in front of police headquarters. I both respected and feared him, and that was exactly how he wanted it.

Chief Guido's ego was the size of headquarters, his sense of self-importance huge. He was a man bent on the settling of scores, reprisal, and power. There was a lot of Tartiglino in the chief.

Run into Guido before lunch—things were fine. After lunch and three martinis—you'd better be ready to duck.

"A book, I can live with a book," he told me. "A movie? Too much, just too much. I'm tired of answering questions from the press about you. I want you gone."

"I want to stay."

He told me that I should go to Vermont and open a hardware store. "I'm not interested in hardware stores in Vermont," I told him. "I'm a detective; it's what I do."

"Really?" he said. "And what could I do with you? You can't testify. Every time you take the stand, it'll be *Prince of the City* all over again. Or worse yet, I send you to a detective squad, somebody shoots you and I have another Serpico on my hands."

He made it sound as though he were in pain.

But at the conclusion of the investigation, I had gone to work every day for five years. I hadn't gone to Switzerland like Serpico.

"Enough time has passed. I'm ready to return to a detective squad and catch cases." I said all this with a certain amount of confidence.

"Bullshit—you could never testify. I want you the fuck out of here, do you understand me?"

On that day there was little constraint in the chief's manner. Given the daunting difference in our ranks, there was little I could say.

"I can do it," I told him. "Give me a chance and I'll show you."

He waved that off. He told me that I was too much of a headache: "Please, do me a favor and pack it in."

When I returned to my office the phone was ringing and the chief was in my ear again, bantering on in that I'm-trying-to-be-nice—and-it's-taking-all-my-self-control style of his.

"You're too complicated," he said. "Look, I think the department has done right by you." His voice was kindly, the dervish doing a spin.

Suddenly I heard myself repeating lines I'd used too many times before. Too many excuses. It strengthened my feeling that in this job, no matter how well-meaning my intentions, I somehow always managed to create problems. I said to myself, *It's over.*

My vanity had told me that I had survived the investigation and then the purge. I'd spun it all out into the idea that I could simply go back to being a detective. The reality was an entirely different story. "Will you wake the fuck up?" Frank Mandato would have said.

It was twenty years to the day since I had been part of a phalanx of gray uniformed recruits marching into an out-of-date building on Hubert Street in lower Manhattan. Twenty years from the time when the weight of a gun belt first felt natural. Twenty years from the time when I was chock-full of wide-awake dreams. Twenty years since all my uniform leather smelled new and my spirit was all eagerness and passion. Twenty years from the time when all us rookies thought we would laugh and live forever. Twenty years.

I walked over to Police Headquarters, handed in my badge and my ID; I kept my gun.

IN NO TIME at all, Sidney Lumet and Jay Presson Allen had deconstructed the book, set up a preproduction office, hired staff, and were interviewing actors. Some were New York–based actors, others had never acted professionally before.

Sidney Lumet was recognized as the ultimate New York film director. From his first film—the courtroom drama *Twelve Angry*

Men—to his more recent efforts—*Network, Dog Day Afternoon,* and *Serpico*—Lumet had been considered a man of exquisite taste. He was a workaholic, a man who was absolutely committed to the profession. Despite, or perhaps because of his early television experience, he was frugal with studio money. Sidney Lumet always brought his films in under budget.

Toward me, he was at all times gentlemanly and gracious. Even more so when I told him that I had no interest in hanging around the set—which of course was not true—but I knew it was wise not to.

Around the same time that I met Sidney, I also met the screenwriter, Jay Presson Allen. She was a garrulous, lively, no-nonsense woman, to the point of almost being intimidating. Jay had created and written one of my all-time favorite TV series, *Family.* She'd also written the play, and then the film, *The Prime of Miss Jean Brodie,* and the film version of *Cabaret.*

Now she and Sidney would take the book *Prince of the City,* and in an amazing feat, write that extraordinarily long screenplay in three weeks.

When I began my own writing, both Jay and Sidney would function for me as critics, mentors, and supportive friends. They would do so for many years. In a world where relationships and so-called friendships have about as much weight, depth, and staying power as a hummingbird feather in an updraft, this is no small accomplishment.

All the same, back then, I was simply the subject of their movie. Someone to be stroked, taken to lunch, and sent on my way. Being sent on my way didn't bother me, wrapped up as I was in a struggle to find the road to an uncertain future. Day followed day, and I desperately missed the police world. It was all I knew, all I had ever known.

In the meantime, I would be the focus of a major feature film. Not something uplifting and inspirational, but a dark, somewhat depressing and painful tale of an episode in my life. I was bound and determined that it would not be the story of my entire life.

Meanwhile, I would try to enjoy it. I just hoped that I had not outlived Babyface—to be reincarnated as *Prince of the City*. And live with that nickname for the rest of my life.

FROM THE MOMENT I met Treat Williams I was impressed. Completely unaffected, he came on as an average guy who just happened to be an actor. Treat was anything but average. Unusually handsome, he was an athlete, intelligent and well read. He drove a motorcycle and had a commercial pilot's license—and he could sing and dance. His performance in *Hair* had been marvelous. And his real name was Treat Williams.

Treat asked smart, endless questions about the life of a narcotics cop. He was polite and listened; every so often he'd glance at me and nod his head, wondering, I supposed, why I did some of the things I had done. Good question.

Around Treat, I tried my best not to make an ass of myself. Sometimes I succeeded, and sometimes I failed. Still, Treat was always kind and never pointed a hurtful finger of criticism toward me.

As a book, *Prince of the City* was a considerable success. There was a huge trade paperback sale and it was the main selection of the Book of the Month Club. As a film, the critics praised its strengths, but the public response was mixed.

The film was not a commercial success, nothing like *Serpico* or *The French Connection*. It is an odd, long, and complex movie. Sidney Lumet and Jay Allen put over a sort of docu-drama—their purpose exactly. They stayed faithful to the material, and the film drew crowds in New York, Los Angeles, and other big cities. It didn't do well in Middle America. As it happens, the film remains a sort of a cult classic in Europe and is played regularly on American television.

Promoting the book and movie, Bob Daley and I did something like twenty-three cities in twenty-six days. Ultimately, I'm sure, apart or together, we appeared on every radio and TV talk and interiew show in America.

All during this time, I lectured frequently at universities, law schools, and police training facilities throughout the country. Alan Dershowitz invited me to his constitutional law class at Harvard. I spoke at the Aspen Institute for the Humanities in Colorado. There, I met CIA Director Admiral Stansfield Turner. He said I should come to Washington and talk to him about a job.

All this traveling was not easy. I had to overcome my fear of flying—being first on the scene of an airplane crash had stayed with me. All the same, the lecturing was important: reliving the story over and over, the ongoing catharsis.

Those long hours in airports and on airplanes did offer one great reward: I began to read in a serious way.

During this time, I was trying to map some sort of future for myself. From the first days of working with Bob Daley, I knew that I wanted to write. And I was presumptuous enough to believe that I had something to say. My formal education was spotty at best. I knew enough about life to understand that there was no magic bullet, that I'd find no success without persistent work. If I wanted to write, I had to educate myself. Reading was the first step.

First there was Wambaugh, and Elmore Leonard. No one captures the milieu of the police like Joseph Wambaugh. He is not only a terrific writer of police stories, he's a fine writer. Wambaugh captures the hilarity, the cynicism, and exposes the demons and dark mysterious world that are the policeman's life. And no one uses dialogue and captures street characters like Elmore Leonard.

I read all their books like a fanatic. Personally, I had material for a hundred novels and a thousand characters. My years of undercover work had given me an ear for all sorts of street dialogue. I certainly had stories to tell. But did I have any talent to write? I began reading more and more. I tried to learn everything, and I had to work very hard to learn something. I threw myself into reading with the same manic passion I once reserved for working a case.

I read police procedurals and mystery novels. I found myself bored with all but the very best of them. Mostly these books were written about imaginary people who I was certain did not live and take breaths in the world that I knew. If they did, I didn't care about them.

Many of those books were best sellers. Then I discovered Jim Thompson, and rediscovered my father's favorite, James T. Farrell. *Well now*, I thought, *here you are*. I read and studied *The Grifters, Young Lonigan, The Young Manhood of Studs Lonigan, and Judgement Day*.

Then I wrote fifty terribly rough pages of a day in the life of a South Brooklyn heroin junkie. It was the beginning of my first novel.

Esther had introduced me to a writer by the name of Bob Reiss. Bob was a first-rate journalist and author. He was doing research on a novel; he needed some police insights.

Young, a casually elegant and a very thoughtful guy, I gave him the insight, and he read my pages. He was flattering, probably far more complimentary than those earliest attempts deserved.

Reiss suggested that I should join him at the Bread Loaf summer writers' workshop. "There will be starting-out writers and a number of published writers as well. I'll be there," he said. "You'll learn something, and you'll have a great time." I went and it changed my life.

IT'S AN ILLUSION, mind you, but illusions can be wonderful. Set in the mountains of Vermont, at Middlebury College, the location of Bread Loaf is stunning. However, it's a fantasy to believe that you'll learn how to write there.

Bread Loaf—its very name is comforting, and that is precisely what it is. Being there was more stimulating to me than anything I could have imagined. Winding mountain roads and pastures and rock walls where chipmunks ran and went into hiding from circling owls and hawks. There were fresh jugs of cold milk in the mornings and crusty dark breads, and a whole lot of pot and booze and singalongs. There were workshops and readings where would-be writers searched for that silver thread that ties one writer to another writer, to another writer, and then to you.

It was a bucolic paradise where I learned the unique and exact way writers looked at things, the way a writer can make the unclear, clear. Suddenly my world was filled with wonder and possibility. *I can do this,* I told myself, *I can tell my police stories—and maybe I can even be good at it.*

Maybe, I thought, I can gain insight into motivation and the dark recesses of my own mind. What makes people tick—what makes me tick.

There was a main house, where most people stayed, but I along with four others settled in a classic four-over-four 1860s farmhouse. There was a porch, and rooms with wide floorboards, a bedroom, a single hard bed, and a writing desk for god knows what. No one wrote at Bread Loaf.

I liked my housemates, two in particular: Bill Jefferson, whom I called Jeff, and George Devoe. Both have remained close friends. A Vietnam veteran, Jeff was doing film reviews for the *Maine Times.* He had reviewed *Prince of the City.* He, like George, was hard at work writing a novel.

Bread Loaf, summer camp for writers. That summer was a banner year for famous writers: Robert Stone, John Irving, Tim O'Brien, Ron Hansen, and Carolyn Forché, to name just a few. There were many others, and many talented writers nearby.

I discovered another man who would turn out to be a lifelong friend, the poet Kit Hathaway. Kit taught me something about poetry, what was—and what wasn't.

The whole idea of the conference was that you would show your fifty pages to a famous writer. Then he or she would give you feedback. My reader was Tim O'Brien. He'd read my pages, then listened to what I had to say, nodded his head, and said I had some talent. Writing was work, all work, and I had to keep at it.

I hardly heard what it was he had to say. I was looking at him—studying him. I'd read his first book, *If I Die in a Combat Zone*, and was immediately captivated. When I read *Going After Cacciato*, I was intimidated and overwhelmed by his abilities.

"You like O'Brien?" Jeff said. "You should try Bob Stone."

I immediately went to the bookstore and bought *Dog Soldiers* and *A Flag for Sunrise*. It took me two days to read *Dog Soldiers*, and soon after I returned home, I finished *A Flag for Sunrise*. I was convinced then, as I am today, that those two books are among the greatest books written in the English language in the past fifty years.

Christ, I had so much to learn, but I also realized that there was only so much you could learn. God-given, exquisite talent cannot be taught. Still, it was okay—I could only do what I could do, and I believed that what I could do could not be done by many.

WE HAD SOLD the Virginia house, and with that, and the money from *Prince of the City*, bought what was for us a big house in Connecticut: five bedrooms, three bathrooms, two fireplaces. It was a big house, on a huge piece of property.

Anthony and Santina went into high school, Gina found a job at Ethan Allan. Through no fault of hers, the marriage was teetering, and had been for quite some time. Even though back then I would never entertain the idea of divorce, it was clear that Gina and I were in trouble.

The past years had been crazed—long separations and dreadful anxieties, bodyguards with her and the children, living apart in other cities and other states. I was never a good husband, focused as I was always on me, me, and me. Now I would at least try to be a good provider.

Gina loved that house, still does; I thought that the Connecticut house somehow would be salve for all the wounds and pain I'd inflicted on the family.

———

I WAS CAPTIVATED by the solitary life of the novelist. You are all alone with books, studying and educating yourself. If you can pay the rent, it is a perfect life.

I have always had my share of detractors, some legitimate and some opportunist, hypocritical, and self-serving. Do I blame them all? Not really. Will I forgive the self-serving and hypocritical? Not ever. Will I strike back? I'll sure as hell try. Within the pages of my fiction, I'll torture them.

I learned that the novelist Robert Stone had a house not far from me in Westport, Connecticut. I searched him out, found his telephone number, and called him.

"Come by," he said. "Sure, we can go for a walk."

I had heard Stone read at Bread Loaf—he'd been subdued then, reserved, almost shy. In person, he was chatty, friendly. He put me immediately at ease. His wife, Janice, was a woman sure of herself and her sense of humor, things being funny and sad at the same time, and her long straight hair was not her only testament to her one-time hippy bonds.

Bob worked in the mornings and went for a walk each day around noontime. As we walked together he seemed as curious about me as I was about him. He asked questions the way a man with the curiosity of a major writer would. We talked about Hollywood, his experiences and mine, and we laughed.

He was doing a book set there and in Mexico. I could come by anytime I liked. Telephone first; then we could walk and talk. He had little formal education, went to sea very young, lived many places, and had seen much of the world.

Read Joseph Conrad, he told me, read Hemingway, Breslin, and Mailer. Read, read, and read some more.

Bob Stone read my pages, gave me advice on this and that. "You're better than you think," he said, "plenty of raw talent, but with work to do."

I enrolled at the New School and studied screenwriting. I

registered at Fordham and studied the history of the rise of man. Esther sold my first novel, and then my second to a publisher who had an imprint at Macmillan. His name was Larry Freundlich, and he was the finest editor I ever had.

I continued lecturing to police, and the catharsis went on. I loved spending time around policemen. They have, after all, unique and matchless stories to tell. I moved into the émigré Russian community in Brighton Beach—spent nine months there and then did a book about a Russian wiseguy from Moscow, called *Odessa Beach*.

In the meantime, I could tell that my writing was improving. I wasn't selling a lot of books, but it was giving me a good deal of personal pleasure, and paying the bills.

It had been five years since *Prince of the City*. With the house in Connecticut, both Anthony's and Santina's college education paid in full, about a thousand dinners in Manhattan, cars, life; the money was gone.

My writing strategy was to attack hypocrisy and work out the complexities of why good people go bad. I wasn't writing hero fiction—characters bigger than life held little or no interest for me. All my stories were character driven; in short, I was not writing the kind of genre books that sell a whole lot. But with Esther's help, I was being published, and making a living. I continued reading, continued to educate myself, and tried to perfect the craft.

When Esther got me a two-book contract to write my fourth and fifth novels, I left Connecticut. The marriage had become unglued. I was not fundamentally unhappy. In many ways, Gina and I were very compatible. But I was constantly lying about where and how I spent my time. Staying away from home when I should have been there. The duplicity was killing me—I thought I had put that all behind me.

I'd had one angioplasty, and then a second. Doctors said, "You have to stop smoking, eat wisely, get some exercise, and reduce your stress." After the third angioplasty, they told me, "Next time it's bypass—or a heart attack—or a stroke."

I found a small village on the water in southern Rhode Island. I rented a house and began spending time around fishermen and sailors, quahoggers and lobstermen.

I left Gina the Connecticut house and all its contents and my police pension to pay for it. All those years of living with me, she'd earned it. I could get along, get by, try to live off my writing. For me, it had never been about money.

I HAD SOLD books in France, Spain, England, Germany, and Croatia, and several times across the ensuing years was invited to writers' conferences in Europe. While there, I traveled to the country of my ancestors. In Italy, I cried heartrending tears for my father, who had died before ever having a chance to see the land his people came from. To feel that sun, smell the lemon trees, and marvel at all the unique and magnificent colors of land and sea and sky. To hear fathers call out to sons, "*Vieni qua*," "Come here," in that same loving tone that he used to call me.

In the north of Spain, in Asturias, I made wonderful lifelong writer friends. We wandered the streets where the revolution to save the Spanish Republic was born. Again I thought of my father, how he would have been awed by it all.

Back in the states, Rudy's star had risen. He was the mayor of New York City. Remarkable. I watched with amazement, concern, and a curious pride the metamorphosis that transformed a rather easygoing, fun-loving guy into a hard-punching political pro.

There had never been much self-doubt in Rudy, for better or worse. He was always a man who could surprise, even shock. A day or two after he'd met Donna Hanover, he telephoned me, and we three met for lunch.

All I can remember with any certainty is that they seemed caught up in those first happy-go-lucky blushes of newly discovered love. Donna was a beautiful woman, with a great tan. She laughed a lot, told funny stories, and made tossing motions with her head. We met and had drinks together two or three more times. It appeared to me that although they seemed well suited, they had different agendas.

Donna was interested in exploring many things—acting, television—she thought that she and Rudy could do the lecture circuit together. She and Rudy—you got two for the price of one. There was no way Donna Hanover was going to sit back and enjoy being Mrs. Rudy Giuliani.

At their wedding, Donna introduced me to Congressman Mario Biaggi and Senator Alphonse D'Amato, a Donna surprise. I knew that Rudy was no fan of these men, but even back then, Donna was an immensely talented bargainer.

In March 2000 Rudy came to Rhode Island to attend a Republican fund-raiser. We managed to sneak off to a small café in Jamestown, where I had dinner with him and Judith Nathan. All over the room people were turning their heads, and one or two clapped hands—everyone trying to draw his attention. He seemed much easier around Judith, and she appeared to accept him on his own terms. In her company, Rudy seemed more his old self. He was relaxed and making jokes about his senatorial campaign (this was before the cancer scare).

His politics had become more conservative, and some both in and out of the media were laying on him the reputation of a perpetually, hardheaded and coldhearted politico. That was not the Rudy Guilani I had known, not at all.

In the old days, he often talked about the battle of the underdog. He'd been a fan of both John and Robert Kennedy. While in private practice, he'd represented coal miners in Kentucky and for three years fought to keep their mine open and safe and the miners working. Unlike so many from the Southern District, he had not come from privilege. He opposed the War in Vietnam and understood the plight of the workingman.

To me, he was always a sensitive, caring, even loving friend. At any rate, he was running for the Senate, and under a well-planned, well-organized attack. Most of the people I knew—just about all the people I knew—were ready to shoulder spears against him. An offense to liberalism, they said. Rudy is an egotist with a stone heart.

"You're wrong," I would say; "I know him, and you're wrong." Rudy competed in a tough arena—the no-holds-barred, no-quarter-given netherworld of New York politics. It was a world where if you didn't develop a hard-faced stance that masked vulnerability, you would not survive.

Sure he has an ego—and he's tough on crime, always has been. Nevertheless, I know him to be on the whole a kind person. I do—I know. I've seen it, and experienced it firsthand; it's no act. Rudy has a good heart.

When he left Rhode Island that night, I promised that I would come and visit at Gracie Mansion. Time was running out—his days as mayor were dwindling.

AS THE SUN rose over Narragansett Bay on September 11, 2001, I was already in my writing room drinking coffee, smoking the only good cigarette of the day, looking out my window through the early light at my neighbor's Morgan horses, which stood like statues in their paddock.

My eyes never got used to the amazing sight of horses standing motionless in the mist at daybreak, just as my eyes never got used to the sight of dozens of swallows all of a sudden soaring out of the barn.

I sipped my coffee, thinking this was going to be a glorious, clear, sunlit New England day. The roosters were out, all five of them. I know less about chickens than I do horses, but I'd learned that roosters crow not only at daybreak but all day long.

This house that I share with Kathy Packard, the woman who also shares my life, has the backdrop of time. It's a four-over-four farmhouse built in the 1860s, very much like the house I stayed in at Bread Loaf.

I began my work for the day. Time flew.

And then the telephone rang.

It was Kathy calling from work, and I expected that she was calling to remind me to keep the chickens out of her garden. Something she did every morning.

"Go put on CNN," she said, "hurry." It was sometime around nine o'clock.

No! One of the two World Trade Center towers was burning. The TV commentator said an airplane had hit it. I watched in bewilderment as the second airplane struck the second tower. It looked like some sort of special-effect movie shot. But this was no movie, this was real—and clearly no accident. This was an attack on America.

Two raging fires were swallowing both buildings. I watched in terror as fire trucks and police cars filled the streets. Sirens, everyone running, there were shadowy shapes in the towers' windows, smoke billowing behind them. Jesus.

I telephoned my daughter, who worked in midtown at ABC News, and couldn't get through. She could be anywhere. Santina often had meetings all over the city. There were thousands of people in those buildings of glass and aluminum—thousands. I phoned my son. He was at home, watching.

On the TV I saw Rudy—jacket off, walking, giving directions, pointing. Calm, in control, as the world around him exploded—Rudy.

I felt a deep, scary sense of dread at what was happening, what I was seeing. Then suddenly, without willing it, I thought of all the times when, with my bodyguards, I had sat for endless days on the fifty-seventh floor of that South Tower, transcribing tapes. On the television I watched as more fire trucks raced to the scene—more police cars.

They said it was American Airlines Flight 11, out of Boston, that struck the North Tower. Boston is an hour and a half from the farm—those terrorists had walked the earth an hour and a half from me—crazy thoughts.

Another news flash—an airplane had crashed into the Pentagon. The Pentagon was burning. Sometime near ten o'clock, the Trade Center's South Tower collapsed. Fuck, it collapsed.

At ten minutes past ten, United Airlines Flight 93 disintegrated on impact in a field in Somerset County, Pennsylvania. Around ten-thirty, I watched the Trade Center's North Tower buckle, then disappear in a monstrous cloud of smoke and debris as it telescoped into the ground, ending all those lives of suffering and terrified human beings.

Later that day, reporters pressed Rudy to estimate how high the death count could be. He told them that there was little value in speculation, but it was "more—ultimately—than any of us can bear." He also said that we would survive. We'd deal with the consequences—find those responsible—and exact justice.

There, I thought, watching the news conference, *that's it, that's Rudy.* That's what he is truly all about. A special kind of strength—a world of empathy, along with conviction of purpose—that's him, that's Rudy.

People say that New York is more reflective of our nation's values than the nation is as a whole. I live somewhere else, and I've traveled extensively throughout the country. I don't necessarily agree with that. I certainly understand its genesis.

Nevertheless, on the day when we needed him most, the country could not find the president. And forget the vice president. So New York offered up its mayor, or rather, its mayor showed up. Putting his life on the line. Rudy was there when we needed him most. He was always there.

AT THE
END OF
THE DAY

'm old now—a grandfather. Babyface is a long time gone. The years between then and now have passed swiftly. South Brooklyn is far away. When I add things up, I've lost many friends and a sweet brother to the drug war and other atrocities of life. Still, I've gained other friends, and others retain the power to withhold forgiveness for the things I've done, perceived or real.

My life is good. I may have entered the writer's life through the back door, but better to enter that way than not at all.

When I think back on it, as I often do, I can still see Frank and me, sprinting through the streets, kicking in doors, rolling around on the ground with drug dealers and other bad guys. What I believed then, and what I know now, are different. I've learned to live with guilt and regret, but I am a different person today.

I read and write constantly—always working on the craft. I am an adjunct professor in the University of Rhode Island's English and Political Science Departments. I continue to lecture to police. This coming month—April 2003—I'm off to Peoria, Illinois. I'll be the keynote speaker at the convention of the Illinois Drug Enforcement Officers Association. There will be six hundred narcotics cops from

Chicago, the Illinois State Police, DEA, and others. This is what I will tell them:

> There are probably those among you who, had they not come to police work, would have been criminals. That minuscule percentage I'm not concerned about. Like terrorists, they will always be among us. We can learn to manage them, protect ourselves from them, but we'll never totally eliminate them. It's the rest of you— the 98 percent of you—that concern me.
>
> Listen to me—those streets you walk have produced many casualties. They are seductive and sensual places, and they will rub off on you. Dope Street is voodooland, a place where it gets real freaky—a world where you can be changed and distorted into something that is foreign to your nature.
>
> Trust me—it can happen to the very best of you. You'll become aware of it—it will be right there for you to see. You'll walk differently, talk differently, and you'll look good—all narcs look good.
>
> The secret to your survival is to not become a reflection of the people you police. Know where you stand, be proud of who you are, what you are. Remember, what you are is the final line of defense. There is, in fact, a drug war—and you are what it's all about.
>
> Now, sit back and make yourselves comfortable. I'm going to tell you a story:
>
> Once upon a time, a time before some of you were born, there walked a narcotics cop just like you. He was a very young man, little more than a boy, and they called him Babyface. . . .

ACKNOWLEDGMENTS

To begin with, to Kathy Packard, my partner in life, who truly understands what this book means to me. To my friend and agent for more than twenty years, Esther Newberg, for all her support and encouragement—and that uphill struggle trying to keep me sane. To the demanding, unforgiving, and gifted editor Henry Ferris, a tireless and brutal critic. Truly an anomaly in today's publishing world. Other writers both commiserate and envy me Henry, and they should.

I owe many people for their generosity and assistance during the writing of this book: My dear friend Tom DiLuglio, a fine lawyer and former lieutenant governor of the great state of Rhode Island, for his counsel and personal support. Andrea Barzvi and Christine Bauch at International Creative Management in New York, and Lisa Nager at HarperCollins—these three women have been especially kind to me.

My gratitude also to the writers Bob Reiss and Tom Zito for reading my pages and offering superb guidance. And to my son-in-law, Michael Asen, another fine lawyer who challenged my thinking and encouraged my work. Finally, to my friend, Emi Bataglia. The loss of her brother, Anthony, to mindless street criminals, is a sorrow shared by us all.